In Lotus-land Japan

IN LOTUS-LAND: JAPAN

UNDER THE PURPLE WISTARIAS

IN
LOTUS-LAND
JAPAN

BY

HERBERT G. PONTING, F.R.G.S.

AUTHOR OF "THE GREAT WHITE SOUTH"

WITH 8 PICTURES IN COLOUR
AND 80 IN MONOCHROME
FROM PHOTOGRAPHS
BY THE AUTHOR

1922
LONDON & TORONTO
J. M. DENT & SONS LTD.
NEW YORK: E. P. DUTTON & CO.

They came unto a land,
In which it seemed always afternoon.
A land of streams! some, like a downward smoke,
Slow-dropping veils of thinnest lawn, did go,
And some thro' wavering lights and shadows broke,
Rolling a slumbrous sheet of foam below.
They saw the gleaming river seaward flow
From the inner land; far off, a mountain-top,
A silent pinnacle of aged snow,
Stood sunset-flushed: and, dew'd with showery drops,
Up-clomb the shadowy pines above the woven copse.

TENNYSON, *The Lotos-Eaters.*

New and Revised Edition 1922

FOREWORD

THIS book is written by a nomad who has worshipped at the shrine of Nature and Art in many lands; who has spent nearly three happy years in one of the most delightful of holiday lands, and who served as a Correspondent with the First Japanese Army during the war with Russia. In it will be found no dissertations on politics, economics or social problems; and he who seeks information concerning Japan's vast textile manufactures, statistics of her progress, or of the rapid growth of her military and naval might, will search its pages in vain.

This volume is intended, primarily, as a guide-book for the traveller; and, secondly, as a means—to those who are unable to roam so far away—to explore a beautiful country through the medium of the lens and observations of one whose camera and note-book have been his inseparable companions in all his wanderings o'er the earth.

During his travels in Lotus-Land, the author's experiences were so many and varied that in writing the book the most perplexing problem has been what to leave out of it, so as to keep its size within reasonable limits. Descriptions of many interesting places and incidents have had perforce to be omitted, but in what has been included herein will be found some account of much that is best about Japan; and, in the hope of bringing some fresh aspects of the country into focus, the writer has narrated experiences which he had far from the "beaten tracks."

When this book was first published, the author was preparing to embark for the Antarctic, as a member of the late Captain R. F. Scott's South Pole Expedition, and it appeared on the day the Expedition sailed. There having been no time to revise the first proofs, the letterpress suffered somewhat in consequence. Notwithstanding this, the book was received with unanimous and generous approval by the Press, and it went through two editions.

The text has now been thoroughly revised; matter of lesser importance has been omitted, whilst much new material has been added, including a brief introductory account of the stirring events which immediately preceded the Reformation —for a proper understanding of many things and places can only be gained with some knowledge of the times with which they were so prominently associated. Also, the selection of illustrations will be found to be better than formerly—a number of new plates having been added, whilst certain less important ones have been discarded.

The photographs from which the illustrations herein are reproduced are all from original negatives taken by the writer. The copyrights of several vest in Messrs. Underwood & Underwood of New York, and in the H. C. White Company of Vermont, U.S.A., whom the author warmly thanks for permission to include them. Some of the writer's original studies, and more particularly those of Mount Fuji, have been copied by Japanese photographers, and by artists and craftsmen working in various metals and textiles. Lest, therefore, there be any who question the origin of these photographs, an extract is appended from a review which appeared in one of the newspapers of Japan when the author's *Fuji-San* was first published.

H. G. P.

"It would scarcely be an exaggeration to say that Mr. Ponting has discovered a new mountain; for no one has ever seen the great quiescent volcano depicted from so many points before, except, indeed, from the pencil of Hokusai. But then, this great painter gave representations that were half true, half fanciful, whereas the pictures before us are pure and unadulterated truth."

The Japanese Times.

CONTENTS

LIST OF ILLUSTRATIONS

LIST OF ILLUSTRATIONS

IN LOTUS-LAND: JAPAN

CHAPTER I

THE LAST DAYS OF FEUDALISM

THE name of Commodore Mathew Galbraith Perry, of the
United States Navy, stands out in the history of Japan above
that of all other foreigners, for it was the action of this American
officer which was mainly instrumental in determining the
Japanese to abandon Feudalism and their policy of isolation,
and to adopt western methods of civilisation and government
as the goal for which they were henceforth to strive.

As early as 1611 a trading agreement had been granted
by the Shogun Iyéyasu to the Dutch, mainly through the
influence exerted on their behalf by the Englishman Will
Adams, who, from the time he was shipwrecked on the shore
of Japan in 1600, to his death twenty years later, was a close
adviser of the Shogun. Will Adams earned the Shogun's
respect and friendship by the information he was able to
furnish regarding foreign affairs, and by his ability to teach
the people shipbuilding and other useful crafts, of which the
Japanese had hitherto but crude ideas.

The agreement with the Dutch was followed, two years
later, by a charter from the Shogun to the British East India
Company, granting them the privilege of trading in any
Japanese port. The Dutch had, however, by that time become
strongly entrenched at Hirado, and a rivalry sprang up between
the traders of the two nations which resulted in the Hollanders
selling goods at a loss in order to drive their rivals from the
market. So great was the enmity engendered by the competition for trade that open hostilities broke out, and a fleet
of armed merchant vessels was sent to Japan by the British

East India Company in 1617. In the fighting that ensued, the advantage lay with the Dutch, and although a peace was patched up, the British retired a few years later from the field, having lost an immense amount of money in their efforts to establish trading relations. The Dutch, however, continued to carry on a profitable business as the only foreign merchants in Japan. The Portuguese endeavoured to establish themselves some years after the English had retired, but the opposition they met with from the Dutch, who were in favour, resulted in the Yedo government denying them any privileges, and they were driven from the country, whilst their successful competitors secured a still firmer footing on the island of Deshima, near Nagasaki, in 1640.

The bickerings and hostility to each other of the European traders only served to make the Japanese more suspicious than ever of all foreigners; and the policy of exclusion now became even more stringent than before; but the learning of the Dutch was respected by all who came in contact with them, and the little colony near Nagasaki was looked upon as a veritable mine of knowledge, for every opportunity was given by the colonists, to those who cared to investigate, for enlightenment regarding the more advanced civilisation of Europe. The Japanese refused, however, at that time to deviate from the course they had laid down as their own, and although repeated efforts were made by America, Great Britain and Russia to open up intercourse, all resulted in complete failure. The Japanese government persistently repelled every attempt at communication, and the monopoly of foreign trade remained in the hands of the Dutch.

The United States was affected more so than any other country by the attitude of Japan. The opening of many Chinese ports to foreign trade, consequent on the treaties ratified at the conclusion of the opium wars, resulted in several schemes for steamship lines from the Pacific States to the Orient. As Japan lay conveniently on the way for coaling purposes, it was imperative for the success of any such enterprise that stations should there be established at which coal could be bought. This necessitated the abandonment of the Japanese policy of isolation. Hence, in November 1852, the United States Government despatched a squadron of four ships—the *Mississippi*, the *Susquehana*, the *Plymouth*, and the *Saratoga*—under the command of Commodore Perry, from Norfolk, Virginia, to Japan, *via* the Cape of Good Hope, to endeavour to bring about this result. Commodore Perry was invested with full power to take whatever course he thought best—force if necessary—to secure certain privileges asked for in a letter which he bore from the President of the United States to the ruling Shogun.

Weak as this small squadron was, the terror which it inspired when it arrived in Yedo Bay was instrumental in securing delivery of the President's letter. Having thus far succeeded in his mission, the Commodore then sailed away to China, stating he would return the following spring for an answer.

For years past there had been brewing in Japan a rapidly-growing revulsion of feeling against the usurpation of the Imperial power by the Shogun, and sympathy for the impotent Mikado, who was little more than a prisoner at Kyoto.

This feeling was manifested openly when it began to be seen that, if the conditions asked for by the United States were not granted, the country would have to prepare for war, after a peace lasting for over two centuries.

Here was a dilemma indeed! To the Japanese, equipped only with obsolete weapons and powerless against a foreign foe, the only alternative to abandoning peacefully their policy of isolation was to engage in a conflict, the result of which was a foregone conclusion. The weight of popular opinion, however, was against the opening of the country, and on all hands preparations were made for war. Forts were constructed, defences put in order, and the manufacture of arms became the order of the day.

About this time the Shogun Iéyoshi died, and was succeeded by his son Iésada, who maintained the policy of his father, and the situation remained unaltered. Affairs then

B

drifted on until the spring, when Commodore Perry, as fore-shadowed, returned — his squadron strengthened by the addition of six ships, a fleet all told of ten vessels of war.

The moral effect of this display of force was sufficient, for the Japanese had never seen anything like it before, and negotiations were at once entered into at Kanagawa, near Yokohama, where a treaty, which obtained for the United States nearly all the privileges demanded, was signed by the Shogun on March 31st, 1854.

This treaty was in the nature of a document preparing the way for future intercourse. It merely provided for the protection of shipwrecked sailors, and the opening of two ports for coaling and provisioning purposes; whilst it was agreed that further meetings should be held between the Shogun's Ministers and the American Commissioners regarding matters appertaining to trade. It was, however, a beginning —the thin end of the wedge that was destined in the end to rend asunder the whole fabric of the Feudal System.

As the treaty embodied the "Most Favoured Nation" clause, the United States was thus ensured that, in the event of any treaty being concluded with any other country granting privileges not contained in this agreement, such privileges should be extended also to the United States without further negotiations. Similar treaties were drawn up with other nations shortly afterwards, and in 1857 and 1858 others followed, securing trading and other privileges.

For over forty years it was under these treaties that inter-course with foreigners was conducted—the ports of Yoko-hama, Tokyo, Osaka, Kobe, Nagasaki and Hakodate being opened to trade, and a duty of five per cent. ad valorem being levied on all goods imported. [Since the conflict with Russia (1904-5) Japan has adopted exceedingly high protective tariffs.]

The above events were the cause of a decade of lawlessness and outrage, due to the inflamed feeling which now became more acute than ever against foreigners.

Political opinion was divided. The supporters of the Shogunate were convinced of the futility of opposing the demands of the western world; whilst the old conservative element which rallied around the Mikado in the Western capital, Kyoto, was bitterly hostile to the new policy entered upon by the Shogun's Government. This, however, was not strange, as the latter had had no opportunity of seeing the might of the foreigners, which had been so strikingly demonstrated to the people of the Eastern capital, Yedo.

The Royalists held that the Shogun had exceeded his powers in signing these treaties, as such privileges were for the Mikado alone to grant; and that the agreements were therefore not legal. They continued in effect, however, and the Shogun's Government was held to answer for the safety of foreigners and the protection of trade, as, having negotiated the treaties, thus assuming supreme authority, the Shogunate had undertaken the responsibility that the provisions contained therein would be observed.

Swashbucklers now swarmed over the land, and deeds of violence were of daily occurrence. Ii-Kamon-no-Kami, the Daimyo of Hikoné—who was acting as Regent for the young Shogun Iémochi, who had succeeded Iésada—was assassinated in 1861 by a band of outlaws of the Mito clan, whose lord had been deprived of office as head of the Anti-Foreign Party by the Regent. Other outrages followed, resulting in the death or injury of members of the foreign legations, the Government being quite powerless to prevent such acts of violence.

Of these unfortunate incidents the most regrettable was that known as the "Richardson affair," in which the foreign victims were to blame, for having, by their foolish action, brought their fate upon their own heads. A brief account of the famous incident will serve to illustrate something of the customs and feeling of the time.

Shimazu Saburo—the powerful acting Daimyo of the province of Satsuma, in the island of Kiushu—went, in the spring of 1862, to Kyoto, to confer with the Mikado regarding the adoption of measures to expel the hated foreign "barbarians" from the land. The Satsuma clan was one of the strongest in Japan, and the great retinue with which the chief was accompanied became reinforced on its way to the capital by a number of ronin—disaffected samurai [1] who had deserted, or been outlawed from, their clans—who were seeking a leader to direct them in their contemplated schemes for ridding the country of the objects of their hatred, the foreigners. These men were desperadoes who were prepared to stop at nothing in the accomplishment of their designs, and their presence in the cavalcade constituted a ruffianly element which the loyal and trained samurai band of Satsuma lacked entirely when it started on the march.

Having met and advised the Mikado at Kyoto, the Daimyo proceeded to Yedo, where he requested a hearing from the Shogun, in order to lay before him plans for the expulsion of the foreigners, and the consequent suppression of the rebellious spirit which was growing daily stronger all over the land.

The Shogun refused him an audience, and the Daimyo started on his return journey smarting with the sting of the failure of his mission.

The highway from Yedo to Kyoto—the old Tōkaidō— passes by the fishing village of Kanagawa; and whilst the long procession—horsemen, foot soldiers and attendants to the number of nearly a thousand men—was passing near the outskirts of this place, it met an English lady and three gentlemen who were riding on horseback.

Japanese etiquette of the road demanded that a Daimyo's caravan should not only have right of way, but that the inhabitants of villages through which it passed should not even so much as look upon it. Notice was usually sent on ahead when a Daimyo expected to pass through a town, or along a road; and that road, or portion of the town, became, for the time being, as in a land of the dead.

Either ignorant of, or disregarding, the course which custom demanded that chance travellers should pursue— namely to dismount, and stand beside the road, and bow to the Daimyo's norimono as it was carried past—the party rode on, until the angry looks with which the soldiers regarded

[1] The samurai were the warrior class of feudal days—the gentry of old Japan.

ON THE OLD TŌKAIDŌ

them convinced two of the riders that it would be wiser to turn aside. But another, Mr. Chas. L. Richardson—a resident of China who was visiting Japan, and who knew little of the Japanese and their ways—would not hear of it, thinking that the people could be treated with the same disdain as foreigners in China exhibited towards the Chinese. As he was about to pass the Daimyo's palanquin without dismounting, a samurai, incensed beyond control by the hated foreigner's wanton insult to his chief, rushed at Richardson, and struck him a fatal blow in the side with a heavy sword. The other two gentlemen, who were also attacked and severely wounded, and the lady, who fortunately escaped unhurt from the blow which was aimed at her, fled to Kanagawa.

It was the unanimous opinion of foreigners in Japan that the victim had brought his fate upon himself; yet an indemnity of £100,000 was demanded by Great Britain from the Japanese Government, and a large sum in addition from the Satsuma Daimyo, as well as the surrender of the assassin for punishment. These demands were refused, and in consequence a British squadron under Admiral Kuper arrived off Kagoshima, the Satsuma capital, in August 1862. Though the Japanese guns killed the captain of the flagship and sixty members of the crew, and a terrific storm raged at the time, the town was shelled and burnt, and the Daimyo's batteries and ships destroyed. The indemnity demanded was then paid; but the assassin was never handed over to expiate his crime, as it was contended his identity was not known.

Just previously to these events occurred an incident which made Shimonoseki famous.

The Chōshu Daimyo, who also was a bitter hater of foreigners, undertook to close the Shimonoseki Strait—which forms the principal western entrance to the Inland Sea— against the ships of foreign nations. Accordingly he fortified the shores and placed warships to guard the channel.

In June 1863 an American steamer, the *Pembroke*, on passing through the Strait, was fired at, though without effect. Two weeks later a French gunboat was attacked and severely damaged. Next a Dutch man-of-war was fired upon; but she returned the fire with interest, and inflicted much greater damage than she received.

On these happenings becoming known, an American warship, the *Wyoming*, proceeded from Yokohama to avenge the hostile act, and on the 16th of July she engaged the Daimyo's ships, sinking one and crippling another. A few days later two French warships appeared; a force of men was landed and the batteries were destroyed.

Negotiations were then entered into by the Treaty Powers to ensure their ships the right to navigate the Inland Sea without molestation. The Shogun's Government evinced its willingness to do all in its power towards granting the demands, but admitted that its impotency rendered it incapable of suppressing the obstreperous Chōshu noble. Hence, a fleet of British, French, Dutch and American warships were sent from Yokohama on 28th August, 1864, to destroy all offensive works found in the neighbourhood of the Strait, and to reduce the hostile Daimyo to a state of subjection.

This result was attained at once, for the Chōshu chief, seeing the futility of offering any resistance against the force, surrendered, and agreed henceforth to act in accordance with the wishes of the Yedo Government.

An indemnity of £600,000 was exacted by the Powers concerned, to cover the cost of the expedition. This was divided between Great Britain, France, Holland and the United States, after the latter three Powers had deducted from the total a large sum as recompense for injury to their ships, and imaginary damage to their prestige.

Seeing that the Yedo Government was in no way responsible for the hostility of the Daimyo, and was doing its feeble best to quell the anti-foreign feeling in the land, the wringing of this great sum from its impoverished coffers, to cover the entire cost of a quite unnecessarily powerful force, stands on record as the most unjust incident that has marked the intercourse of the Foreign Powers with Japan.

[To the credit of the United States, the American Government twenty years later refunded to Japan its entire share in the indemnity—*i.e.* the principal, without interest; but up to the present time none of the other Powers has shown any disposition to follow this righteous example.]

Lessons like this served to convince the staunchest supporters of Feudalism the futility of contending against the foreigners on anything like equal terms; and the conviction rapidly grew, that if Japan was to remain an independent power, she must abandon her present unsatisfactory methods of government, begin at once to purchase modern ships of war, and adopt a military system based upon that of western nations.

Such were the main events which led to the abandonment of the dual government.

The Shogun Iémochi died on the 19th of September, 1866; and on the 3rd of February, 1867, the Mikado Kōmei died, and was succeeded by his son Mutsohito, who was fifteen years of age.

Disaffection and strong party feeling grew stronger day by day throughout the land until the new Shogun Yōshinōbu resigned, having been urged to do so by the Daimyo of Tōsa, one of the sagest and most diplomatic nobles in Japan. He represented to the Shogun that the cause of the nation's troubles lay in the fact that it was divided in twain by reason of the lack of unity and harmony of action between the rival governments; and that if the Japanese were to become a homogeneous people, the dual government must be abandoned, and the affairs of the nation henceforth be administered under one head.

Even after this radical change was effected, much fighting ensued, for several Daimyos were bitterly opposed to it and devoted to the cause of the Shogun whom they desired to reinstate. These, with their samurai, rallied round Yōshinōbu, who was in retirement at Osaka, where, whilst he had nominally abdicated, he still continued, at the request of the young Emperor Mutsohito, to direct the administration of foreign affairs. But this excited much jealousy among the Daimyos who supported the Royalist cause. They desired to see the Shogun shorn of all power whatsoever, and this they finally persuaded the Emperor to effect. Consequently the early months of 1868 were days of continual strife between the Royalists and the Shogun's troops. The most serious of these collisions occurred near Kyoto at the end of January, and resulted in the complete rout of the rebels. The ex-Shogun escaped, a fugitive, to Yedo, and his stronghold, the castle of Osaka, the strongest in all Japan, was burnt down to its massive stone foundations.

More fighting ensued in the north, but the victory always lay with the Royalist forces. Finally, however, the partisans of the Shogun saw the futility of resisting the growing power of the Mikado, and laid down their arms.

The events of that period form some of the most interesting reading in the history of Japan. Those were days of stirring heroism and self-sacrifice: of the struggle of brave men for all the traditions they most loved and cherished. Old Japan was dying and they knew it, but the changed conditions which the foreigner had brought made the onward march of events irresistible.

On the 8th of February, 1868, the last remnant of the fabric of Feudalism fell when the Emperor officially notified the foreign representatives that henceforth the reins of government would be held by him alone.

Thus was the Reformation effected, and the period of MEIJI, the "Enlightened Era," established.

CHAPTER II

TOKYO BAY

FROM the time we left San Francisco's fine harbour behind us, few had been the daylight hours when the heavens were not mirrored in the ocean. The sun sank each evening in a cloudless sky ahead of us, only to reappear next morning in a cloudless sky astern, and each successive day had been a repetition of the lovely day preceding it. It was a record voyage for weather. No one on board could remember the like. The end of it came at last, however, as it does to all good things; but to the final hour of the voyage the kindly fate that had befriended us never deserted us, and the last evening was even more beautiful than all the others had been, for the moon was full, the night as romantic as a night at sea can be, and the very air seemed laden with the spirit of the land of our dreams that would soon be a dream-land no more.

I was up next morning long ere the first streaks of dawn had dimmed the brilliancy of the moonlight. We were due to anchor at Yokohama soon after daybreak, and, as I came on deck, soft, balmy breezes, borne of our rapid progress, whispered gently in my ears, and bore on their wings the scent of land. I went up to the bow, and saw that as the sharp prow parted the glassy waters which mirrored the starry heavens, feathers of spray leaped high along the vessel's trim and tapering sides, and burned with a ghostly light which spread around the ship, so that she seemed to be gliding through a sea of fire. Seldom have I seen the ocean so phosphorescent in any part of the world.

We were steaming just off the entrance to Tokyo Bay, and now and then a junk, or some smaller fishing-boat, loomed suddenly out of the night, drifted like a phantom across the

silvery path of the moonlight, and passed on as suddenly
again into the dusky shadows. As the day began to break,
these craft increased in number and distinctness until many
hundreds of them were to be seen, homeward-bound after the
work of the night. The great sails of the junks looked silken
as they hung listlessly in a hundred tiny festoons that threw
soft shadows on the white; and the smaller boats, the sampans
—with the half-nude figures of the fishermen swinging to and
fro against the background of the moonlit water, as they
worked the long sweeps, called yulos—formed a novel and
delightful picture which filled me with anticipation of what
was to come.

Whilst my attention was absorbed with the fishing-boats
the morning rapidly grew, and now the delicate outline of that
loveliest of all mountains of the earth—that wondrous inspiration of Japanese art, Fuji-san—was softly painted on the
western skies.

The grey of dawn was shot with pink, and blue, and amber,
and high in the iridescent azure, far above the night-mists
clinging to the land, the virgin cone of Fuji hung from the
vault of heaven.

Then in the blushing east there was a flash, and the great
red sun rose slowly above the hills of Bōshu, tinging the skies
with a ruddy glow, and staining all pink and rosy the snows
on Fuji's crest. Over the holy mountain the moon was paling,
and innumerable junks, with idle sails, lay becalmed on the
mother-o'-pearl waters of the Bay.

Many times since then I have seen the peerless Fuji.
Under every condition of sunshine, storm, and snow, and at
every hour from dawn till sunset, in spring, summer, autumn
and winter I have gazed at it from a score of places within
twenty miles of its base; but never did the great sacred mountain appear lovelier than during that first hour I spent in
Japanese waters.

So this was Japan! My fondest dreams had created no
such scenes as these from which to form my first impressions,
and from that day it has always seemed to me that if the fitness

of things could be more strikingly exemplified than in the adoption by the Japanese of the red disc of the rising sun as the emblem of their empire, it would be in their having the outline of the sacred Fuji on their flag instead.

Twice since this, my first visit, I have entered Tokyo Bay in drizzling rain, and had I not known what there was behind the mists, I should have had but a doleful idea of my dream-land. Japan is a wet country in the spring-time, and Fuji so chary of displaying its charms that the mountain sometimes sulks for weeks together in impenetrable banks of clouds. Those, therefore, who arrive when the sun is shining, and Fuji is in complaisant mood, may deem themselves favoured of the gods—at least the Japanese gods—and should be thankful for the honour.

CHAPTER III

MOST visitors endeavour to arrive in Japan in spring, in time to see the Cherry-blossom Festivals.

Reverence for flowers is one of the most charming characteristics of the Japanese. They are not flower-lovers, however, in the sense that Europeans are, for they care not for every flower. They love only a few; but these few they love in a different way from any other people. Their love amounts almost to worship. They hold great festivals in honour of their favourites, and they flock to famous spots to view them by hundreds of thousands.

For a brief week or two each year, all Japan is a very shrine to Flora, as any one who has been there in spring-time can affirm. It is a land of azaleas and cherry-blossoms. The face of the country smiles with them, and the latter are far more symbolical of the Empire of the Rising Sun than the chrysanthemum, which forms the Imperial crest.

If trees be included in the category, the flower-festivals of Tokyo begin with the first day of the year, when everybody goes round visiting his neighbour to wish him "Shinnen o médétō gozaimas"—the equivalent for our own greeting at that season. New Year's Day is the festival of the bamboo and the pine, and every house-door is decorated with these evergreens—the one emblematical of straight and honourable dealing; the other of long life and good fortune.

The real flowers begin with the plum-blossoms, which burst late in February and bloom well on into March. In Tokyo, Kameido is one of the most famous places to see them, for in the gardens of this old Shinto temple are gnarled and tortured veteran trees that creep, and writhe, and twist them-

14

selves into amazing contortions along the surface of the ground
before they raise their heads; and because of their reptile-like
shapes they are called the "Recumbent Dragons."

Tokyo can scarcely claim to rank among the most beautiful
cities of the world, yet there are times when the Japanese
capital glows with beauty. These are the occasions of the
Cherry-blossom Festivals; and of all Japanese floral displays
none can compare with April's glorious pageant.

It must be a sorrowful or spiritless soul that does not fill
with gladness in the sweet Japanese spring-time. The joy of
it is in the very air. The thrill of it lends a glitter to every
eye. The whole land awaits breathlessly the opening of
the favourite buds, and important newspapers devote long
paragraphs to their notice.

In 1905 I asked a Japanese friend if he observed much
excitement among the people over the near approach of the
Russian Baltic fleet.

"They are already too excited about the cherry-blossoms
to think of it," he answered.

If you are fortunate enough to be in Tokyo in early April,
the stream of eager humanity which surges eastwards across
the broad Sumida-gawa will surely gather you in its vortex.
From every side the people come, and the crowds grow thicker
as the Azuma bridge is approached. They are hastening to
see a truly beautiful sight, for on the left bank of the river is
Mukōjima—an avenue of cherry-trees, a mile long, which is
one glorious mass of blossom. Japanese cherry-blossoms are
pink, not white like ours, and from a distance the trees resemble
a bank of clouds softly flushed by the evening afterglow.

Under this exquisite canopy Carnival is King, and from
morning till long after midnight the avenue rings with music
and shouts of revelry and laughter, for Mukōjima is the festival
of the *bourgeoisie*. The river is crowded with house-boats,
and under the spreading branches the avenue is lined with
impromptu tea-houses and refreshment stalls. Saké is in
evidence everywhere. Nearly every one of the merry-makers
carries a gourd of it at his belt, and the crowd is beaming

with rubicund saké faces. Everybody is good-natured, for the intoxication set up by the insipid rice-distilled spirit does not seem to make for contentiousness, but only to render the carouser's spirits more convivial and hilarious. Reeling saké-drinkers offer their gourds to every kindred spirit, and constantly replenish them from the hogsheads at the wayside stalls, whilst people who have never seen each other before are in a minute the best of friends, and cementing their vows of lifelong amity with draughts of the national beverage, as they hang on each other's necks. False moustaches, whiskers, and noses make caricatures of the revellers, and wandering geikin and samisen players set every one into merry peals of laughter, as they pick their way through the crowd, twanging accompaniments to their comic and topical songs as they go. The crowd is warm with humanity, joyous with humour, and amiable with courtesy. No irascibility or pugnaciousness mars the merriment, and roughness is conspicuous by its absence, for the Japanese crowd is a lovable crowd—the best behaved and tempered in the world.

At night-time each tree and tea-house is festooned with paper lanterns, and the dainty, fairy-like screen of pink overhead is suffused with their soft glow, which falls on the gay kimono of many a butterfly geisha in the passing throng below.

One season, prompted by the sight of the people's joy, my old friend Professor Edwin Emerson of Tokyo was inspired to paint the gladsome throng in verse. Before the blossoms had fallen he presented me with a leaflet, fresh from the press, bearing the following lines, which describe the merry scene with a grace that a mere chronicler in prose can only envy as he quotes them:

THE CHERRY-BLOSSOMS AT TOKYO

Oh! just see the people go;
Old and young, the fast and slow,
Haste to see the splendid show
Of the lovely cherry-blossoms.

How the crowds pass blithely by,
Cheered by the resplendent sky!
Eager as the birds that fly
    Swiftly to the cherry-blossoms.

Larger crowds are seldom seen;
Nothing rude, or low, or mean
Mars the pleasure of the scene;
    Lovers these of cherry-blossoms.

What a mass of flowers at hand!
So distinctive of this land;
Raptured groups of people stand
    Spell-bound by the cherry-blossoms.

Worshippers of nature's grace,
Love of flowers marks this race;
Highest joy beams in each face
    At the sight of cherry-blossoms.

Flowers—how divine the sight;
Earth's own stars in colours bright;
With sweet fragrance to delight;
    Charming are the cherry-blossoms.

Verses hanging from the trees
Flutter with each passing breeze;
Vows, and hymns, and odes are these,
    Prompted by the cherry-blossoms.

Just as Mukōjima is the people's festival, so Uyéno in
cherry-blossom time is the resort of the *élite*. Uyéno is a
magnificent old park, where the bodies of six of those great
military rulers of feudal Japan, the Shoguns, lie entombed,
beneath massive monuments of bronze, in the grounds of
gorgeously-lacquered memorial temples that are among the
finest architectural features of the land. The approaches to
these shrines are gravelled avenues of great width, lined with
cherry-trees which spread their branches wide and form a
veritable sea of diaphanous blossom. Whichever way one
looks, great foaming billows of soft pink fill the view, and
from the billows a delicate perfume falls. Along the smooth
roadways dainty Japanese ladies drive in carriages and motor-
cars, dressed in soft greys, and fawns, and quiet neutral tints;

whilst under the great spreading trees the pedestrians walk with dignity and decorum. This is the *Bois* of Tokyo, and neither when the cherry-trees are blooming, nor at any other time, are there the gay and festive scenes that characterised the saturnalia by the river.

Besides the two celebráted places named, there are many others within the city precincts where the show is of almost equal beauty. The Edo-gawa, a river running through the eastern portion of the town, has both its banks lined with avenues of trees bearing the lovely double blossoms. The moat around the Imperial Palace—beautiful at any season— in April is a lake in Arcady. The British Embassy looks out upon a forest of cherry-trees. Asakusa is embosomed in another clump. Shōkonsha becomes a perfect fairyland. The lovely Shiba Park—filled with temples raised centuries ago in memory of departed Shoguns: temples which rival in beauty and grandeur the far-famed shrines of Nikko—is a forest where the cherry-blossoms gleam, in contrast to the deep-green cedars, with a beauty indescribable, and where every courtyard is fragrant with the flowers that fill it. Then every private garden has its cherry-tree or two, and Atago-yama, the city's Prospect Hill, is crowned with them. The gardens of the Government Offices are filled with them. The Crown Prince's Palace is buried in them, and every noble-man's mansion is surrounded with them. Even great modern breweries have so far condescended to pander to the national sentiment as to grace their compounds with the tree on which the beloved flower grows. Tokyo, in fact, for its whole length and breadth, in April beams with the joyous blossoms. The entire city is one great show of them, and for that month at least the Japanese capital is probably the most beautiful city in the world.

The peony is the next to reign, and holds its levees every-where. At many a florist's garden shows are held, where magnificent blooms are to be seen. Then the azaleas set the gardens at Ōkubō on fire, and make each famous mountain-resort a blaze of glorious colour.

KAMEIDO

Early May is heralded by the most graceful and delicate of all Japanese flowers, and with the blossoming of the wistarias one feels that summer is indeed at hand. The gardens of Kameido are again the favourite spot, and thousands go to see them. The grounds of the old temple, sacred to Tenjin-sama, are an enchanting sight, for the pond winding amongst the islands is completely surrounded by tea-arbours, from the trellised roofs of which depend miracles of white and purple floral stalactites.

Many of the pendent blooms are of almost incredible length—a yard or more—and above them a dense canopy of foliage grows, shutting off all direct light from the sky. But the blossoms all hang downwards, and under these lovely bowers æsthetic flower-worshippers sit in the cool, scented shade, and meditate and improvise poems which they tie to the floral wonders by which they are inspired. Merely to rest for hours on end in this flower paradise and gaze and think in silence is pleasure enough to thousands of the quiet, well-conducted nature lovers; and at Kameido one sees none of the Bacchanalian merriment attendant on the April scenes at Mukōjima.

One absorbed observer had brought his opera-glasses, and, though he sat but a yard below the blossoms, was busy surveying them from that distance. In another place an excited group could scarcely contain their glee over the movements of a bumble-bee that buzzed from flower to flower above them. Everywhere these busy creatures were loading themselves with honey. One of them tried to settle on a pretty little child near me. I told her it was because she was so sweet, and the compliment caused a merry ring of laughter from all who heard it.

Bands of schoolgirls and schoolboys are conducted round the gardens, the beauty of the flowers being dilated on by their teachers. Hundreds of soldiers and sailors come out to view the blossoms, too. As each fresh party arrive they hang over the bamboo rail and clap their hands; but clap they never so loudly, it is all in vain, for the huge carp, which live in the

c

green pond below, loaf under the projecting verandahs, gorged
with the cakes that everybody throws them, and deaf to all
appeals to feed. Occasionally, however, a great red beauty
glides out lazily and unconcernedly to gobble in another mouth-
ful; or, seemingly infected with the prevailing epidemic of
gladness, dashes up from the depths and leaps out of the
water, to the intense delight of the picnickers. Sometimes a
tortoise comes paddling to the surface, causing an equal diversion; but, like the carp, though cakes and mochi be showered
at him, he is obdurate, and can seldom be cajoled to touch
them. May is certainly the month of months for the carp and
tortoises of Kameido.

Everywhere about the gardens there are rapt individuals
composing verses, and painters faithfully depicting in water-
colours the beauty of the scenes; whilst strolling players roam
the grounds playing pretty catching airs upon the geikin.

Busy little neisans run about replenishing tea-pots, or
bringing fresh supplies of cakes, and, if the day be warm,
glasses of shaved-ice and fruit-syrup are called for by everyone.

There are toy and nick-nack sellers, whose stalls display,
amongst other dainty things, wonderfully natural paper wistarias, and pretty pins for the hair adorned with tiny silken
sprays of the flower. There are also sellers of paper carp, and
merchants whose stalls are all a-glitter with tiny globes of
goldfish. Then there is the tortoise-man at every few yards
you go. He has a score of the shelly creatures, hanging by
their legs, and, if you like, you can buy one for a price ranging
from a penny to threepence, and by returning it to the pond
earn a little grace from Tenjin-sama. Many of these creatures
have been fished out and sold some scores of times, and have
thus earned quite a nice little sum for those who have the
right to catch them.

Stone lanterns and curiously-trained trees are scattered
about the temple grounds, and there are semicircular moon
bridges—so called because the reflection makes a perfect
ring—to cross which is no mean feat for a foreign lady visitor
if she happen to be shod with dainty high-heeled shoes. She

A WISTARIA ARBOUR AT KAMEIDO

will accomplish the ascent easily enough, but wait till she has finished viewing the pretty scene from this elevated point of view and starts to descend! Just wait a little and watch her, and watch the Japanese faces too, and see how amused they are at the dilemma of my lady! She reaches terra firma without a fall, but her descent is not exactly dignified, and she has amused the interested flower-worshippers vastly with her antics. There is a level footway beside the arch, but to take the more difficult path over the bridge to the temple is a meritorious act, and young people skip nimbly over it all day long, whilst even the old and shaky do not always shirk the task.

At dusk every arbour and tea-house is hung with pretty paper lanterns, for the night phase of the flowers is admired as well as the daytime effects, and the last visitors do not pass out under the grey old temple gateway until well on towards the small hours.

There is no sweeter season in Japan than "when May glides onward into June," for under the gentle influence of the sunny days that warm the earth another of the fairest flowers of the East bursts into blossom, and the first week of Summer is marked by the Festival of the Iris.

To see this stately flower at its best you must go along the Mukōjima cherry-avenue—now all green with leafy shade—and turn to the right at the end of the long parade of trees, when you will find yourself among the gardens of Hori-kiri. This is the most famous place in Japan for irises: many acres are covered with the elegant beauties.

Sprinkled about the gardens, on tiny hill-tops and in pretty nooks, there are rustic tea-houses, from which, as you sip the golden beverage that is never wanting for two consecutive hours in this land, you can look out upon a vari-coloured sea of such irises as were never seen before.

Many are of truly regal proportions, measuring a foot from tip to tip of the petals, and all are grown in serried ranks —vast battalions of floral Amazons, marshalled into regiments of complementary hues. Most of the flowers are white, but there are reds, and yellows, and blues, and a dozen shades of lilac and purple, and some are shot and streaked with colour, whilst others have coloured spots and blotches.

Along the narrow pathways that divide the beds admiring Japanese ladies walk, fairer still to look upon in their pretty native costumes than the flowers themselves; and from the bordering tea-houses the tinkling of samisens rings out across the gardens, for many can only enjoy to the full such festive occasions when sharing them in the companionship of the merry geisha. Black-haired, brown-eyed little Hebes flit about among the flowers with trays of tea and cakes to the various summer-houses; and the clapping of hands, which summons the busy maids, with their answering shouts of "Hai," come from all directions. Nobody is in a hurry except these smiling lasses, and all can well afford to wait their turn when there is so much beauty to wonder at. Artists are sketching everywhere; foreign tourists snap away yards and yards of film to help to swell the Kodak dividends, and a dozen spectacled Japanese photographers are getting pretty "bits" for post-cards. Every visitor, as he pays his bill, is presented with a few budding spears by the little maid who has waited on him. These he proudly bears home in his rikisha as a token of a happy hour or two spent at Hori-kiri.

Nothing could be more appropriate than that the Emperor's birthday should be the 3rd of November, as the season of the glorious chrysanthemum is then at its height, and the chrysanthemum is the Imperial crest. There are people of lesser degree who also boast the flower as their family device, but not the chrysanthemum of sixteen petals. Others may have fourteen, fifteen, seventeen, or as many more or less as they like, but to use the sixteen-petalled chrysanthemum as a badge is the exclusive prerogative of royalty.

Regal as the chrysanthemum is, both in appearance and as an emblem, it is yet held only second in general esteem. The cherry-blossoms easily surpass every other flower in popular favour. But the cherry-blossoms are Nature's work, whilst the chrysanthemum is a toy with which the Japanese gardener plays with as he wills—and play with it he does in

manner truly marvellous. He accomplishes veritable miracles. At the Temple show in London, or at any other horticultural display in Europe or America, you may see great shock-headed beauties as large in diameter as a dinner plate; but the Japanese master-gardener of to-day laughs at such easy triumphs. "Who would find any difficulty in producing such?" he asks. "You have but to carefully tend and feed a plant, and let it concentrate its whole productiveness into yielding one enormous blossom, and the thing is done." The Japanese gardener has long since passed the stage when such successes satisfied him. Instead of producing one towsled monster on a single stem, he will make that stem bear such a number of creditable blooms as, unless one has seen the result with one's own eyes, sounds utterly incredible. However, "seeing is believing," and when once I had the privilege of being conducted by Count Okuma to view his unrivalled display, I counted on one huge plant over *twelve hundred chrysanthemums growing from a single stem,* and few of the blossoms were less than four inches in diameter. The main stem was as thick as my thumb, and the branches of the plant were carefully trained on a light bamboo framework into the form of a cone, the bottom ring of which was eight feet in diameter and had about a hundred blossoms in it, whilst each higher ring decreased in size and the number of flowers it contained, until the apex was formed by a single bloom.

That was the most convincing proof I have ever seen of the mastery which the Japanese gardener attains. Such astonishing results as this are rare, however, even in Japan, as only those who have reached the highest pinnacle of skill can achieve them.

The great popular Chrysanthemum Festival of Tokyo is held at Dango-zaka; but it is less beautiful than curious, and is as much a Madame Tussaud's or an Eden Musée as a flower show. One does not go there only to see leviathan blooms, nor yet the result of efforts to produce hundreds of average-sized blossoms on a single stem. The show is a perfect fair of oddities.

The road up Dango hill is lined with booths and tents,
filled with composition-faced figures clothed from head to
foot in tiny chrysanthemums. The figures are life-size, and
made out of a network of cane. Concealed from view, behind
and within this framework, the plants are placed with roots
packed in damp earth, moss, and straw, and the flowers are
drawn carefully through the interstices to form a smooth and
even face on the front of the figure. The heads and hands are
made wonderfully life-like out of composition, but all else is
made with flowers. No leaves, or stems, or anything but
flowers are visible, and these continue to bloom for several
weeks under the care of the gardeners who water and trim
them as required.

Staged in this manner you may see famous scenes from
history and legend. Perhaps one booth may have a scene from
the tragedy of the Forty-seven Ronins; the *pièce de résistance*
in another may likely enough illustrate the finding of the Robe
of Feathers; or the great swordsmith Masamuné forging a
blade; or any one of a thousand well-known and oft-depicted
incidents such as appeal to everyone. Before these groups the
people stand riveted to the spot with admiration, and the
tents re-echo with many a "Naruhodo!" [1] from the slowly
passing crowd.

Then, again, celebrated landscapes are sometimes reproduced in miniature, the whole scene being worked out in tiny
chrysanthemums of many colours. As you leave each booth
a score of touters shout invitations to you to visit their shows,
and hold expectantly before your eyes printed sheets giving
an outline of the attractions to be seen within. One can see
half a dozen shows for a shilling, and a shilling's-worth of
Dango-zaka will last most people for a lifetime.

Behind the waxwork shows there are sheds where flowers
sent for exhibition and competition are displayed, and here
one can see overgrown prodigies looking very aristocratic and
dignified on their lonely stalks, or a happy family of a few
hundred blooms springing from a common stem.

[1] An expression of appreciation or wonder.

IN A LOTUS GARDEN

To see the greatest marvels of the Japanese horticulturist's art, however, you must seek the goodwill of some enthusiastic grower and be a guest at his November garden-party.

But the regal chrysanthemum does not hold the stage alone in the final tableaux of the year's floral pageants. There is yet another scene—the dying maple-leaves, which are thought by many to be the most beautiful sight that Japan has to show. They certainly share the honours of autumn with the Imperial flower, and are so beloved as to hold full floral rank. Japanese maples are a beautiful sight at any season of the year; they are always warm with colour, and even in spring-time form contrasts to the bright surrounding greens; but when the first breath of winter tints them deeper still the maple-trees are lovely as though decked with blossoms. The glen of the Takino-gawa, at Oji, in the northern suburbs, is a particularly gorgeous sight at this season. Almost every tree is a maple, and from the river to the bordering hill-tops the woods are resplendent with russet, red, and gold. Great paper-manufacturing mills, near by, disturb the stillness of the peaceful glen with their continuous roar, and stain the autumn skies with the smoke from their ugly chimneys. Such things are but some of the penalites of progress, and Japan has long since found that progress has its attendant evils.

There is still another flower, but though it unfolds its glory in the height of summer I have left it until the last, because, of all the flowers that the Japanese mostly love, it alone has no festival. It is the lotus—the flower whose physical and symbolic beauty inspired the title of this volume.

There is no gladsome fête for the lotus, for it is no flower of joy and frolic. The lotus is a food. Its roots and seeds are eaten in Japan. Besides, too, it has a deeper, allegorical meaning. It is a Buddhist emblem—the symbol of triumph over self; of extinction of the fires of passion; of abnegation and self-control. The delicate blooms are also the token for all that is best in man and woman; for, because the plant thrives best when growing in the foulest mud, and raises its great pink blossoms high above the poisonous slime below to open petals of surpassing beauty to the morning sun, they typify a chaste and noble heart—unstained, unsullied, and untouched by the insidious breath of evil with which life is permeated—opening to the light of truth and knowledge.

People are to be seen astir early in the garden where the lotus grows. They come to see the great blossoms, which close at eventide, unfold their petals to the rising sun. But few come to the garden of the lotus in festive mood. Most come to watch, and meditate in silence, and to pray; for the holy flower, beautiful as it is to the eye, brings often only memories of sorrow to the heart. Who that has not sounded something of the soul of this people can know anything of the pain that sometimes wrings the heart of the Japanese when visiting the garden of the sacred flower "that shrinks into itself at evening hour"? The subdued demeanour and sad faces of the early wanderers too often show that they are nursing grief within, and plainly tell of sorrowful memories recalled by the blooms; for the lotus is not only the token of truth, and light, and purity, but is also a symbol of that grim Reaper whose path is wet with tears. It is the Buddhist emblem of Death. For a few weeks only the flowers display their glory. Then the ponds become all unkempt, bedraggled, and forlorn with dying stalks and leaves. They are a sad, depressing spectacle in the midst of summer joys, and remind the thoughtful Japanese that beauty is but evanescent, and life but a passing dream.

CHAPTER IV

CONCERNING JAPANESE WOMEN

ONE of the most charming features about travel in Japan is that one cannot pass a day without being more or less under the gentle influence of woman.

In China or India one may travel for months and never have occasion to address anyone but a man, as the women do not enter into the foreigner's life at all. But in Japan it is different—and how much pleasanter! For woman is a great power in Japan, and her sphere is a large one. The home is woman's province; so is the inn. Little soft-voiced women fill your every wish and make you feel how indispensable they are to very existence from the time you enter a hostel in Japan to the time you leave it. Life at a Japanese inn has, to *bona fide* travellers who seek really to *know* the people of the land, a charm that at first they cannot define. Perhaps they do not try to. They know they find it fascinating, but they do not ask themselves why. Certainly it is not the degree of comfort that pleases, nor is the unsatisfying food particularly to their taste. Yet they find they prefer to live at native inns instead of "foreign-style" hotels. Why? If you ask yourself the question, the answer is easy. It is because you feel the gentle influence of woman the moment you enter a Japanese house. That is the charm. With all its beauty, Japan would not be the fascinating holiday-land it is were it not for the amiable little women who minister to your comfort and every need; whose faces are wreathed in perpetual smiles, and who cheerfully fly to do your bidding at any hour of the day or night, the moment you clap your hands to summon assistance.

Whatever woman's position may have been in the past,

and whatever it may even be to-day, outside the inn—I cannot say home, because I have had little experience of Japanese home-life, though I suspect it does not differ very much in this respect from life at an inn—there can be no two opinions about the part woman plays inside the household. She is an autocrat, and a clever one, for she rules even where she does not really pretend to rule; but she does it so tactfully that, whilst the husband holds the reins, he simply follows wherever she chooses to lead.

But woman is not only pre-eminent in the house; she is fast becoming a very important factor in the whole social and industrial system of the country, and whatever may have been the relative status of man and woman in Japan in days gone by, there is little doubt that another generation or two will see the sexes as much on an equal footing as they are in almost any other country, for women are proving themselves fully as competent as men in many occupations. One now sees female assistants in all the large Tokyo shops; female clerks in post-offices; female operators at telephone exchanges; female ticket-sellers at the railway stations; and, in a score of other occupations, women doing work formerly done only by men.

The Japanese girl is no longer content to remain a pretty chattel of the home. Her emancipation is progressing by leaps and bounds, and she now expects, and is allowed, such freedom as must rudely shock her grandmother when the old lady thinks of the days when she was in her teens. Healthy athletic exercises at school are fast changing the entire physique of the modern Japanese girl, and she is already bigger, and heavier, and longer-limbed than her mother. She demands fresh air and country rambles, and the habit of going un-attended to school has bred in her an independence that enables her to go out alone—which she does without fear of molestation.

From the standpoint of the older people this change is not altogether for the good, for she is losing some of that feminine charm which caused Lafcadio Hearn to describe her as "the sweetest type of woman the world has ever known." The submissiveness, which was one of the Japanese girl's principal attractions, is less noticeable in the present generation than the last—so I am told by Japanese friends, who look upon American notions of school training with pious horror. Modern progressive ideas, and the higher education, are encroaching more and more into the family circle, and undermining the Confucian foundations on which it has rested for centuries. The Japanese girl of to-morrow will perhaps consider herself as good as her brother, and may even not hesitate to match her opinions against his. But the time is far distant when Japanese women will clamour for votes, though it has come, and passed, full circle, when they were able to demonstrate to all the world that their services were almost as vital to the country in time of war as were those of the men.

Even though the Japanese girl grow less passive under the modern system of education, she is never likely to lose her place among the daintiest and most refined of her sex, for the inuring processes that have gained it for her will never be omitted from her training, no matter what new features are introduced.

The position which the Japanese wife occupies in the respect and affections of her husband is even to-day but little understood by foreigners, for so much misinformation has been disseminated about her that a wholly wrong impression is generally held of one who is among the most amiable of man's helpmates in the world. The Japanese home is perhaps the most difficult of any to gain intimate access to, yet almost every globe-trotter who dashes through Japan is a self-constituted authority on the Japanese woman, and most make the unpardonable mistake of classing the modest, retiring lady of the land—whom probably they never even see—with tea-house girls and the popular favourites of the capital and the Treaty Ports.

Even the humbler members of the Japanese feminine world—such as waitresses and hotel servants—have been too

often maligned, and represented to be what they never at
any time were, as their artless, unaffected ways are often
misunderstood by those who come from lands where customs
are so different, and who cannot speak the language. "Too
many foreigners, we fear," says Professor Chamberlain, "give
not only trouble and offence, but just cause for indignation
by their disrespect of propriety, especially in their behaviour
towards Japanese women, whose engaging manners and naive
ways they misinterpret. . . . The waitresses at any respectable
Japanese inn deserve the same respectful treatment as is
accorded to girls in a similar position at home."

No class of Japanese womanhood is more misunderstood
by foreigners than the geisha. Frail she may be, but the geisha
has no counterpart in Europe: she is a purely Japanese creation. The word geisha when mentioned to people unversed
in matters Japanese often causes side glances and suggestive
smiles. This is because she is too often, and quite wrong-
fully, confounded by globe-trotters with the inmates of the
Yoshiwara.

When European ladies wear Japanese clothes, or array
themselves as "Japanese geisha," they often make the most
glaring errors—wear elaborately embroidered kimonos, stick
many long pins in their hair, tie their sashes in front, and, in
short, make themselves resemble neither geisha nor ladies.
Japanese ladies *do not* wear embroidered kimonos; they never
wear a halo of long pins in their hair, nor do they tie their
sashes in front. Neither do geisha. These things are the
badges of the courtesan.

The geisha is an entertainer. She is trained from childhood
in the arts of music, dancing, singing, story-telling, conversation, and repartee. No Japanese dinner in native style is
ever given without attendant geisha. There is usually one
geisha at least to every guest. It is their function to see that
the guests are never for a moment dull; to ply the saké bottles
and watch the cups, lest at prescribed moments they should
be aught but full; and at appropriate intervals during the
meal to enliven the diners with music and dancing. Compared

with a high-class native "dinner" in Japan the orthodox European one must, to a Japanese, be the most boresome experience imaginable.

The geisha, too, is in great request for boating and picnic parties, and no company of merry-makers intent on a spree —such as the annual "opening" of the Sumida River at Tokyo, or a visit to the Gifu cormorant-fishing—would dream of going without the companionship of geisha. Whenever two or three jovial spirits are gathered together for an evening's fun at some tea-house, geisha are hired to furnish the music and to liven the occasion with their wit and songs.

Apart from the unique social place she fills, the geisha is simply a woman—neither stronger nor weaker than others of her sex the world over, exposed to the same temptations— and many have made brilliant marriages.

An author who has devoted a volume to the story of a *liaison* he formed with a Nagasaki *fille de joie* has done much to harm the Japanese woman in the eyes of the world. It is the exception to meet a tourist, Japan bound, who has read the book, who does not believe every Japanese girl to be a potential "Madame Chrysanthème." A more recent writer has done still more wrong to the good name of the Japanese woman by weaving a romance round the most sordid and degrading aspects of life in Japan—aspects which the Japanese are endeavouring to eradicate; aspects which no visitor to the country will ever see unless he search them out. There are muddy under-currents in the life of every country, and each traveller sees what he looks for. In Western lands vice walks undisguised; but not so in Japan! In Japan it must be sought for. Other writers have equally, though less seriously, mis-represented the Japanese woman in the "pidgin English" they have made her speak. She may speak broken English, but "pidgin English" *never*. She does not say "velly" for "very"; and for "like" she does not say "likee" but "rike." The Chinese replace "r" with "l" when speaking English, but not so the Japanese, for their syllabary has no sound "l," whereas "r" is one of the commonest sounds in the language.

Therefore they turn all our "l's" into "r's," until they have learnt to pronounce the unfamiliar sound.

Moreover, the Japanese girl does not suffix her English verbs with "ee." She does not say "talkee," "walkee," "thinkee," "speakee," etc. She never talks this "pidgin" jargon of the Chinese ports, but such English as she knows she speaks, perhaps brokenly, but very prettily. English is now compulsory in every school, and taught correctly; when, therefore, one reads this gibberish, as samples of a Japanese girl's conversation, one knows the writer has never seen Japan.

To those who really wish to *know* this dainty creature, the Japanese lady; who would learn of the whole order of her life, from the time she wears her swaddling clothes to the day she is wrapped in her shroud; who would see the pretty Japanese child grow into happy girlhood, and the happy girl gradually develop into budding womanhood; who would see this sweet woman grow sweeter still as she becomes a mother; who would see this gentle mother rear her family, and each day be more honoured and respected until she attains the height of her fondest ambition and power as a grand-mother; to those who would, in fact, follow the Japanese woman from the cradle to the grave, I would say read Miss A. M. Bacon's book, *Japanese Girls and Women*, for in the pages of that delightful volume you will find so charming an account of family life in the Land of the Rising Sun that, when you have read it, you will know the Japanese lady *far* more intimately than you would be ever likely to by travelling in the land.

Miss Bacon's opportunity was unique, and fortunately she was more than competent to embrace it to the full. Her book is a classic; for a similar chance can never come to any one again. Japan is rapidly changing, and the Japanese girl of to-morrow will be quite a different creature from the Japanese girl Miss Bacon wrote of yesterday.

The traveller to far Japan must not expect to find home life there an open book. A Japanese visiting Europe, furnished with good letters of introduction, would be welcomed with

A MAID OF FAIR JAPAN

open-hearted hospitality into the family circle of his newly-found acquaintance; and every member of the household would do his or her best to contribute to the enjoyment of the guest. After a round of such visits the traveller from the East would be well qualified, on his return home, to write about the home life of the English lady.

But how different is the case of the European bearing letters to the Japanese! The very most he can expect is to be invited to some club; perhaps a Japanese dinner, with its accompaniment of geisha-dancing, may be arranged in his honour at the Maple Club; or in some exceptional cases he may be invited to see the house and gardens of his host. In still more exceptional instances he may be presented to the wife and daughters; but he will *never* be invited to stay at his host's house, and, for the time being, become, as it were, a member of the family. How, then, can the passing globe-trotter ever hope to see the Japanese lady in her true perspective, when foreign residents, who have passed their lives in Japan, admit that even they have only formed their estimate by a series of fortunate glimpses, few and far between?

It is the exception to meet a foreign resident who seems to have any desire to cultivate an intimate knowledge either of the country or the people. I have met many who have lived years in the land who could not express their simplest wants in Japanese. On the other hand the most interesting foreign residents I met were those who loved the land and liked the people; who talked the language and understood the meaning of all they saw.

Owing to the nature of the mission that took me on one of my journeys to Japan—as a correspondent during the war with Russia—I had the honour of meeting several Japanese ladies of the highest social rank in their own homes, and the good fortune to see certain phases of the character of the women of Japan, which the Western world hitherto had not known they possessed. For what I then saw I shall honour the Japanese woman always, for she stood revealed to me in all those qualities that men mostly esteem in the opposite sex. She was sagacious, strong, and self-reliant, yet gentle, compassionate, and sweet—a ministering angel of forgiveness, tenderness, and mercy.

I cannot, in the limits of this essay, give more than a few vignettes of this most feminine of women; but I hope to show that she is something more than a "pretty butterfly," [1] as she is generally thought to be by those who do not know her. When duty calls, there is no woman in the world who obeys more readily and capably; and the best of Japanese manhood respects her as truly as any other woman in the world is respected, even though he loves her less demonstratively. Close observation, during three years of travel in this land, has clearly shown me, too, that the women of the Japanese peasant and poorer classes are accorded such courtesy from the opposite sex as is quite undreamt of by women of the corresponding classes in Europe.

Would that one could speak as warmly of *all* Japanese men as of their mothers, wives, and daughters! My own experience, however, but corroborates that of my friend Chamberlain. Writing of Japanese women, he says: "How many times have we not heard European ladies go into ecstasies over them, and marvel how they could ever be of the same race as the men! And closer acquaintance does but confirm such views."

I witnessed many sad scenes in Japan, during the war with Russia. Many a time I saw a soldier bidding his last good-byes to wife and mother before embarking for the war; but I seldom saw any tears. Often there were even smiles, for in Japan the smile is a mask which hides the agony of the heart. The women exhibited a front so firm and unquailing as it seemed well-nigh impossible such gentle little creatures could show. And there were no caresses at parting, but many and many a bow, and sweet, oft-repeated "Sayonara." And as, the

[1] There is nothing the Japanese girl, or woman, resents more than to be compared to a butterfly. The cho-cho does not appear to Japanese as we see it—a beautiful summer insect—but as a fickle, restless creature that is ever flitting about from flower to flower, never content to stay anywhere long. The butterfly is, therefore, an emblem of inconstancy, and a Japanese girl is indignant at being compared to one.

farewell over, the little wife and mother turned back to her husbandless home, if nobody cared to know of the fear she nursed in her bosom, certainly nobody would ever divine it from any betrayal in her features; for her face, like that of her husband, who smilingly went forth, perhaps to die, was a mask: a disguise born of blood trained for centuries in the mastery of the feelings.

I saw tears sometimes, however, for not every Japanese woman is a Spartan, and the poorer people cannot always restrain their feelings as do those of better blood; but I did not often see such human emotion shown.

The self-control of the Japanese women, when troops were leaving for the Front, was misunderstood by many foreigners. They were called cold, and lacking in sympathy, and indifferent; but this was far, far from the truth, for they are full of such feminine instincts as sympathy and fellow-feeling. On such occasions as a husband going to the war it is almost a point of honour to control oneself; but I have *often* seen an act of kindness bring tears to Japanese eyes, and I have seen a whole theatre-full of people—women and children, and men too—sniffling and sobbing audibly as a touching tragedy was being played. The Japanese are an exceedingly emotional people.

The Japanese smile, too, which is so often belied by the heart, takes long to understand; but when one knows what it often means, one's heart is sometimes wrung to see it.

A Japanese friend with whom I travelled for many weeks frequently spoke to me of his sister, to whom he was deeply attached. He showed me her picture—she was a pretty girl, just turned eighteen—and he told me much of the happy days he and she had spent together. Her parents had taken her to Dzushi, a seaside resort for consumptives, for the dread scourge of Japan had settled on this young life. One day when we arrived in Kyoto, after a long tour in the country, a letter was placed in his hands as we entered our hotel. He tore it open and read it, and then turning to me, remarked, with a broad smile that I shall never forget, "Ha, ha, my sister is dead already!"

D

As his features assumed the ghastly mask, and he uttered the cold-blooded words, a chill of repulsion swept over me; but it quickly changed to sympathy, for, though there was not a quiver of an eyelash, I knew that the smile was a lie, and that his heart was filled with sorrow at the unexpected blow. He went at once to his room, and I saw him no more that day, for I respected his evident desire to be alone ; but friendship warmed towards him, as I knew that the tears he refused to show in public were shed for many bitter hours in the solitude of his chamber.

Desiring to observe the working of the Japanese Red Cross organisation during the war with Russia, I secured permission from the War Department to visit the Reserve Hospitals at Hiroshima.

Hiroshima, capital of the province of Aki, a beautifully-situated town near the mouth of the Ota River, which flows into the Inland Sea, ranks as the seventh city of the Japanese Empire.

From the standpoint of its relation to the war with Russia, Hiroshima stood in importance second only to Tokyo; it was practically the rear of the Army as far as the wounded were concerned, for they were sent back there from the Front in a week, with their first-aid bandages on.

When I arrived at this place I began to realise something of the real horrors of war, and the true nature of the terrible task on which Japan was engaged. In the time that I spent in the hospitals I learnt, too, more than I could otherwise have learnt in a lifetime about Japanese women; for I saw there what a noble part they played in the greatest crisis in the history of the nation.

For nearly three weeks I spent the greater part of each day in the various divisions of the hospital, where over twenty thousand wounded soldiers were being cared for; and having, later, spent a week in the Russian prisoners' hospitals at Matsuyama, I can truly say that, to friend and foe alike, the Japanese nurses were angels of mercy. Their tender solicitude; their quiet ways as they moved quickly, yet like phantoms,

GEISHA

about the wards; their readiness and willingness to obey instantly the calls of their charges; their untiring energy and devotion; their patience and earnestness; their courtesy to their patients, and their gentleness in washing and bandaging them—all showed that these Japanese ladies, who had responded so nobly and whole-heartedly to the call of duty and humanity, were as instinct with all the finest virtues of their sex as any women in the world.

I saw many pathetic scenes during those weeks at Hiroshima; but I think the incident that touched me deepest was when the pupils of a primary school for little Japanese girls visited the principal wards. There were perhaps fifty in all, in the care of their lady teachers, and as they tripped silently, in their soft white socks, into the ward where I was sitting by the bed of one of my wounded friends, they all courteously bowed several times to the patients on one side, then several times to the patients on the other. Every soldier who could returned the courtesy, and those who could neither sit nor stand inclined their heads or raised their hands to the salute.

The principal lady teacher, in sweet, gentle tones, then quietly addressed the men, telling them how great was the honour that she and her pupils felt to have the privilege of visiting so many gallant soldiers who had helped to gain a glorious victory for Japan. Here the fifty little heads all bowed in mute approval of their teacher's words; and she went on to say that she hoped every soldier would soon be well, and perhaps able to fight again, but that those who had been too severely wounded to return to the Front would always be honoured for the part that they had played in the war. The childish heads were ducked, with one accord, again.

Turning to the little girls, who now all stood meekly, with downcast eyes, the teacher then addressed her charges, reciting briefly the story of the great battle in which these brave fellows had fought, and how it was won, and how bravely they had done their duty. She continued that it would be a proud moment for their parents when these, their sons, returned to their homes, bearing the honourable scars of war. No woman could have a higher ambition than to be the mother of sons to fight for Japan, and she hoped that when these little girls grew up, and had sons of their own, they would teach them to be as brave and loyal subjects of the Emperor as the soldiers now lying maimed before them. The tiny lassies here all bowed again in silent resolution, and then, with several parting bows to right and left, they proceeded to another ward.

To me the incident was a stirring object-lesson of how Japan loses no opportunities of educating her children. Those little girls would remember all their lives what they saw that day; and the words of their school-mistress, I have no doubt, sank deep into each of those childish souls. As years pass by, and those little girls become mothers, the exhortation of that soft-voiced teacher, made under such impressive circumstances, will sound again in their ears; and sons of Japan, as yet unborn, will grow up to be better and braver men because of words their mothers listened to when they were little more than babies themselves.

At Matsuyama the wounded Russians were loud in the praises of their gentle Japanese nurses. The looks with which the fallen followed every movement of their little guardians told a simple tale, and more than one gallant fellow left his bed pierced by an arrow that wounded him deeper than the bullet which had laid him low.

Never in history did foeman have a kinder and more generous adversary than did Russia in that struggle, and never did women of any land play a nobler and more tender part than did the women of Japan.

It must not be thought that because Hiroshima was a hospital town it was necessarily a doleful place. Like most garrison towns, it was gay. Indeed it was the gayest of the gay. My hotel bordered on the river—one of the five streams that form the delta of the Ota-gawa. On either side of it were other hotels, restaurants, and tea-houses; and on the opposite bank of the river similar conditions obtained. These places were all crowded, according to their class, with military officers or soldiers, billeted there for a day or two prior to their departure for the Front.

As soon as night settled on the waters, the sound of the samisen rang out from every house beside the moonlit river. As surely, too, as the light on the paper shoji changed from that of day without to that of lamps within, the plaintive cadence of the geisha's song wailed out on the evening air.

Night after night I listened to her songs of revelry, of love, and of despair. There was something weirdly pathetic about her often sorrowful lay—for the geisha is at her best when singing of some stirring incident that lives for ever in history.

One night, as a singularly beautiful voice broke on the night air, the samisens and other sounds were silenced, one by one, till naught but that one woman's voice could be heard. Every window within earshot was thrown open, and every reveller on each side of the river crowded to the balconies to listen, for the singer was one of the most famous in Japan, and the song she sang was the Ballad of Dan-no-ura.[1]

Inspired by the impressive silence, impelled by her art, she sang with magic power the terrible story. In accents wondrously moving she told of Tokiwa's pleading for her mother and her children, and in piteous tones of the dishonour of the famous beauty. Then in tragic crescendo she sang of Yoritomo's lust of vengeance for his mother's ruin; and in a frenzy of passion of the great Minamoto leader's resolve to stamp the Taira clan from off the earth. She sang of how the tide of battle waged, first this way, then that, in the great historic conflict, till it ended in the extermination of the rival clan—even to the slaughter of women and children—and over the sadness of the final lines of suffering and death her voice grew infinitely tender, and culminated in an outburst of passionate sobs. I have never heard anything more stirring than that geisha's wonderful song.

On the balcony, listening beside me, there were several Japanese officers, and tears were coursing down their cheeks,

[1] See page 57.

for even Japanese soldiers can easily be moved to emotion by histrionic art, and the story is the most famous and bloody in Japanese annals—one that will live in the hearts of the people when the war with Russia is forgotten.

As the voice of the singer ceased, only her sobs for some moments broke the silence; then from every balcony and window on both sides of the river there burst forth a storm of applause and loud shouts of approbation.

At Hiroshima it was always this dainty creature, the geisha, who made merry the last evenings of the officers ere they went forth to the war; and she was always the last to cheer them on their way, pledging them, in tiny sips of saké, health, victory, and a safe return. Truly it is almost as hard to imagine how Japan could survive without the geisha as without the army itself.

That the sterling qualities of the Japanese women were appreciated by the officers of the Army I had daily evidence during the time that I was attached to the First Division in Manchuria. One of the first questions asked me by every officer whose acquaintance I made was, "What do you think of the Japanese women?" and the following incidents serve to show something of the regard in which they were held by the leaders.

On one occasion, at Mukden, when I went to pay my respects to the Commander-in-Chief, Marquis Oyama, and to General Baron Kōdama, I met the latter outside his head-quarters—a Mandarin's yamen.[1] Kōdama was a handsome man, rather American than Japanese in appearance, with a deeply-bronzed face and dark-brown eyes which sparkled with the love of fun. He was the most celebrated wit in Japan, and even during the heat of battle his jokes, I was told, never ceased. I had previously met him at Tokyo—the day before the departure of the General Staff for the Front. I was in his drawing-room, when General Baron Terauchi, the Minister of War, called, with several other exalted officers. Instead of the conversation being of a serious turn (seeing that such moment-

[1] The mansion of a Chinese official.

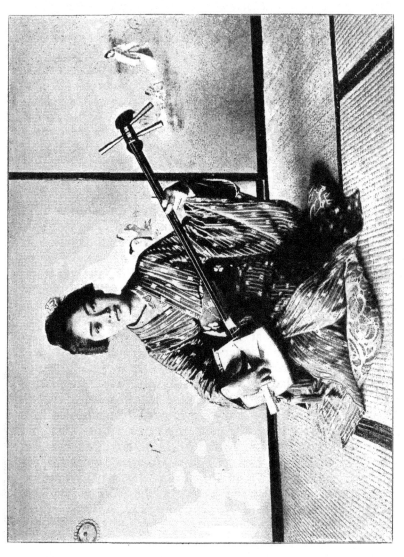

A GEISHA PLAYING THE SAMISEN

ous events were portending), it was, on the contrary, of the most jovial nature, and the impression I shall always have of General Kōdama on that occasion was seeing him leaning back in his chair, convulsed with laughter at the fit of the War Minister's riding-breeches.

When I met him in Mukden he at once invited me to enter his house, and holding aside a bamboo portière that hung in the doorway, and pointing ahead, said, "There! what do you think of that?" in Japanese. I looked, and saw a large kakemono [1] of a Japanese girl, painted in modern style and nearly life-size. I congratulated him on being such a connoisseur of feminine charms, whereupon he laughed merrily, saying, "You see I'm not very lonely here with such a lovely girl to look at. *Beppin-San des, ne?*" ("Isn't she a beauty?") Then he laughed again more merrily than ever.

I found his apartments luxuriously furnished in Chinese style. What, however, most attracted my attention was a tall, slender Chinese table of blackwood—perhaps ten inches square and three feet high—on which stood the most beautiful doll I have ever seen. The figure was about twelve inches tall, and marvellously life-like. It was dressed in a mauve silk kimono, with a rich gold-brocade obi; and every detail of a Japanese lady's toilet was carefully worked out, even to a tiny jewelled obi-domi [2] and the pin in her hair. It was, in fact, a perfect miniature of a Japanese lady, and a work of high art. "She is my mascot," said this great General, who was known as the "Brain of the Japanese Army." "She is my mascot, and goes with me wherever I go. She has brought me much good luck." Such was General Kōdama's tribute to the women of his land.

A few days after this incident I was sitting next to General Kurōki—Commander of the First Division—at a General Staff dinner at the Front. General Kurōki is one of the samurai

---

[1] Picture that rolls up like a scroll.

[2] A small clasp, attached to a narrow silken band, that holds the obi, or sash, tightly in place.

of the old days—the knights of feudal Japan—and the following
episode will show something of the mould in which his gallant
soul is cast.

He spoke no English, but conversation was made through
the medium of that lightning interpreter, Captain Okada, who
translated each sentence the moment it was spoken.

Having a fair working smattering of Japanese, I mustered
up courage, after a glass or two of wine, to address the General
in his native tongue. I was equal to the following simple
sentence, and voiced it: "Anata sama wa Eikoku no kotoba
hanashimasen ka?" which means, "Does not your honourable
self speak English?" It was simply a plain, unpolished speech,
but the effect on General Kurōki was electrical. Turning to
me with sparkling eyes and raised eyebrows, he replied,
"Eikoku no kotoba hanashimasen; anata wa Nihon no kotoba
yoku wakarimas, so ja arimasen ka?" ("I do not speak English;
you understand Japanese well; is it not so?")

I replied that I only knew very little indeed, and then asked
General Kurōki what part of the country he came from.
He replied, "Satsuma."

I told him I had read that Satsuma had always been a
famous province for producing fighting men, and cited the
names of several.

"You have studied Japanese history, then?" he asked.

"Yes, a little, and I have found it exceedingly interesting,
and not unlike our own. Your feudal days are fifty years old,
whereas ours are five hundred; that is the principal difference,"
I replied.

From this we got on to various phases of Japanese history,
and I mentioned the bombardment of the Kagoshima forts
by the British under Admiral Kuper, in 1862.[1] Captain Okada
had stepped in as interpreter, never hesitating for a word, as
the conversation had got beyond my linguistic powers after
the few sentences which had served to start it.

The old General's face became a study, and his eyes a
blaze of light, as he replied, "Yes, I was there, I was there

[1] See page 7.

at the time! I was a boy of eighteen, and helped to serve one of our guns!"

So excited did he become as he began to tell me of this affair, and warmed up to it, that he made a plan on the table —using glasses and plates, and anything that was handy, to mark the positions of the various forts—whilst the staff officers crowded round to see. A large ornamental vase on the table was the island, Sakura-jima, and a number of wine-glasses were used to show the position of Admiral Kuper's ships.

He told me, what I had already read, that a fierce hurricane raged throughout the day, and that some of the ships had to cut their cables and put to sea; that the captain and sixty members of the crew were slain on the flagship, and that although the squadron succeeded in setting fire to the town and dismantling the forts, they departed much the worse from the effects of the Japanese guns and the ravages of the storm.

After a long pause the old General continued: "Those were dark days for Japan—when all the land was rent with strife; when we were yet in ignorance of what would be the outcome of it all; when we seemed beset with enemies, and England was the most terrible of all. How different it all is now! How different it all is now! England is our warmest friend, and has taught us most of what has brought us success. How could we ever foresee at that time that the trials through which we were passing were but the fire heating the steel which the events of later years have tempered?"

It was one of the most interesting hours of my life when that old Satsuma samurai stepped out from the pages of Japanese feudal history, and, with eyes sparkling, and hands illustrating on the table, told me of that day which marks one of the deepest of England's injustices, and the darkest stain on her early dealings with Japan. The staff officers were as interested as I in the General's story, and when he had finished, the impressive silence showed how deeply all were stirred.

Immediately afterwards we were engaged in a discussion

on the praiseworthy qualities of the Japanese soldier—his indifference to hardship, his endurance and bravery, and what he had accomplished.

General Kurōki after a time spoke thus: "When we speak of the achievements of the Japanese soldier, we must not forget that it is not the men of Japan who are solely responsible for these deeds. If our men had not been trained by their mothers in the ethics of Bushido—that everything must be sacrificed on the altar of duty and honour—they could not have done what they have done. The Japanese women are very gentle and very quiet and unassuming—we hope they may never change—but they are very brave, and the courage of our soldiers is largely due to the training they received, as little children, from their mothers. The women of a land play a great part in its history, and no nation can ever become really great unless its women are before all things courageous, yet gentle and modest. Japan owes as much to her women as to her soldiers."

When General Fujii, the Chief of Staff, proudly added to the words of General Kurōki, "Let us drink to the Japanese women, for I think they are the best in all the world," I remembered again the words of the immortal Lafcadio Hearn, and I knew that no one who had seen what the women of Japan really were, could affirm that any women were truer to their duty in any land on earth.

BY THE KARAKAMI

CHAPTER V

THE HOUSE AND THE CHILDREN

ABOUT the tatami and hibachi of a Japanese household an entire volume might be written, for on and around these important essentials of the home revolves the whole domestic life of the nation. The tatami are the mats which cover the floors of Japanese houses, and the hibachi is a brazier for burning charcoal in—the fireplace of Japan.

The Japanese spends the greater part of his life on tatami. He is born on them, walks on them, sits on them, eats on them, sleeps on them, and dies on them. They are at once the floor, the table, the chairs, and the bedstead of Japan, and as such are deserving of more than passing notice, for they reflect much of the character of the people with whose life they come into such close daily contact.

Tatami are of many qualities, but of only one size—six feet by three. The area of a room is therefore always estimated by the number of mats required to cover the floor: thus an apartment measuring fifteen feet by twelve will hold ten mats, and is called a "ten-mat room." Any Japanese hearing it described thus, knows its size, because, whatever be the arrangement of the mats, the floor will be covered by ten of them. Rooms are sometimes so small as to have but three mats, or even two, whilst a little chamber of four mats is quite common. Tatami are two inches thick, made of rice-straw, tightly pressed and sewn, with rectangular corners and edges, and covered with closely-woven white matting made from rushes. The six-feet sides are bound with broad tape—usually black, but sometimes white—which laps over on to the surface, forming a border one inch wide. Coloured matting, such as is exported to America and Europe, is not used in Japan.

The floors of any well-kept Japanese household present

45

a scrupulously neat and clean appearance, and thus they are a faithful mirror of the people who live on them. They are also yielding and noiseless, especially as Japanese people never wear boots in their houses. Boots are cast off at the threshold on entering the house, and slippers are left on the polished wooden floor of the passage outside the room. You can always tell by the number of pairs of boots, or sandals, on a doorstep how many visitors are at a house, or by the slippers outside a room how many people are within it.

In the best households the mats are re-covered twice a year, so that they are always fresh and white, with even a tinge of green in them; or the covering may be turned, as both sides are alike, after six months' use, and renewed completely at the end of the year. The matting becomes yellow with age, and in poor households it is used until worn out. No household, however, is so poor that it cannot afford tatami of some sort, though the tape binding is sometimes dispensed with. The arrangement of the mats is altered occasionally, and the appearance of a room can be completely changed by a fresh grouping of the straight black lines.

A ten-mat room is a very convenient and even large-sized apartment in middle-class houses; but in the houses of the wealthy and the nobility rooms double this size are quite common, whilst rooms for entertaining a number of guests may have as many as fifty mats or more. At a Japanese inn at which I stayed in Gifu I was shown to an immense apartment, the floor of which took no less than seventy-eight mats to cover it, but my selection fell upon a chamber of more modest dimensions.

If an apartment be found too small for the use for which it is required, the sliding doors (fusuma, or karakami), dividing it from the next apartment, can be quickly removed, and thus two rooms are thrown into one. If the house be a large one, a number of rooms can be opened up *en suite* in this manner, should a large hall be required for entertaining purposes. The karakami, which are often adorned with paintings of landscapes or figures, do not reach the ceiling of the room. They are six feet high, and above them there are usually a few panels of open wood-carving, which serve as a ventilator. These are called ramma. The sides of the room facing the passage-way and open air are filled with sliding screens, covered with rice paper. These are the shoji, and they admit a soft, diffused light into the room. Wooden shutters, called amado, protect the shoji at night-time or in wet weather.

The principal part of a Japanese room is the tokonoma, a raised recess at one side, usually made out of beautifully grained woods. There the single kakemono (picture which rolls up like a scroll), which the room contains, is displayed, with invariably some object of art beneath it, such as a bronze or porcelain flower-vase, a piece of carving, a dwarf tree in a handsome pot, or a curious stone in a dish.

The furnishings of a Japanese room are of the simplest. They consist of a hibachi, and a cushion or two to sit on. There are no tables, or chairs, or any of those aids to comfort that help to make life bearable elsewhere. The tatami do duty for all these things. Conspicuous, therefore, in all this emptiness is the hibachi, and there is much of interest about it.

Hibachi are of many kinds. Sometimes it is a curious stump; or gnarled excrescence of a tree; or a piece of wood of beautiful grain; or it may be of stone, or earthenware, or porcelain. More frequently it is of brass or bronze, often exquisitely carved. Its shape varies almost as much as its composition. It may be round, or square, or oblong; or it may be polygonal in design. Sometimes the hibachi is built into a small chest, a foot high, in one end of which there is a set of drawers, the top of which serves for a table. This kind is, however, only seen in the general domestic living-room of a house or inn, and never in the guest-chambers or private rooms.

The hibachi is filled to within a few inches of the brim with ash, which should be carefully heaped up into a truncated cone, the top of which is hollowed a little. Into this depression a few embers of glowing charcoal are placed. That, in a nut-shell, is the *modus operandi* of the hibachi; but about the management of the charcoal and the ash, and the etiquette of the hibachi in general, much of interest may be said.

For instance, in the best households the ash may be covered with several inches of calcined oyster-shell, called kaki-bai, which is a powder, white as driven snow; no common fuel is burnt in it, but cherry-wood charcoal is used—so cleverly charred that even the grain of the bark is intact. Each block is about two inches long, and in diameter according to the size of the branch. It is sawed neatly and without any breaks. Two or three of these little blocks, heated to a glow in the kitchen fire, are carefully buried in the little crater, with the top of one block just showing. These will burn without attention from dawn till dark. The better the ash is heaped up round the charcoal the longer will the latter burn, but if it be desired to increase the heat, with consequent rapidity of consumption of the charcoal, a depression must be formed in the lip of the crater to allow air to enter at the bottom of the fire, and thus form a draught. Not only must the ash be evenly graded into a cone, but there is a little serrated-edged brass scraper used for this purpose. This has the effect of leaving the slopes of the miniature volcano seamed with shallow furrows which converge towards the summit.

The charcoal is managed with a pair of brass or bronze tongs, called hibashi, often as delicately wrought as the brazier itself. These are manipulated by the fingers of the right hand in the same manner as chop-sticks. At inns the common grade of charcoal usually supplied requires much attention, as the cheaper the charcoal the more rapidly it is consumed. Moreover, at inns one never sees anything so expensive as oyster-shell ash, though I have occasionally seen burnt lime used as a substitute.

It is a great breach of etiquette to throw cigarette ends or anything into the hibachi which will make it smoke. A small receptacle is always provided in the tabaco-bon[1] for this

---

[1] A small wooden tray containing a tiny hibachi for lighting pipes and cigarettes at, and a small section of bamboo, called hai-fuki, for the reception of expectorations and stumps of cigarettes.

WRITING A LETTER

purpose. At inns, however, no such niceties are observed, and after a meeting of several friends the hibachi usually bristles with cigarette ends sticking in the ash. When the party has dispersed the neisan removes these, and each morning, before renewing the charcoal, she carefully sifts the ash through a wire sieve to separate all lumps left from the previous day, and any foreign substance that may be in it.

At high-class Japanese inns the guest-room to which I have been shown has sometimes been of such immaculate cleanliness that I have stood on the threshold hesitating to enter it, for to tread such snowy mats with foreign socks instead of soft white tabi seemed almost like sacrilege. The karakami would be adorned with frescoes; the ceiling made of beauti-fully-figured, unpolished wood, and the whole apartment illumined by a flood of soft, mellow light that came through the paper shoji.

There is no prettier or more characteristic picture of Japan than such a room, with gleaming black-bordered tatami and a fine old hibachi, at which a Japanese lady is sitting. Perhaps the fire has become disarranged or burnt low; so with finished grace she takes the hibashi between her taper fingers, deftly clips the pieces of charcoal and piles them into a tiny pyramid. Around this she draws the ash with the scraper until she has made a miniature Fuji-san. She does not do this from a superstitious belief that the nearer she approaches in her arrangement of the fire to the shape of the sacred mountain the better it will burn—as I remember once reading in some globe-trotter's book—but because she knows the draught is better so; and still further to aid combustion she burrows a little hole below the lip of the tiny crater to admit the air. When my dainty lady has completed this to her satisfaction, she rests her pretty wrists against the edge of the brazier, and holds her palms outstretched to warm them.

The hibachi has several important appendages, chief of which is the kettle used to heat the water for tea. These kettles are of every conceivable shape and design, and of such beauty that the collector burns with desire to add each fresh specimen he sees to his household gods. They are made of silver, bronze, brass, shakudo, shibuichi, and iron; but of them all the iron ones are the most fascinating. They are very thick and heavy, often weighing four or five pounds—the philosophy of this being that thick metal cools slowly. Some are round, some square, some squat, and some tall, some are plain and some are carved—and in the carving every whim known to the Japanese artist is to be found. There are dragons, flowers, landscapes, seascapes, gods, goddesses, animals, legends, historical incidents, and geometrical designs depicted on them. One never sees two alike. These kettles are called tetsu-bin, meaning "iron-bottle."

The tetsu-bin is placed over the hibachi fire on a little contrivance consisting of a circular hoop of iron, which lies buried in the ash. From this three little iron uprights spring, when required, to support the kettle. This device is called the san-toku, or "three virtues"—the virtues desired being that the fire may burn slow, clear, and hot. Sometimes a wire screen is placed on the san-toku, on which small cakes can be toasted. This is called the ami, or net; and in the case of the special screen, on which the glutinous rice-bread, or mochi, is baked, it is called mochi-ami.

Around the hibachi circulates not only the domestic but also the social life of Japan. All warm themselves at it; tea is brewed by means of it; guests are entertained, chess played, and politics discussed beside it; secrets are told across it, and love is made over it. The hibachi, in fact, is accessory to so much of the thought and sentiment of this land that it is easily the most characteristic object of Japan.

It is quite astonishing how quickly a cold room can be warmed by a hibachi well supplied with charcoal. The reason is that a charcoal fire gives out great heat, none of which is wasted—all the warmth generated by the fire being diffused into the room. There is no danger whatever of asphyxiation when the better grades of charcoal are burnt; only the cheapest kind gives off any poisonous fumes. The hibachi, however, is not left in the room at night, for any

BEDTIME IN JAPAN.

carbonic-acid fumes that may be freed naturally sink to
the floor, and Japanese people sleep but a few inches above
the mats. It is therefore removed and a small tabaco-bon
substituted for it. The tabaco-bon is a *sine qua non*, for the
tiny brazier that it contains holds a choice piece of cherry-wood
charcoal which glows all night. Whenever a Japanese awakes,
he or she must have a whiff or two from a pipe, as a solace,
before sleep comes again; the tabaco-bon is therefore placed
close by the bedside.

Beds are made of thick padded quilts, called futons, spread
on the floor. There may be one or several of them, and another
is used as a covering. These futons are very warm—and very
much esteemed as safe and comfortable retreats by Japanese
fleas, which are the most robust and energetic of their kind.

The makura, or pillow, used by men is a small round and
rather hard bolster. This makura is very difficult for a foreigner
to manage. Though I have spent many months at Japanese
inns, I have never mastered the knack of keeping it from
rolling off the futon and letting my head down with a bump.
Invariably I had to put my large camera-case at the head of
the bed to keep it in place—much to the amusement of every
neisan who saw it there.

Women sleep on quite a different pillow. They use a little
lacquered stand with a soft pad on top which just fits the neck.
The head does not come into contact with this device at all.
It projects over it, so that the elaborate coiffure is not disarranged. In the base of this pillow-stand there is a tiny drawer
for the reception of hair-pins and other such little feminine
requisites.

"A delicate affair is beautiful hair" in most lands, but in
Japan it is a very serious matter. The dressing of a lady's
tresses may take an hour or two, and can only be done by a
professional kami-yui, or *coiffeuse*, who visits the house for
this purpose. When, therefore, the hair has been arranged,
it is carefully kept in order for several days, with merely a
little prinking up each morning. If, however, the hair be worn
in the pretty foreign-style modified pompadour, now affected

E

by many Japanese girls, the services of the *coiffeuse* are, of course, not required.

Enormous spiders, called kumo, haunt Japanese houses. Their bodies are as large as a filbert, and the legs fully four inches from tip to tip. They are quite harmless, but have a distinctly unpleasant look as they walk across the walls. One of the most "Japanesey" pictures I ever saw was a pair of tiny youngsters, with arms round each other's necks, standing in the passage-way watching the peregrinations of a kumo which was creeping on the other side of the semi-translucent shoji, its body throwing a deep black shadow on the paper from the light of a lamp burning in the room. Rats are a great nuisance in Japanese houses, because of the noise they make as they scamper over the thin resounding boards comprising the ceiling. But though I have often been disturbed by them, I have never seen one in any native inn.

Walls have ears in Japanese rooms, and even a *sotto voce* conversation held in an adjoining chamber can be heard. Not only have they ears, but they have eyes as well, and it is not an unknown occurrence for a bright feminine one to be seen peeping through a hole in the paper shoji. Occasionally you may detect a finger in the act of making such a hole, or enlarging one already made. The paper is fixed to the framework so tightly that when a finger is poked through it, it makes a very audible "pop"; so to obviate this the tip of the finger is moistened, and a slight twisting motion enables the hole to be bored quite noiselessly. More than once I have caught the offending finger as it entered, and always found the owner to be some laughing, mischievous maid. Once when I was staying at an inn in a country district I noticed a peculiar noise at night as I lay in bed, but put it down to mice. A suspicion, however, crossed my mind that it was something larger when I distinctly heard a whisper, so, jumping out of the futons, I threw open the shoji—to see three pairs of white-socked feet flying down the corridor as fast as they could go, whilst shouts of laughter filled the narrow passage from the merry little neisans who owned them.

THE PICTURE-BOOK

The frailty of Japanese houses necessitates the children being brought up from infancy to be careful; but Japanese children seem instinctively to respect such delicate things as paper walls and windows. Seeing the gentleness and care of their elders, they grow up to be solicitous of everything, and the most delicate things may be left about without fear of being harmed.

During festival occasions I have seen thousands of paper lanterns hung from frail bamboo poles along streets which were filled with vast crowds of merry-makers. Yet these delicate things were never harmed. This alone speaks volumes for the gentleness of the people and their bringing up; those who can be so heedful for other people's belongings may well be trusted to take good care of their own. Yet this daintiness and frailness of their surroundings does not make the people mawkish or effeminate, as recent history has clearly shown. The national love and daily use of dainty and beautiful things tends to make a people high-spirited and refined of nature, and such qualities will carry a nation further than mere brute courage and animal strength.

When I was staying at a hotel in Kumamoto, in Southern Japan, a Japanese banker and his family had the adjoining rooms to mine. The family consisted of two little girls, aged seven and nine respectively. We soon made friends with each other, and every day the pair came to visit me in my room. In everything they did those two little girls were the model of well-bred courtesy and elegance, and self-consciousness or shyness was unknown to them, though they were full of sweet childish modesty. They taught me their games and I taught them new ones, and at every visit they asked to see my photographs of Japan. These they would examine as they sat on the tatami, laying each picture, as it was done with, aside with care. And when their mother called them, these two delightful little creatures would bow their heads to the mats, as they voiced the prettiest thanks, and with a happy "sayonara" instantly run to obey the mother's bidding, never waiting for a second summons.

But not all Japanese children are as attractive and winning as are those of the middle and upper classes. The children of the peasantry are often more repelling than engaging, as too often they have the dribbliest of noses and other unattractive distinctions. A great percentage of them suffer from a skin affection which covers their shaven heads with a mass of scabs. No attempt is made to cure the ailment, as to let it run its course is said to ensure stamina and vigour later on in life. The infection is possibly conveyed from poll to poll by means of unclean barbers' brushes, but Miss Bacon [1] offers the explanation that it is due to the sudden change from mother's milk to adult food. Japanese children are not weaned until four or five years old, when they are at once put on to adult diet, there being no middle course, for special feeding of children is considered unnecessary. The natural consequence is to upset the stomach completely; therefore it is about the age of weaning that the disfiguring complaint usually breaks out, and it lasts for years. In some villages more than half the children suffer thus, apparently without any inconvenience.

It is quite remarkable how the children of adjacent villages differ in appearance. At Boju, a village within the outer crater walls of the volcano Aso-san, I noticed that the youngsters playing on the roads were neat and comely; whereas at Miyaji, another village not two miles away, they were dirty, ill-kempt, and ugly. The children of the well-to-do, however, are usually the very dearest little creatures, and as different from the peasant youngsters as are the children of Kensington from the gamins of Poplar.

One of the most delightful characteristics of Japanese children is their courtesy, not only to strangers but to their parents and each other. It is certainly charming to see school children greeting each other at the school gate with a bow, and to see the respect which the young, one and all, pay to the old.

Not only are children gentle and courteous to their elders

[1] *Japanese Girls and Women.*

EVENING IN JAPAN

in Japan, but their elders are also gentle and courteous to them.
Courtesy is mutual. Children do not get "spanked" and
"sat upon" in Japan. They do not need it. Their bringing
up is such that they do not become "smart" and precocious.
There are no *enfants terribles* in Japan. Young and old pull
together. The old folk never forget that they themselves
were at one time young, and the young seem to divine
instinctively what is due to age. There is mutual consideration as well as mutual courtesy. From infancy Japanese
children are taught that self-restraint is one of the greatest
of virtues, and this teaching manifests itself in a total
absence among all classes of the irritableness of many
Europeans. Japan has been called a "Paradise of Babies,"
and Professor Chamberlain has offered the comment, "The
babies are generally so good as to help to make it a paradise
for adults."

The fact is, Japan is a pleasant land for every one, for
consideration is the birthright of one and all. What could be
more convincing evidence of this universal goodwill than
New Year's time? This is the season for the battledore
and shuttle-cock, and every street is filled with youngsters
playing the game. Not only do the children play it, but the
elders join in too. Father and mother come out to play as
merrily as the young ones, and even grandfather unbends
his rheumatic legs and makes a few dabs at the flying
shuttle-cocks. Sometimes the passing postman chips in as
he jog-trots by, and I have even seen the police-officer,
whose deportment is usually more dignified than a beadle's,
playing as gaily as any of the rest with a score of children
and soldiers.

That Japan is a children's paradise is quite apparent from
the hour one arrives in the land. Comical little people romp
about the streets quite regardless of the passing traffic.
There are no side-walks, and the roadway is the common
property of all. The children seemingly have as much
right to play their games there as have the kurumaya
to run with their rikishas, and the latter avoid the former

much more assiduously than the former trouble about the latter.

The way Japanese children of tender years run and play about with babies on their backs is one of the first things noticed by a foreigner. It seems a reckless thing to trust a baby of a few months old to a child of four on the open street, yet this is what may be seen anywhere. Every child is trained to carry another child from the time it begins to walk. At the age of two it has a large doll tied to its back, and the doll is replaced by a larger one later on; thus, when baby sister arrives, baby brother of three or four is already "broken in" for riding, and little sister is lashed to his back, without more ado, the very first time she takes the air. In this way, from earliest infancy, Japanese babies associate with their elder brothers and sisters in all their games; thus they are cultivating an intelligent interest in all around them, at a time when babies in other lands are still prattling in their cradles.

The children have two special yearly holidays—one for the girls and one for the boys. The girls' fête is held on March 3rd, when every little maid in the land brings out her dolls for one great annual party. Some little girls have hundreds of them, which are carefully placed away for the rest of the year. Many of the dolls are heirlooms that have given pleasure to mother and grandmother, and great- and great-great-grand-mother before them; and many are wonderful and costly works of art. The boys' holiday is the 5th May, its great feature being a long bamboo pole outside every house where there is a boy. Hanging to the pole are several large paper or cotton carp, which float in the breeze and resemble the fish swimming in the water. They are hollow, and have round, open mouths, through which the wind blows and keeps the body firmly bellied out. "The idea," says Professor Chamberlain, "is that as the carp swims up the river against the current, so will the sturdy boy, overcoming all obstacles, make his way in the world and rise to fame and fortune."

A LOTUS-POND

CHAPTER VI

THE nearest provincial point of interest to the port of Yoko-hama is the ancient city of Kamakura, which owes its historical fame to Yoritomo, the founder of the Shogunate, who chose it for his capital in 1192.

For generations prior to that time the high-spirited aristocracy of Japan, tired of the effeminacy of the Mikado's court, had seethed with impatient desire for more manly dominion. Eventually this unrest broke out into open warfare between the two greatest families in the land—the Taira and Minamoto clans—and during the latter half of the eleventh and the whole of the twelfth century the heads of these clans alternately rose to almost Imperial power, as the fortunes of war favoured the one or the other.

Yoritomo, a scion of the illustrious house of Minamoto, was born in 1147, and thirty-eight years later the vendetta of his clan with the Taira, which had filled a hundred and fifty years with bloodshed, culminated in the battle of Dan-no-ura, which was fought on the Inland Sea near Shimonoseki. This conflict, in which some accounts state Yoritomo completely exterminated his rivals and their whole army, putting even women and children to the sword, is the most famous in mediæval history, and an epic of Japan.

The name of Yoritomo, great as it is, is yet one of the most hated in Japanese history. But his crushing victory over his enemies, even though he pursued it to such extremes, is not responsible for this feeling. The odium in which he is held is due to his inhuman treatment of the popular hero Yoshi-tsuné. For his terrible vengeance he had a personal cause;

but for his inhumanity to Yoshitsuné he had none. Yoshitsuné
was his half-brother by the famous court beauty Tokiwa
Gozen, the favourite concubine of their father Yoshitomo.
When Yoritomo was a boy of twelve, and Yoshitsuné but a
baby in arms, the Taira clan were predominant, and their
menace developed into a massacre in which no quarter was
given, so that the Minamoto were threatened with extinction.
At this point in Japanese history there occurred a dramatic
incident which later entailed the forfeit of thousands of lives.
Tokiwa escaped from the massacre with her sons; but Kiyomori, the leader of the Taira—a crafty and tyrannical autocrat,
who made every beautiful woman he fancied serve his pleasure
—numbered among his captives Tokiwa's mother, for whose
ransom he would accept only the surrender of Tokiwa and
her children. Filial duty being the greatest of Japanese virtues,
he knew well that the daughter would sacrifice herself to
save her mother.

On hearing of her mother's capture, Tokiwa, who was
in hiding under the care of a pitying Taira soldier, at once
decided to yield herself up, and appeared before Kiyomori,
appealing by her beauty that he would spare her mother and
her children. Unfortunately for his kinsmen and their offspring
as yet unborn—for he himself died before the vengeance
fell—Kiyomori granted her request, conditionally that she
submitted to his embraces.

Twenty-six years later the historic battle of Dan-no-ura,
and the extermination of the rival faction, was the penalty
exacted by Yoritomo for this dishonour of his mother.

Yoshitsuné was his elder brother's right hand in the fight;
and it is said the laurels of victory were really his, for it was
he who, by his braver, stronger, and kinder nature, was beloved
by every one, and he thereby gained support for his brother
in the great position which the latter filled. This ever-growing
popularity Yoritomo feared, and planned his brother's destruction; but Yoshitsuné escaped, and fled to Northern Japan
with his faithful henchman Benkei, the companion of his
boyhood. Yoritomo's spies pursued the pair, and one account

says that they were treacherously murdered on the banks of the Koromo river in Yezo. Another account states that when they found all was lost they disembowelled themselves. Both reports, however, agree that Yoshitsuné's head was sent to his brother at Kamakura, preserved in a tub of saké; and to this day the hero is worshipped as a god by the Ainu aborigines in the northern island.

Though Kamakura was once the first city of the land, and the capital of the Shoguns for over two hundred and fifty years, it is now but a shadow of its bygone greatness. It can still, however, show many famous buildings to attest its former glory. Its one-time population of over a million has shrunk to but a few hundred souls; yet no other city in Japan can boast a more stirring record. In its day the city was the scene of constant strife. Over and over again it rose from ashes, for it was repeatedly sacked; and tidal waves devastated it utterly more than once. These disasters and cataclysms the city survived, but as Yedo became the Shogun's capital and rose to prosperity, Kamakura fell into ruin, until to-day it is little more than a pretty hamlet.

One of Kamakura's finest sights is the Hachiman temple, which was rebuilt in 1828 after a conflagration seven years previously. Hachiman is the Chinese name under which the Emperor O-Jin—who on his death in A.D. 313 was deified as the God of War—is worshipped. The shrines are most beautifully situated on the side of a wooded hill, with an avenue of stately old pine-trees, in which the ravages of time and tempest have left many gaps, leading straight up to the temple stairways from the seashore. In this avenue are three very fine old stone torii,[1] whose simple lines and dignified proportions have a severe and solemn beauty, harmonising perfectly with the restfulness of the stone-bordered lotus-ponds and bridges and broad flights of stone steps in the temple grounds. They were wonderful artists, as well as architects, who could so plan the approaches to such old Japanese sanctuaries that even a foreigner becomes deeply impressed and subdued in

[1] See page 219.

spirit by their influence long before the temples themselves are reached.

At the base of the great main stairway at the end of all these torii, bridges, and lotus-ponds, there is a giant old icho tree, which is believed to be over a thousand years of age. Whether it has the power to spray water from its leaves in the event of a conflagration, like its mate in the Nishi Hongwanji temple at Kyoto,[1] tradition does not say; probably it has not, since it allowed some of the buildings to burn a hundred years ago.

Once I visited this temple of the god, who understands so well his business, the day after the news of the fall of Port Arthur, during the war with Russia, was received. Its usually almost deserted avenues and stairways were thronged with people. Young men and maidens, old men and women, and children of every class of society, with one accord were visiting O-Jin's shrine to return thanks for the victory he had vouchsafed to the Japanese arms. Quietly they came, and quietly they went away. There was no elation in their bearing, for, in this their hour of triumph, dread was gnawing at their hearts. These were fathers, mothers, wives, brothers, and children of those gallants who, across the seas in a foreign land, were risking all for Emperor, home, and country; and as yet many knew not whether their dear ones had fallen in the strife. This only they knew, that success had been gained at terrible cost; and my heart ached for those gentle wives and aged parents, who, with humble mien, and heads bowed in the agony of suspense, flocked to the War-god's shrine to pray.

A few months later I stood on 203-metre Hill at Port Arthur. As I looked over its scarred and shell-torn slopes, and across the surrounding hills and valleys, they were furrowed with trenches as far as the eye could reach, and littered with the broken impedimenta of war, whilst four great battleships, two fine cruisers, and a fleet of smaller craft lay sunk in the harbour, their upper works rising above the waves.

[1] See page 214.

A SHINTO PRIEST

Near me a long trench had been filled in, and at each end of it there was a post with the simple inscription in Japanese, "A hundred soldiers of Japan are buried here." Close to it there was another trench, and the inscription, nailed to a cross, was in Russian, "Here lie a hundred faithful soldiers of the Czar." There were many such trenches, and the air was filled with a nauseating stench from the buried corpses.

Friend and foe lay side by side in death, and as I stood with bared head on that historic ground, I thought of the scene I had witnessed at the War-god's shrine at Kamakura —of those young wives widowed, and those gentle old folk bereaved of perhaps their only sons and bread-winners. I thought of Japanese homes bereft; of mothers, daughters, and sweethearts mourning in silent anguish; of wrinkled grand-mothers and stooping grandfathers bending in sorrow before the household shrine—their hearts rent with grief, yet swelling with pride, for, though grief be bitter, it was sweet to have bred sons who scoffed at death and suffering when the Reaper's scythe was whetted on the stone of honour.

During the war with Russia a great deal was written by correspondents about Japanese soldiers being eager for death, and their wives and parents sending them forth hoping that they might die for their country. Such articles were produced by writers who were in Japan for the first time, who neither understood the people nor the language, and who allowed their own enthusiasm for a picturesque land and people to run away with their pens. It is impossible for aliens who cannot speak Japanese to gain more than a superficial knowledge of the people; and many foreigners, who have spent a life-time in the land, admit they are little nearer to compre-hending the Japanese heart than when they first came. Though I have talked with numerous parents, and with numbers of Japanese soldiers—at home, and in the field, and in the hospital—I have never met a single Japanese soldier who wanted to die, and I never met any father, or mother, or wife so inhuman as to hope that their son or husband might be killed.

Life is just as sweet to the Japanese soldier as to any other, and perhaps sweeter than to many, since he lives in such a scenic paradise.   He is naturally anxious, therefore, to prolong that life as much as possible.   Like any other soldier, he wants to kill as many of the enemy as he can, but he hopes to keep his own life safe, and body intact, in doing so.   He does not fear death, but he does not court it, for he is far too sensible to forget that it is live men, not dead ones, who win battles.

Among the relics of Yoritomo which are preserved in the Hachiman temple there may be seen a gleaming strip of steel, before which every Japanese soldier bows, and reverently sucks his breath between his teeth, for it is regarded as something almost sacred.   It is a sword which has helped to carve Japanese history: a blade by Masamuné, the greatest swordsmith the world has ever produced.   Soldiers, armourers, and all who live for the art of war are Hachiman's special protégés; and the sword, the weapon of old Japan, was so venerated in feudal days that in the interesting study its history affords much insight can be gained into the feelings which sway the Japanese mind.

In 1876, the eighth year of Meiji—the Enlightened Era —the Imperial Edict went forth that from the 1st of January, 1877, the wearing of the sword would be a punishable offence. That the proclamation was received without a murmur speaks volumes for the unanimity and enthusiasm with which the Japanese, to a man, had come to recognise the new order of things.   It was the signal that the very last remaining threads of the old fabric of Feudalism had snapped.   Prior to that time every Japanese gentleman wore two swords, and his father had worn two before him; and his ancestors, for generations going back into hazy antiquity, had done likewise.   The wearing of the sword was one of the oldest institutions of the land, yet such had been the moral effect of Commodore Perry's ships; the signing of the treaties; the opening of Yokohama, and the bombardments of Shimonoseki and Kagoshima, that, when the edict went forth, not a protest was raised, not a blow was struck, not a murmur was heard throughout Japan. It was as if the people were dazed by the rapid sequence of events, which, like a flood, was bearing them along on its bosom they knew not whither.

It had been feared that the samurai would rise in revolt against this decree, which dispossessed them of the most precious insignia of their rank. To the amazement of all, however, they did not wait to be stripped by force; and, if they did not beat their swords into ploughshares and pruning-hooks, they cast into their lumber-rooms, or sold to the curio-shops, unhesitatingly, weapons that a few months before they would "less willingly have parted with than with life itself."

"The sword is the living soul of the samurai," said the great Shogun Iyéyasu. To wear it was the most cherished privilege of the feudal knight. Even as a tiny boy at school, struggling with intricacies of the Chinese ideographs, he wore a dirk in his girdle—for was not this the outward and visible sign of the proud indomitable spirit within: the external badge of the fighting blood that ran in his warrior veins? As he grew to man's estate not only did it serve to protect his life wherever he went—and in a land where the slightest breach of a rigid etiquette might hold a life as forfeit, there were times when death might lurk in any shadow—but it served to protect what was dearer to him still, the life of his liege lord, the Daimyo to whom he owed allegiance.

Seeing, then, that his sword was loved by the samurai as his own soul, it is not strange that the craft of the sword-smith was esteemed the highest in the land; and that those who were able to forge a blade which would stand every test without turning edge, gained for themselves high distinction, if not social position, and won renown in the annals of Japan far eclipsing that attained by any one in any other craft. The names of the greatest of these are as immortal on the scroll of fame as are those of Kōbō Daishi, the talented Buddhist saint; Yoshitsuné, the half-brother of Yoritomo; or Oishi

Kuranosuke, the leader of the Forty-seven Ronins. There is no schoolboy in Japan who does not know them.

About the end of the thirteenth century Masamuné lived at Kamakura, and practised his craft. A highly-esteemed Japanese friend told me of an incident of the great sword-maker's life, which I relate as showing something of the heart of the man, hard and unrelenting as the steel he forged, and his temper, keen and flashing as his blades.

Masamuné had a son who assisted him in his work, but whom he had enjoined never to pry too closely into his methods. The son was, however, of a curious and inquiring nature, and was continually searching for the key which would unlock his father's secrets. The swordsmith had forbidden him ever to put his hand into the water in which the blades were hardened. Thinking that here lay the solution to the mystery of the marvellously-tempered edge, which, before it was whetted, would rebound uninjured from a two-handed blow given by a strong man against a bar of cast iron, Masamuné the younger, one day whilst his father's back was turned, dipped his hand into the vessel which held the water to ascertain its tempera-ture. At that moment the master, with an unfinished blade in his hand, turned round. Without a moment's hesitation he dealt a slashing blow, from which his son only escaped death by leaping aside. But though the blow missed the head at which it was struck, it severed the right arm at the shoulder; and to this day the son, who also rose to some distinction in the craft, is known in history as Hidari Masamuné or Left-Handed Masamuné.

The names of the three other greatest sword-makers of Japanese history are Munéchika, who flourished in the tenth century; Muramasa, towards the end of the fourteenth century; and Yoshimitsu, who was a contemporary of Masamuné. All the existing weapons which they made are now in public or private collections, and the domicile of every blade produced by these renowned swordsmiths is known. There are not many of them. Masamuné's output in particular was very small, for he broke every blade which did not please him.

AMIDA, THE BUDDHA

Other swords by the great masters may be seen at the military museum at Shōkonsha, Tokyo. These old Japanese swords have no rivals in the world. They excel even the celebrated blades of Toledo. At the famous factory on the Tagus I have seen wondrous marvels of the cutler's art: blades of temper so true that they might be bent point to hilt and would spring back straight as before; and if you ran your eye along the razor edge you would find it neither swerved to left nor right by so much as the breadth of a single hair. I have seen there, also, a little round box into which was coiled what looked like a thick clock-spring. It had nothing to do with the life of a clock, however, but could play havoc with the life of a man, for, on being released, it sprang out with an angry hiss, as though raging at the confinement in which it had been kept, into a beautiful sword, straight and true as an arrow.

But the Japanese swords will not bend. They were made of soft magnetic iron combined with hard steel, and the heating or tempering was done in a charcoal furnace. The making of a blade often took as long as sixty days, and was, in the case of renowned makers, accompanied by much etiquette, and even looked upon as a religious ceremony. When tempering the blade the smith donned a black cap; and in the process the back and sides of the blade were protected by clay, only half an inch or so being left exposed. The edge of this fireclay cover was moulded by each maker into a particular design, which, in the hardening, transferred itself to the metal. These patterns are now among the surest means of identifying an unsigned blade.

Baron Terauchi, the former Minister of War, and the late Prince Ito—whose collections of swords I had the honour of being shown by the owners in person—as they tenderly drew each blade from the simple sheath of plain hinoki-wood in which it was kept, would invariably draw my attention to the pattern of the tempered edge. There were designs of Fuji, and of pine-trees bending in the wind, and various landscape scenes, and so forth.

The Japanese literature of the sword is most voluminous.

In the study of his beautiful country house at Oiso, where Prince Ito kept his sword-racks, I noticed that one end of the room was entirely covered with hundreds of volumes on shelves. "They are all books about swords; it would take a lifetime to master them," the famous old statesman told me.

As the weapon of old Japan was looked upon by its owner as his richest possession, and was loved by him as his own life, it is but natural that, in a land where love of art is innate in every breast, the sword and its furnishings should have been considered suitable objects for the reception of embellishment in its most highly-skilled forms. "Artists of the highest attainments spared nothing to render it an article of the highest artistic value."[1]

"Daimios often spent extravagant sums upon a single sword, and small fortunes upon a collection. A samurai, however poor, would have a blade of sure temper and rich mountings, deeming it honourable to suffer for food that he might have a worthy emblem of his rank."[2]

There are probably no people more conversant with the history, mythology, and legends of their country than the Japanese. This is because history forms one of the principal subjects in the school curriculum; and Japanese history is such a continuous record of tragedy, romance, self-sacrifice and heroism, that artists have found in it most of the motives by which they have been inspired.

Japanese mythology sometimes becomes almost as beautiful as that of the ancient Greeks, and the legends, which are woven about every famous place in the land, are so charming that the study of them is an inexhaustible feast of high-spirited sentiment and poetic thought. Enlightened in this fascinating lore at his mother's knee, the Japanese boy has seen it, and almost every romantic episode of history, depicted so often in every phase of art, that, as the years pass by, they become so interwoven with his life as to seem an integral part of his own existence.

[1] M. B. Huish, *The Art of Japan*.   [2] Griffis, *Mikado's Empire*.

Need one wonder, then, that artists so loved to depict their ideals of these things; and that craftsmen, skilled in the art of working in metals, put forth their finest efforts in applying them to the adornment of the sword?

In the zenith of its history Kamakura was the home of these and many other arts, and the blades in the Hachiman temple are relics of those prosperous days.

In the old days, too, many of the famous metal-workers lived at Kamakura, and here was cast the finest of the numerous statues of Buddha in Japan. The Daibutsu, or Great Buddha, has passed through many vicissitudes in its eventful history, but never was the danger of annihilation more menacing than when an American visitor, whose scent for a business deal was keener than his reverence for ancient monuments, offered thirty thousand dollars for it, as material for the melting-pot. Though the offer was more rational than the proposal to transport Stonehenge across the Atlantic, it was fortunately declined, and Japan's greatest work of art was thus saved from an ignominious end for the praise and prayers of future generations.

The measurements of the Daibutsu, as given in a booklet sold by the priests, are much exaggerated. Every writer on Japan has accepted the Japanese figures without question, and they have frequently been quoted. But a cursory glance at the photograph herein proves the guide-book figures incorrect. It was made with a sixteen-inch lens from a distance of fifty yards, so that there is no distortion. The distance from knee to knee is quoted as thirty-five feet, eight inches—which is correct. The height is given as forty-nine feet, seven inches; but the height is almost exactly the same as the length from knee to knee. The length of the face is given as eight feet, five inches, which is about right. This is approximately a sixth of the stated height, whereas, as the photograph clearly shows, the face is almost one-fourth of the total height of the figure, not including the stone pedestal. The width of face from ear to ear is said to be seventeen feet nine inches—more than double the length; but the length and width of face are very nearly identical. I have often estimated the height of the figure, when inspecting it, as about thirty-six feet, and examination of the photograph confirms these figures. The height as given by the Japanese, and quoted by Murray's *Handbook*, is an exaggeration of nearly fourteen feet.

The eyes are said to be of pure gold, and the wisdom boss on the forehead composed of thirty pounds of silver. This information may, or may not, be more reliable than the measurements. Who can say? But through the narrow slits between the nearly closed lids such parts of the eyes as can be seen appear to be of dark green bronze, like the rest of the figure.

It is not, however, by mere bulk that the Daibutsu impresses, but by the truly wonderful manner in which it symbolises the teaching of the Buddhist faith; the pose is no less beautiful than the expression. There is something supremely sad in the gentle drooping of the head, but to realise the beauty of the pose one must stand near and look up into the face. To do so is to feel subdued and awed by the infinite compassion, and peace, and understanding, written in the serene and tranquil countenance.

There are four of the works of man in the East that have left indelible impressions in my memory. They are the Shwé Dagon Pagoda at Rangoon, the Taj Mahal at Agra, the Great Wall of China, and the Kamakura Daibutsu.

About the Shwé Dagon—that tapering golden finger piercing the turquoise sky by the great Irrawaddy—there is a delicious dream-like atmosphere, as one listens to its thousand tiny gongs, all tinkling in the heavily incensed air, and sees the fairest maids of Burma match their palms in prayer at its base each evening as the sun goes down. The Taj Mahal—that love-tale in marble and rare stones—pearl of India's buildings, and mirror of a great king's heart—seems also like some palace of a world of dreams. Before the Great Wall one has an indescribable feeling of awe, as the eye follows its interminable meanderings across the barren hills and sun-baked wastes of China. But the Daibutsu—that wondrous

A PRIEST OF BUDDHA

embodiment of Buddhist ideals—seems to be vestured in the very cloak of peace, so subtly has the hand of man clothed it with serenity and spiritual calm.

Although the name of the artist who designed it is unknown, none but a master could have conceived it, for every line of its moulding contributes to the repose the figure seems to emanate. Yet the god is not in repose, for scrutiny shows that the nearly closed eyes are watchful and alert, and the attitude is not that of ease, but of repression and self-control. It is Amida, the " Ideal of Boundless Light," wrapt in meditative calm, concentrated in the extinction of all earthly desire.

At the top of a short flight of steps, approached by an avenue of pine-trees, in a beautiful garden with soft lawns, lotus-ponds, and sōtetsu palms, the image rests, like some great guardian spirit, "sitting for ever waiting for the world to die." For six and a half centuries the Daibutsu has stood the ravages of time, and twice (1369 and 1494) it has breasted, without injury, tidal waves which swept the great sanctuary that sheltered it, and the city of Kamakura, off the earth. It dates from 1252, and was cast in seven separate layers, which were welded together and finished off with the chisel. Four centuries and more of exposure to the weather, since the temple was last destroyed, have stained the bronze to a brownish green. The great building which formerly enshrined the image was fifty yards square, and its roof was supported by sixty-three immense wooden pillars resting on stone bases, many of which may still be traced. For many years the priests have been collecting funds to rebuild the temple. It is to be hoped, however, that the money may be applied to some other purpose, for, even though the site is not an ideal one, the image is far more impressive framed with palms and pines and cherry-trees, than it could ever be imprisoned in a building—judging by the effect achieved at Nara, where another and larger, though much inferior, Great Buddha is to be seen in the Tōdaiji temple.

Owing to the silly and irreverent pranks of foreign visitors, who used to climb up on to the hands of the Daibutsu, it is

now only with great difficulty that one can obtain anything
better than surreptitious snapshots of it, unless one buys the
photographs sold by the priests and others. An elaborate
formula must be gone through. Not only is the consent of the
custodians necessary to use a camera, but one must go to
them armed with a permit from the naval headquarters at
Yokosuka before they will consider the matter. Some time is
necessary to secure this concession, and even then a substantial
donation must be made to the building fund before the priests
will endorse the naval document with their acquiescence.
Not that there is anything to grumble at in this, for the
authorities are, of course, justified in making any terms they
please. If one does not desire to make studies of one's own,
one can go to any photographer's in Yokohama, and there
buy, for 20 sen, a photograph of the Daibutsu as proof of
what spectacles one's countrymen sometimes make of themselves when abroad. Many of the negatives of these photographs were taken thirty years ago, when conditions were
less stringent; and as the courteous priests then permitted
liberties, which are now denied, some visitors abused the
privilege by clambering all over the image, which to the Japanese is sacred, and were even photographed, often in ridiculous
poses, on its hands and arms. Looking at such photographs,
one wonders why the Japanese do not insist on all foreigners
carrying a properly verified certificate of sanity before allowing
them to go anywhere at all.

It is a remarkable thing that some people, when abroad,
seem to treat the natives of the lands they visit as creatures
quite apart from fellow human beings, and conduct themselves
as they would never dream of doing at home. I once saw, at
Kamakura, a tourist and his wife, both of whom were past
middle age and old enough to know better, standing before
a Japanese policeman and discussing him as if he were graven
in stone. The policeman tried hard to look dignified as he was
carefully examined and commented on from the peak of his
cap to his well-polished boots, but he stood the ordeal well
until the man took hold of the hilt of his (the policeman's)

sword, and drew it from the scabbard, before the latter realised that such an act was contemplated. The officer snatched his weapon back, not having the slightest idea of the foreigner's intention, and replaced it in its sheath without a word, though his eyes were blazing with anger. No one unfamiliar with Japan could imagine the magnitude of such an insult, for there is plenty of the old spirit remaining, and many of the police are of samurai blood. To the samurai of old even so much as to touch his sword would have meant a matter of life or death, and as for drawing his blade unasked—such a thing was unknown. An interested crowd of spectators laughed at the policeman's embarrassment, for he was quite at a loss what to do, courtesy forbidding him to interfere with a foreigner accompanied by a woman, though he evidently regarded him as not responsible for his acts. An American friend, with whom I had watched the incident, went to the officer's assistance at this juncture, and when he had told his compatriot what he thought of him, in language ungarnished with any flowers of speech, and asked him how a New York constable would be likely to treat any inquisitive foreigner who tried to snatch his baton away, the now shamefaced offenders were glad to flee from the laughter of the crowd (who had understood the meaning of the altercation, if not the language in which it was couched), and the policeman, grateful at being helped out of an awkward situation, thanked my companion with many salutes and repetitions of "arigato gozaimas" ("I thank you very much").

The Daibutsu is hollow, of course, and one may go through a door cut in the bronze lotus-petals on which the figure reposes, and climb a ladder to the head, in the back of which there is a window. There is also a shrine inside, dedicated to the Goddess of Mercy; but it is better to leave all this unseen, as it is too disenchanting.

High on the slopes of one of the most densely wooded of Kamakura's lovely hills, facing the morning sun, and commanding a glorious view, stands Hasédera, sacred to Kwannon, Goddess of Mercy. In spring-time its heavily-thatched old roofs and balconies peep out from a veritable forest of cherry-blossoms; whilst in the autumn, the hillsides above, below, and all around the temple burn with crimson maple leaves. Long flights of grey old steps, all spotted with moss and lichens, lead upwards, and from the weather-beaten and time-worn balconies one looks over rice-fields, covering the land like mosaic work, to yellow towering cliffs. Away to the right the mighty Pacific spends its force in a line of foam on a crescent bay of silver sand. All is beautiful. Everywhere is peace.

An old priest came out to greet me, and to show me what there was to see. At the entrance to the temple my attention was arrested by a printed notice in English. The English was so perfect, and the language used so beautiful, that I quote it herewith *in toto*:

PROPOSED RESTORATION OF HASÉDERA

It is my earnest desire, and the one wish and object of my whole life, to put this ancient temple (which is dedicated to the Goddess of Mercy) into good and lasting repair, and towards that end I have worked steadfastly for many years, but the money collected is far below the total sum required, and, owing to the poorness of my parish, the restoration fund accumulates very slowly. I therefore appeal to and entreat all friends, whether Japanese or Foreign, entering this Sanctuary, to assist me in proportion to their means with funds to restore and preserve an Historical Landmark and Church to Prosperity; in order that, when time shall have blended the present living with the bygone dead, Hasédera may still stand in Kamakura to point a moral to future generations, and to serve as a place for the Everlasting and Immutable Law whose doctrines, given to the world by the "Light of Asia," the blessed Sakyamuni, have pointed the way through many a dark and troublous age to the Holy Path and the Pure Land, and guided the feet of countless weary pilgrims to the "Haven of Eternal Peace in Nirvana."

BUDDHISM is no narrow creed confined to one community or nation. It is the Law of the Universe, which was before beginning, and is for ever without end: it is the Law of Cause and Effect, and it teaches of a Divine and Transcendent Power in Nature, vast and boundless as eternal space, and yet governing the most trivial circumstances of men's lives, and providing means of Salvation and eternal happiness, benevolent and welcome as light in a dark night.

WE ADORE THEE, O ETERNAL BUDDHA.

Meiji 25th year 5th month (May 1892).

THE SUPERIOR (Minister of the Jodo Sect).

The image of Kwannon stands in an apartment behind the altar. For a fee of 50 sen the old priest conducted me into this chamber, in which the darkness was Cimmerian until he struck a match and lighted a candle. For a moment or two I looked for the image in vain. I could make nothing out of what little could be seen. Then, finding that I was only looking at its feet, I raised my gaze gradually until it was lost in the darkness above. Lighting another candle, and placing them both in iron frames, the priest then drew them slowly up the figure, lighting its different parts with weird effect, until they finally stopped before the face, thirty feet above us. In that narrow chamber the goddess was of truly colossal size, and must surely be most awe-inspiring to the pilgrims who come here, whose faith is the light of their lives. To them the *séance* must be almost overpowering.

The figure is said to be carved out of a single bole of a camphor-tree, lacquered and gilded. One of the huge hands holds a staff of shakudo, and the other is uplifted, holding a lotus-bud in the fingers, with a rosary hanging over the arm. The image is in excellent preservation, and, of course, legend has been busy with it. It is one of a pair carved by the gods, which they threw into the sea. This one floated into Sagami Bay, and was brought to Kamakura by two fishermen 1200 years ago.

The ever-busy Kōbō Daishi[1] carved an image of Daikoku, the God of Wealth, which squats on the right of a gilded Kwannon on the temple altar. The work is rough, but very curious, all the effects being gained with single slashes of the knife. There is also a pair of very fine old Ni-Ō[2]—well bespattered with the spit-balls of the faithful—which, curiously enough, are inside the temple, a most unusual place to find them. Outside the sanctuary the naughty old Binzuru[3] expiates his indiscretion in disfigured and meditative solitude, as at Kiyomizu in Kyoto.

There are many more fine old temples at Kamakura: Enkakuji, with a monster bell; Kōmyōji, with its sixteen

[1] See page 83.   [2] See page 254.   [3] See page 202.

pools where Kōbō Daishi bathed; Kenchōji, with Yoritomo's
war-drum, magnificent old juniper-trees, crumbling buildings,
and still stately gateway; and Ennōji, with its celebrated image
of Emma-Ō, the god of the Buddhist hells. This figure is
diabolical—which perhaps is not surprising seeing that it
was executed by one Unkei, a carver of gods, who, having
died, was summoned in due course before the Satanic deity,
who expressed much dissatisfaction at the portraits Unkei
had made of him. He commanded Unkei, now that he had
seen him, to return to earth and carve a better likeness. So
Unkei returned and executed this image, which is known as
"the work of Unkei redivivus." The image is kept behind
curtains, which the priests draw back suddenly, disclosing
the hideous god in a frantic tantrum, with gleaming eyes and
teeth, and malignant dark red face; but he is no more awe-
inspiring than the Hindu Ganesh.

The advent of the foreigner has been a godsend to Kamakura. Thousands of transient visitors come annually to see
the Daibutsu and other shrines, and many English and American merchants, as well as Japanese, have villas there, to which
they fly in summer from the heat of Yokohama and Tokyo.
Not that Kamakura is a cool place; but the frequent breezes
from the Pacific, and the ocean view and splendid bathing,
even though the sea be tepid, offer change and relaxation from
the greater heat of the cities. There are excellent hotels in
both native and foreign style, and, altogether, Kamakura is a
pleasant place to spend the summer, if business ties prevent
one going up to the lakes, which lie farther afield. Kamakura
is not an hour's journey from Yokohama, but Hakōné, the
nearest lake, is a good six hours away.

There is a village named Katasé four miles from Kamakura. Electric cars run the distance, but at every season of
the year the walk is lovely. The road skirts the glistening
sands of Sagami Bay, where great rolling billows come curling
in from the broad Pacific's purple hazes; and, when the sun
is shining, the green transparent waves are all shot and streaked
with blue, as, dragging long ribbons of kelp within them,

they raise their crested manes to dash them into snowy foam upon the strand.

This road teems with historical associations. At one place Nitta Yoshisada, a captain in the army of the deposed Mikado Go-Daigo, marching on Kamakura to attack the forces of the Regent Tōkōyori—head of the Hōjō clan, who had usurped the Imperial power—found his passage barred by cliffs, defended by the Hōjō army and a line of war-junks lying a few hundred yards off-shore. Nothing daunted, Yoshisada addressed a prayer to the sea-gods for help, and, drawing his sword, cast it as an offering to the waves. Thereupon the waters parted, just as the Red Sea did for the hosts of Israel, and Yoshisada's army marched in triumph into Kamakura. This dramatic episode has become immortal in song, and is to be found illustrated in every phase of Japanese art and craft.

Just before Katasé is reached there is a little village called Koshigoé. At this spot Nichiren, the Buddhist saint, miraculously escaped death by execution, to which he had been sentenced by Tōkōyori for his excess of zeal. Kneeling upon the silver strand, and repeating the formula "Namu-Myōhō-Rengé-Kyo"—which is the invocation of his sect to this day —upon his rosary, he bowed his head for the executioner's sword. The headsman raised his blade to give the two-handed blow, when a blinding flash of lightning rent the heavens, breaking the sword in pieces and striking dead the headsman, whilst the holy priest remained uninjured. Hōjō Tōkōyori, in his Kamakura palace, heard the crashing thunders, and saw the lightning flash in the cloudless sky. Terrified by these signs of the anger of the gods, he sent a messenger with a pardon for his victim; whilst at the same moment a runner was despatched to the palace from the execution ground to ask for further instructions. The two men met at a little stream that crosses the road, which to this day is called the "River of Meeting"; and every Japanese child who passes it is taught the whole seven-hundred-years-old story.

Katasé is a little fishing village of no greater importance than hundreds like it round the coasts. It is not, however, to study the fisherman's life that thousands come here annually, but to pass on to the sacred isle of Enoshima, one of the loveliest spots in all the Japanese archipelago. In this land of fascinating fable, where every pretty spot is enshrouded in mystery and legend, it is only right that Enoshima should have received its fair share of such lore. Like many other isles, especially beloved, it sprang out of the ocean-bed one night, about twelve hundred years ago, during violent contortions of the great fish, on the back of which Japan rests, whose wriggling causes the earthquakes. This particular upheaval was due to the wrath of Benten, the Goddess of Luck, who visited the spot to put an end to the ravages of a fierce dragon that dwelt in a submarine cave and devoured the maidens of the near-by village of Koshigoé. On the goddess appearing over the spot, the sea-bed rose to meet her. Descending from the clouds, she met and pacified the monster, and seems to have found him more amiable than she expected, for she forthwith married him. To this day a deep cave at the water level, which is sacred to her name, bears witness to the virtue of the story, and in a hundred forms of art you may see Benten and her dragon soaring away in the clouds. What further proofs of the truth of the story than these could any rational folk require? This incident in the life of the goddess has been dealt with in pleasant variety by native artists, but the most up-to-date of the changes that I have seen rung on it was a large poster depicting the deity and her dragon mate sitting on a cloud, exchanging broad smiles of satisfaction over the possession of a bottle of Japanese lager beer.

Enoshima is enchanting enough, however, without its charming vesture of legend. You enter the holy isle through a fine old bronze torii at the water's edge, with tortoises climbing up wave-washed rocks carved at the bases of the uprights. It is a steep path to the summit, but as interesting as steep, for the road is bordered with curio-shops and quaint inns. This is the place to see all the wonders of Japanese conchology and the strange things of the sea. There are shops where shells of every imaginable kind and colour are displayed, and corals and rope-sponges too; and you may buy shell toys and ornaments, and pretty paintings on the halves of iridescent bivalves, and even natural sprays of cherry-trees with the tiniest and pinkest of testaceans cunningly clustered to form the petals of the blossoms. There are monster crabs, too, fearful-looking creatures—with small bodies, but with claws that measure ten feet from tip to tip—of a species which, it is said, has been known to attack living human beings, and even kill and devour them. These gigantic crustaceans are the bogies of the island children, who believe that they emerge from the sea at night and scour the rocks, searching for little girls and boys.

On the hillside above the shops there are maple woods, with tortuous paths under red old pines; and at the summit of the island there are restaurants and tea-houses, with beautiful vistas through the bristly branches of trees which lean at impossible angles over the cliffs, as though courting destruction in the waves below. On the southern horizon, Oshima, an island volcano, sends leaden smoke-wreaths to the clouds, and on the bosom of the sunlit Pacific the sails of junks and sampans gleam "like blown white flowers at sea."

The proper thing to do at Enoshima is to have one of the fish dinners for which the place is noted. You can have it at the Kinkiro, or some other of the excellent inns; or if you prefer, you can have it served in some quaint look-out on the verge of a beetling precipice, with glorious scenery around you. Some of the concoctions are not tempting to the foreign palate; but there is delicious pickled cuttle-fish; and a kind of whelk—broiled in butter, in the shell, over a charcoal fire—is a delicacy which will please the most fastidious taste if prejudice can be overcome sufficiently to try it. The Bordeaux snails, so esteemed in Paris, are delicious when one musters up the courage to try them, but they cannot be compared with the Enoshima whelks.

Down on the rocks below, the wrinkled veterans of the island earn a living by waylaying visitors to the Dragon's

Cave, and inducing them to throw small coins into the water, for which they dive and catch them as they slowly sink. They also dive for shell-fish, and infallibly bring one up from the clear green depths. Noticing that every time a diver plunged in he first retired to the cave for a moment, I became suspicious, and, stopping one old fellow, just as he prepared to plunge, found he had a crayfish concealed in his breech-clout. This exposure of the trick caused uproarious merriment.

One day I resolved to play them a deception. I went down to the rocks to have a swim, and a small crowd gathered round to watch me. The sea was ruffled by a breeze, so that one could not discern anything below the surface. Taking a long, deep breath I dived in, and, swimming under water, came up behind a rock about thirty feet away. I peeped over the top and saw the crowd peering down into the water. A minute went by and they became anxious. Two minutes passed, and still I did not reappear. Then several of the divers plunged into the water, and all were beside themselves with excitement, believing me to be drowning. I allowed another minute to pass and then slipped quietly back into the water behind my sheltering rock, and, going deep down, came up again, puffing and blowing, under their very eyes. They never suspected the truth, and followed me back to the village telling every one about the feat. Months afterwards when a friend visited Enoshima it was related to him how a foreigner had, one day, dived in and had stayed below *ten minutes*!—whereas I had not really been under water more than a minute altogether.

The Dragon's Cave is not at all spectacular. It is nearly 400 feet long, about 30 feet wide at the mouth, and narrows to but a yard or so at the end. A slender platform of plank and bamboo is fastened to the wall, along which to walk, and beneath it the waves surge in and demolish the staging altogether when the Storm-god rages and lashes the sea to fury. A few little shrines, before which the guide lights sputtering candles, are all that now do honour to the glory of the goddess Benten.

CHAPTER VII

MIYANOSHITA AND LAKE HAKŌNÉ

THERE are few pleasanter spots in any land, for those who love a ramble o'er hill and dale, than the Hakōné district of Japan. Its lovely woodlands and mountains, ringing with the sound of rills and rivers, cascades and waterfalls, make it a veritable paradise for a holiday. Of all places within easy reach of Yokohama, Miyanoshita, the chief village of the district, is the favourite week-end resort for foreign residents of the seaport.

A journey of two hours from Yokohama on the Tōkaido railway brings one to Kōdzu, where a change is made for Yumoto into an electric car, on which "parsons infected, introxicated, or lunatics will not be allowed, children without attender too," to quote one of the Company's Regulations as displayed in the cars. There is usually a wait for some ten or fifteen minutes before the car starts, and the proper way to fill this interval is to have tea at one of the near-by cha-ya. Whether you want to or not, you cannot help conforming to the custom, for buxom little country maids appropriate your luggage, see it on the car, procure your ticket, and look to it that everything is well, before you have hardly time to take your bearings; and long before these services have been rendered tea has been prepared for you.

Midway between Kōdzu and Yumoto is the ancient town of Odawara, and as the tram speeds for two miles through the straggling thoroughfare which is its main street, the whole household system and life of the inhabitants are revealed through the open doors and windows. The town, it is said, was the scene of constant strife in feudal days; in fact the whole country hereabouts teems with the most sanguinary historical associations. Yumoto is the terminus of the tram-line, and from here to Miyanoshita a mountain road winds for four miles along the gorge of the Hayakawa, the "Rapid River." Rikisha-runners from the hotels are always here to meet the trams, three or four of them being necessary for each vehicle, as the road is very steep; but it is quite an easy tramp for a good walker, and the scenery is lovely all the way.

There is a pretty cascade near Yumoto, where a hundred feathery streams gush out of the mountain-side, and tumble in the sunlight like a shower of flashing gems from rock to rock. The Japanese, who have poetical names for every beautiful feature of the land, call it Tama-daré-no-taki, the "Waterfall of Falling Jewels." The jewels drop into a limpid pool, where monster gold carp lazily glide about in shoals, or loaf in the shade of the stone bridges and over-hanging maple-trees.

A little farther up the road, the picturesque village of Tonosawa lies deep in the heart of the glen, with noisy waters all around it, for another torrent comes plunging along to join the parent river. There are hot sulphur-streams in the moun-tain overhanging the village; these have been tapped by tunnels, and their waters piped to a dozen different hotels which are popular week-end resorts for residents of Tokyo and Yokohama.

The scenery becomes finer at every turn as the road winds up the leafy mountain-side. Rocky cliffs give way to maple-woods, and then to bamboo-groves, whose graceful shoots lean outwards, forming lovely canopies overhead. The Haya-kawa fills the valley with the murmur of its waters, and down its banks and precipices many a streamlet tumbles and leaps into the gorge below. This road is lovely at every season of the year. In April "the cherry-trees are seas of bloom and soft perfume"; sweet May then comes and makes the hillsides burn with red azaleas; in drowsy summer a myriad cicadas strive to hush the murmur of the river; autumn sets the forests ablaze with fiery glory; and "when winter's hand spreads

THE WATERFALL OF FALLING JEWELS AT YUMOTO

wide her hoary mantle o'er the land," they are more beautiful than ever, for the feathery bamboos leaning across the road bow deeper still, weighted down with the snow that lies on their slender branches.

Miyanoshita's one street is a bazaar of pretty things. It is the centre for the Japanese wood-mosaic work—known all over the world. Inlaid boxes, and articles for every conceivable domestic use, are here for sale, all made out of the choicest and most beautifully-grained of woods, at prices that are irresistible.

The Fujiya Hotel stands at the head of this street. Here, amidst the loveliest of scenery, one lives in the lap of luxury and comfort. The table is of the choicest, the service unsurpassed, and the daintiest little maidens of Japan, with soft white tabi on their feet, tread silently to anticipate one's every wish, or run to do one's bidding.

But the baths! One almost lives in them! Hot volcanic water, with just a trace of sulphur in it—enough to make it soft and soothing—is piped from the solfataras, several miles higher up in the hills, to huge tubs, which one can enter any hour of the day or night, and use the water as one pleases. But that is not all. At the back of the hotel, out in the open air, there is an immense swimming-bath, from three to ten feet deep, with spring-boards and diving-stages, and hot and cold water laid on, so that its temperature may be fitted to the season.

With pleasure and appreciation I recall the courtesy and kindness always extended to me by the proprietress, Madame Yamaguchi, whilst staying at this hotel. No thought or attention was omitted to add to the enjoyment of my stay, and many a picnic excursion we arranged to lovely places in the hills. With genuine enthusiasm the charming and accomplished châtelaine of the house would sometimes even chaperon the pretty little waitresses to distant spots to pose and give a touch of beauty to my pictures. The Fujiya Hotel sets the standard of highest excellence in all the East. Comfortably housed at this hospitable place, surrounded by every luxury in one of the fairest places of Japan—where the air is so recuperative and invigorating that one is tempted to wander for endless miles over the hills—it is easy to understand why those who come here for days stay for weeks; whilst those who come for weeks, extend the weeks into months, and then leave this enchanting spot with many regrets, and the firm resolve to return at the earliest opportunity.

There is no end to the number of delightful places within less than a half-hour's walk from the hotel—Dogashima, a tiny village in a cool ravine with a cascade such as wood-nymphs love; Kiga, and the "Gold-fish Tea-house," with its pretty garden, and waterfall, and fountain, and golden carp; Jakotsu-gawa, the "Stream of the Serpent"; Miyagino, a rustic village by the river-side, with a picturesque old mill and water-wheel; and a score of other little gems of beauty-spots. But, charming as are all these beauty-spots, the favourite excursion from Miyanoshita is to Lake Hakōné.

The road leads along the left bank of the Hayakawa for some distance, and thence strikes off up a steep pathway into the Ashinoyu mountains, through the village from which they derive their name. This is a bald, uninviting locality, but is famed far and wide for the curative properties of its sulphur springs. Native sufferers from skin diseases flock to the place in summer; whilst foreigners, afflicted with rheu-matism and kindred complaints, come here and spend pre-scribed hours of their time, immersed to the neck in the malodorous waters, which come hot from the bowels of the earth. One of the baths is so powerful that those who enter it have to do so inch by inch, so as not to agitate the water and free the fumes, which will quickly overpower the strongest. Even to smell a sponge soaked in the water will make a strong man faint, it is said. When any one enters the bath an attendant closely watches him whilst he is in it, and many a time it would have claimed a victim, had not the bather, when overcome, been taken out at once to the open air. Ashinoyu is 2800 feet above the sea, and is always cool even in the hottest weeks of summer.

From here to the lake it is a gradual downward slope through hills thickly covered with dwarf bamboo. On the way there are some famous carvings to be seen. The most interesting of these is an immense bas-relief, cut in the face of a wall of rock, of Jizo, the Buddhist god who watches over the souls of little children, and to whom women about to become mothers offer up their prayers.

The sentiment surrounding this deity is a very beautiful one. It is the popular belief that when children die they descend into purgatory, and are compelled by a cruel witch to pile up into cairns the stones of the Sai-no-Kawara, or "River-bed of Souls"—the Japanese Styx. This labour is unending, for bands of angry demons, called oni, rise from the river and destroy the heaps, and the terrified children would have to toil for ever rebuilding them, were it not for the gentle, compassionate Jizo. He comes to their help, drives away their tormentors, and hides the little ones in the great sleeves of his kimono. Hence, those who pray to Jizo deposit a stone or two about the shrine, as thus they lighten the toil of their little ones who have passed away.

This image is said to be the work of Kōbō Daishi, a Buddhist saint who lived in the eighth century, and he is credited with having accomplished the feat in a single night. If Kōbō Daishi did all that the Japanese say he did, he must certainly have executed this work in the time allotted; for otherwise, had his days exceeded those of Methuselah, he could scarcely have effected all the wonders for which the Japanese gave him credit.

Having spent some years mining in western America, I did a little figuring on this achievement, and estimated that if two good Californian miners had worked, with the assistance of modern explosives, in blasting out the rock alone, without attempting any carving, they would have well earned good wages if they had completed the work in a week.

Kōbō Daishi was a man of great attainments. His sympathies were many, and his talents manifold. He was the most famous of all Buddhist saints of Japan. He was a great traveller, and, amongst other endowments, excelled as a painter and

G

sculptor. His writing was of such beauty that the eyes were dazzled on beholding the characters, and at the age of thirty-five he invented the syllabary of the land. To such great dexterity did he attain in the art of calligraphy that he was able to write equally well with five brushes at once, one in either hand, one in each foot, whilst the fifth he held in his teeth. There was no medium upon which he was unable to record his handwriting, and it is told that on one occasion he traced characters which thereupon appeared in the heavens, and that at another time he wrote upon the flowing waters of a river. But even this was not the limit of his skill, for he would take a brush and shake it, and the drops of ink, as they fell, became transformed into characters exceeding in beauty any hitherto seen. It is not strange, therefore, that his renown is great throughout the land, and that he is the most deeply venerated of Buddhist saints.

The road all the way from Miyanoshita, like other mountain roads in Japan, was well bestrewn with worn-out waraji, the straw sandals which are the only footgear used in the hilly districts. They are very cheap, costing but two or three farthings a pair, and will last an entire day. Even horses are shod with waraji, specially made to fit their hoofs, which would otherwise speedily become cracked and broken on these rough and stony paths. At every house we passed these useful articles were sold.

There are three ways of making the journey to Hakōné, which is about six miles—on foot, on horseback, or in a yama-kago, or mountain basket. The latter method is that by which all Japanese ladies, and many men, travel in mountain districts.

The kago is a light bamboo litter, hung on a single pole, which is carried on the shoulders of two or more bearers. It is well adapted for native use, as the Japanese are accustomed from infancy to sit with their feet tucked under them. How comfortable European or American ladies can make themselves is largely a matter of personal temperament. I have only tried this method once, when disabled by a sprained ankle from

walking, and I found it comfortable enough. If one be not prone to cramp, or pins-and-needles, or sea-sickness, it is an easy way of travelling, as the back is arranged at a convenient angle, and there are soft cushions to sit on. The motion is nauseating to many people, but the Japanese seem to find it soothing, for they generally go to sleep. The bearers are wonderfully sure-footed, and two can carry a Japanese lady all day, with occasional spells of rest and changes of shoulder.

The lake bursts suddenly into view a short way past the Jizo image, and the road zigzags down to it. A fine torii stands at the top of the steep, and Moto-Hakōné is the name of the picturesque village by the lake.

One Christmas Day as I reached this point the view was more than usually lovely. The bamboo thickets sparkled with hoar-frost crystals in the sunlight, and the lapis-lazuli lake lay snugly bosomed in mountains of gold—all yellow with the ripened kaia-grass. Beyond the rugged barrier range on the western side, the peerless Fuji-san, thickly shrouded with newly-fallen snow, raised its proud crest high into the heavens —"a stainless altar of the sun."

Hakōné is the name of the mountain region comprising the entire southern portion of the province of Sagami. The lake is called Ashi-no-umi, the "Sea of Reeds," though why such a name was given is not easy to comprehend. Japanese names are usually most apposite, but in this case there seems to have been a misfit, for with the sole exception of a shallow place at the northern end of the lake, where there are a few reeds, the shore descends abruptly into water many fathoms deep.

The Emperor has a summer residence here on a peninsula. There is also a fine old stone torii by the waterside; a famous Shinto temple; an avenue of cryptomeria-trees, and everything is fairly cloaked with legend and mantled with historical memories.

One day when I was strolling through the village, I purchased, at a little shop, a curious guide-book. It was a small

blue volume, embellished with a golden outline of Fuji—a
translation from a native work into English by a Japanese,
Mr. C. J. Tsuchiya. I found the quaint language of the
volume so interesting that I quote some of the author's
descriptions of this region by kind permission.

Speaking of the beauties of the place, he says: "Owing
to toilsome ascent many difficulties must be endured by
travellers. The result of toleration is pleasure. There the
Imperial Palace stands; Hakōné Gongen, a Shinto temple,
adorns itself with perpetual unchanging dress of forest; the
Ashi lake spreads the face of glowing glass reflected upside
down the shadow of Fuji which is the highest, noblest and
most glorious mountain in Japan; and the mineral hot springs
warmly entertain the guests coming yearly to visit them during
summer vacation. The purity of the air, the coolness of summer
days, and the fine views of landscapes are agreeable to all
visitors; for these facts, they do not know how is the summer
heat and where is the epidemic prevailing."

"Whenever we visit the place, the first pleasure to be
longed, is the view of Fuji mountain and its summit is covered
with permanent undissolving snow, and its regular configura-
tion hanging down the sky like an opened white fan, may
be looked long at equal shape from several regions surrounding
it. Every one who saw it has ever nothing but applause. It
casts the shadow in a contrary direction on still glassy face of
lake as I have just described. Buildings of Imperial Solitary
Palace, scenery of Gongen, all are spontaneous pictures. Wind
proper in quantity, suits to our boat to slip by sail, and moonlight shining on the sky shivers quartzy lustre over ripples of
the lake. The cuckoo singing near by our Hotel plays on a
harp, and the gulls flying about to and fro seek their food in
the waves. All these panorama may be gathered only in
this place."

Hakōné was the scene of many fierce conflicts in feudal
times. The latest battle is described thus:

"At May of the first year of Meiji, about thirty years ago
from the present, two feudal and military chiefs engaged in

battle on Hakōné mountain. One of them was Ōkubo Kagano-Kami, the Lord of Odawara-Han, and the other was Shonosuké Hayashi, Lord of Boshu; and the former belonged to Imperial Army and the latter was in Shogun's side. One time, Hayashi staid at Numadzu and held a good many soldiers. Leading them, he passed Mishima and came to Hakōné. He requested to the guardsmen of Barrier Gate to let his army pass through it. At that time, the guardianship of the gate was in the hand of Odawara-Han, and the request was not permitted by its master Kagano-Kami. He durst to pass through it by military power. Then the battle was instigated, and instantly guns were fired. All of dwellers of Hakōné were so frightened that they fled out of their dwellings and hid into mountains or valleys. After short struggle, the guardsmen could not conquer him, and retired to Odawara to shut themselves up in the castle for its defence. Taking advantage of victory, he advanced his army to destroy them. He missed unexpectedly his cogitation. He was defeated very badly, and retired to Yumoto. Secondly, he ran back to Hakōné, defeated by enemy. By violent pursuit of Imperial Army, he was finally obliged to run to Ajiro about four miles south from Atami and thence to escape to his own previous dominion. Thenceforth, the construction of perfect Imperial government by the revolution of Meiji, placed the nation out of impetuous struggles of Feudalism. And this ruin was remained to endless fancy."

The eight principal sights of Hakōné are summed up in these words:

1. "The snow-crowned view of Koma-ga-dake."

2. "The evening twilight of Tōga-shima."

3. "The flowing lanterns on the waves of Ashi lake."

4. "The wild geese flying down near Sanada-yama."

5. "The moonlight shining on Kurakaké-yama."

6. "The blossoms of azalea, or tsutsuji, flowering upon Byōbu-yama."

7. "The ship putting firewoods into when the weather snows."

8. "The wild ducks swimming about Kasumigaura in light-hearted manner."

"It was already described that all the mountain sceneries in Hakōné are very agreeable to us, but especially these eight sceneries may be picked out."

This is the style of the little volume from beginning to end.

If the author's language be quaint and flowery, let his readers bear in mind that he is trying to turn Japanese poetic thought into English prose. Though the sentences are high-flown, it is yet remarkable how nearly every word secures the desired effect, and leaves exactly the impression intended.

Jikoku-toge, the "Ten Province Pass," ten miles south of Miyanoshita and 2000 feet higher, offers the widest prospect of any vantage-point in Hakōné; the view is exceeded in grandeur only by that from Otome-toge—described in the chapter on Shōji.

At the summit of the pass there is an enormous boulder, called the "Ten Province Stone," because from it may be seen on clear days a panorama extending over no less than ten provinces of the Empire. "Bays, peninsulas, islands, mountain-ranges lie spread out in entrancing variety of form and colour," says Murray's *Handbook*. It is indeed a magnificent scene, with the great Fuji mounting high above all the other peaks —making them look quite unpretentious by comparison— and Sagami Bay, a thousand yards below, and but two miles away, a lovely azure contrast to the yellow autumn hills.

The abrupt descent to the sea is fringed with bamboo thickets wherein are to be found little groups of time-stained granite gods; and magnificent camphor-trees, the largest in Japan, spread wide their twelve-hundred-year-old limbs in the grounds of Kinomiya temple at the foot of the steep.

As we descended the mountain a cloud of steam shot sky-wards in the middle of the pretty town of Atami, which nestles in the sunshine on the shore of a little artificial-looking bay.

It was the geyser that has made Atami famous. Once every four hours it spurts, and its salty steam is said to be so efficacious for throat and lung complaints that the town is practically supported by those who come here to undergo the geyser cure.

Atami has no sights. It is simply a little restful gem of a place, which the hand of winter never touches; where plum-blossoms deck every nook and temple-ground whilst Tokyo is all a-wallow with icy slush; and where every hill-side that rises out of the sea is yellow with orange-groves. It is a little peaceful Eden where the sick come and find renewed health and strength, as they loaf about in the warm, sunny gardens during the winter, whilst, not twenty miles away, the Tōkaido may be white with snow.

CHAPTER VIII

SHŌJI, AND THE BASE OF FUJI

ONLY to see Shōji, and the scenery at the sacred Fujiyama's base, is worth the journey to far Japan.

The little hotel by Lake Shōji in the province of Koshu, on the north side of Fuji, certainly suffers, in the patronage it receives, from being so far from the railway; and yet, to those who have found this delightful retreat, its isolation is one of its principal charms, for the place has not yet become hackneyed. A hundred or so visitors, who do not begrudge their sole leather, find their way to Shōji annually, and never one returned who was not full of praises for the scenery, and enthusiasm for the plucky, enterprising English-born subject of the Emperor who discovered the spot, and invested all he had in founding a hotel there. Thus he opened up one of the fairest districts of Japan, and made it accessible to that class of tourist who only travels where he can sleep each night in a foreign-style bed.

To Hoshino San (the news of whose death, to my great regret, I received a few months before I wrote these lines) and his kind and clever little Japanese wife, I owed some of the pleasantest weeks I spent in Japan.

The Shōji trip is usually extended into a journey round the entire base of Fuji—one of the most beautiful scenic tours in Japan. Lakes, forests, rivers, and waterfalls succeed each other in turn, and always there are new and bewitching vistas of the matchless mountain which dominates the background, each seeming even more beautiful than the preceding views.

Though I have made this journey at each season of the year, I cannot say that at any one time it was more charming than at any other. Certainly nothing could exceed the beauty

of the scenery in the depths of winter, when Yamanaka plain
was two feet thick with snow, and Shōji lake locked in the frigid
embrace of the Frost King. As we tramped through the woods,
the sunlight, glinting through the frosted branches, studded
every tree with a myriad sparkling gems, and our boots
creaked and squeaked on the hard snow crystals that flashed
like diamonds underfoot. Fuji was covered to the forest-line
with a shroud of white, and the sharp, invigorating air made
one glory in the possession of vigorous health and for the
opportunity to enjoy this lovely face of Nature. The ice on
Shōji lake—which is the only one of the five sheets of water
at Fuji's foot that freezes—was so hard, and clear, and smooth
that only the sharpest skates could bite it; and we revelled in
the finest of all exercises amidst scenery of such beauty as
can well defy the world to excel it. Few people find their way
so far from the well-worn paths in winter, except a few permanent foreign residents of Yokohama who know the attractions of the place, and hasten there every year as soon as the
welcome news reaches them that "Shōji is frozen."

In summer the mountain is no longer white, being almost
entirely snowless, but there are many pleasures to compensate
for the absence of the beauty of the snow-cap. The woods
are at their best, ringing with the song of the cicadas, and the
air is soft and warm, yet bracing; whilst, to those who are
fond of fresh-water swimming, Shōji is a paradise.

Perhaps, if any months are more suitable than others to
see the lakes, May, October, or November should be chosen.
Then Fuji's crest is well covered with snow, and the woods
are clothed in their fairest dress.

There are three different places, accessible by rail, from
which to reach Shōji. They are Kofu, Ozuki, and Gōtemba,
but very few visitors go *via* either of the two former routes.
Gōtemba, the starting-place for the ascent of Fuji, is the most
convenient of these three points, being on the Tōkaido railway
—the beaten track to all the principal towns from Tokyo.
The trip, however, may be most delightfully combined with a
visit to Miyanoshita, where English-speaking coolies can be

obtained, for the modest sum of three shillings a day, to conduct one the entire distance. These Miyanoshita coolies are the best in Japan. Their backs are broad and muscular, and with a load of fifty pounds strapped to their shoulders they will easily cover as much ground per day as a good walker.

The way lies over Otome-toge, the "Maiden's Pass," up which there is a steep bridle-path of some three-quarters of a mile as a climax to a beautiful seven-mile walk. The pass is 3333 feet high, and between it and Fuji there are twenty miles of space; yet in clear weather the great mountain seems, from this altitude, so tremendous and overwhelming as to be scarcely more than a league distant. No words can convey the grandeur of the scene as Otome-toge's summit is reached and this vast prospect of seemingly illimitable expanse abruptly opens out to the vision. During the entire walk from Miyanoshita the barrier range of Hakōné is a natural wall that completely conceals the presence of the majestic mountain beyond. You toil slowly, and perhaps impatiently, up the zig-zag pony-path, that lies deep between the banks of yellow kaia-grass which rise high on either side, entirely blotting out every prospect for the last half-mile or more. This is one of the conceits that Nature loves. So that none of the effect she has arranged so carefully shall be lost, she takes cautious heed lest you should see aught else to claim your interest, and shuts out everything for a while before displaying this climax of her charms. Then suddenly she snatches the scales from your eyes and says, "There!" and you are nearly dazed by the loveliness she reveals to you.

To see Fuji for the first time like that must surely be one of the moments of one's life; those who can say that such was their experience are indeed to be envied: they will certainly never forget it.

The miles of intervening space give the lower slopes an exquisite lilac tint, which merges ever so softly and gradually into the green of the velvet valley below, and as timidly gives way to the petals of the great snow-blossom that hang from the skies above.

It is a glorious sight, but one before which the art of man is powerless, for the scene is too vast and too far-reaching for him to reproduce it by any craft he knows. Six miles away, and a thousand yards below, a thin winding line, looking like a thread on the velvet, is the Tōkaido railway; and just beyond it, the little hamlet of Gōtemba nestles snugly amidst the surrounding fields. On a clear day it seems that one could almost toss a biscuit into the village, and one would vow that a stone set rolling from Fuji's crest would never stop until it reached the valley floor—so cleverly does Nature delude us with the enchantment lent by distance.

With the exhilaration of so much beauty to delight the eye, one's feet speed down the mountain-side as though shod with the winged sandals of Mercury, instead of waraji, and Gōtemba can easily be reached by any active walker well within the hour.

The next eighteen miles is the least interesting part of the circuit of Fuji, though not by any means lacking in really fine scenic beauty. At Gōtemba one can either charter saddle and pack-horses, or engage a basha, as I did—for a miniature tram system traverses the whole distance to Kami-Yōshida. A special express vehicle, to which all others must give way, can be engaged for a few yen.

Subashiri, with its grey old temple, deep in a cedar-grove, was the only point of interest passed during the first hour, and through the straggling village the basha-man gaily drove the hide-bound abortion of a quadruped which passes for a horse in these parts, tooting incessant blasts on a horn to clear the way. The rickety vehicle creaked and rattled at every step, all its joints being loose, and it seemed a miracle that it could even hold together.

Just beyond Subashiri the ascent of the hill called Kago-zaka, or "Basket Hill," begins. This is very steep, and is ascended by many twists and turns which remind one of the Mount Tamalpais Railway in California, or the line up which the tiny train climbs the Himalayan foothills to Darjeeling. This, and all the surrounding hills, are composed entirely of ash from Fuji, which is piled up in waves and hummocks, in some cases many hundreds of feet deep, over the underlying rock. We left the basha at the bottom of the zig-zag and walked up a deep gully, cut by the rains, to the top, thus saving the horse the labour of dragging the weight of myself and the coolies up three miles of incline. The gradients are skilfully engineered so that one horse can pull a tram full of people up quite easily, but on the downward journey the cars run by gravity, and the speed they get up is sometimes dangerously fast.

On a subsequent occasion when coming down this place, as the vehicle raced round one of the bends in the track at a speed of twenty miles an hour, we found ourselves confronted by an upward-bound basha, not fifty yards away. The driver jammed the brake on, whilst the passengers on the upcoming car fled helter-skelter out of it, tumbling over one another as they did so. The other driver made frantic efforts to pull his horse off the track, but it would not budge, and for a moment or two it looked as if it must be crushed, as the track was single at this place. Fortunately the brake acted in time, and the car was brought to a standstill as the footboard gently touched the frightened horse's forelegs. Our reckless driver looked very shamefaced under the tongue-lashing he received from my coolies and from the occupants of the other car who had made such an unceremonious exit to safety, and he finished the rest of the journey carefully enough.

On the present trip, as we reached the summit and began the gravity run to Yamanaka, after taking out the horse and leaving it in charge of a boy to bring down more leisurely, the basha-man started on a wild career, rounding the bends at obviously dangerous speed. He took an acute outward curve at a truly startling rate, for if the vehicle had left the track it would have leapt into space. I opened the door to stop his madness, but before I could do so we were at another curve —fortunately an inner one—and the car jumped the rails and collided with the bank with such force that it was badly damaged. The undergear was not hurt, however, and we soon had it on the rails again, for it was very light; but I insisted on taking the remainder of the journey at a more reasonable pace until we got away from the curves. It is little wonder the rolling stock is in such a rickety condition if this is the treatment it has to submit to.

Loudly tooting his horn, to apprise the unwary of his approach, the basha-man brought us without further mishap to Yamanaka.

Mika-dzuki-Kosui, or "Three-Days'-Moon Lake," which lies north of the village, cannot compare with any of the four lakes farther on for beauty. The whole district hereabouts is bleak and desolate; in fact it is one of the most inhospitable in Japan, for the winds are almost constant and very trying, and the climate in winter is exceedingly severe. The great Fuji, the heart of which is but fifteen miles away to the south-west, spreads its skirts to the very village, and blocks out much of the winter sunlight. I have seen Yamanaka plain several feet thick with snow, yet on the western side of the mountain, a few days later, it was so warm that children were playing in the sunny fields, and it almost seemed like summer.

The whole southern side of the lake is destitute of trees, and the barren, wind-swept wastes around it are such sterile ground that no crops can be successfully raised there. The peasantry of this district are hardy, but extremely ugly. Only the fittest survive, and those who reach maturity have all pretensions to looks withered out of them before they arrive at that state.

As I went down to the lake to take a photograph, a curious mushroom-shaped cloud obscured the mountain-top. This effect is one that the Japanese greatly admire. They call it Fuji no Kasa, or "Fuji's umbrella," and I was very pleased to be able to add this phase of the mountain to my series of its portraits.

Changing into a fresh basha, we continued the journey. Soon after leaving the town a little woman by the wayside hailed us, but the driver shouted to her that this was a private car and that she could not enter it. She was obviously tired and disappointed, so I told the coolies to make room for her and get some of the baggage out of the way. She said she was very weary and had been hoping for the last hour that a basha would appear. She was dressed in her best, neatly and prettily, and told me she was going to Yōshida to sell some pieces of silk that she herself had woven. Undoing the furoshiki—a large handkerchief—in which she had the product of her skill, she asked me to accept a piece in return for the favour I had done her. Demur as I would, she would hear of no refusal, and fairly compelled me to accept a small square of beautifully-figured blue silk, for which she would not hear of accepting any payment. Nothing could have exceeded the grace of her manner when she bid me "Sayonara"[1] at our destination, nor the courtesy of the phrases in which she voiced her thanks; yet she was but a simple country-girl, and the balance of favour was all on her side, for the piece of silk was worth many times the small sum she would have had to pay for a basha fare in a public car.

Yōshida's one and only street is a mile or more in length. In the midst of it there is a fine old stone torii which makes a splendid foreground for Fuji, towering up beyond. On a subsequent tour of this district, when I visited the ancient village temple, I thought I had never seen so truly depressing a place. Save for the bright red torii at the entrance all was dismal indeed, for a drizzling rain was falling, and the tall cryptomerias, in the midst of which the rickety old temple stands, threw deep gloom over everything. Great drops falling from their branches splashed on to the row of mossy stone lanterns that stood below, and shivering crows, with ruffled feathers, sat above, emitting hoarse croaks and croupy caws.

In the temple a priest was mumbling in sepulchral tones what sounded like a dirge, now and again punctuating the weary monotony of his recitation with a drum-tap, whilst swirling clouds of mist swept through the tree-tops and wound themselves about the temple like a shroud. The whole place seemed redolent of death and spirits of the past, and I was glad to leave it and get back to my room with its warm hibachi,

---

[1] Good-bye; literally: "If it must be."

for the chill of the weather and the abject dreariness of the place sent cold shivers down my spine, and set me wondering how any human beings could spend their lives in such a lonely, cheerless, ghostly spot and still retain their reason.

Whilst I was dining on grilled eels and rice—a dish for which this place is noted, as the eels caught in the lakes are of a particularly delicate flavour—mine host entered, with many prostrations, and presented the register for my name, age, occupation, and other information such as the police require. An inspection of this volume indicated that these officials must be sorely puzzled at times to decide where truth ends and humbug begins. For instance, an American authoress, and a lady artist from San Francisco—both of whom I had met on a Pacific steamer—had described themselves as "ballet girls," aged sixty-seven and seventy-five respectively; and amongst the notabilities who had recently visited the district was "Abraham Lincoln," whilst another visitor, according to the book, was a veteran of 107 years. One brilliant wit had described his residence as "a dog kennel," to which some other traveller had added the appropriate line, "A very proper domicile for such a silly pup."

The landlord told me that such trifling with his register caused him serious trouble, and in the case of the two ladies mentioned, a police-officer had been sent all the way to Shōji to warn the hotel proprietor that "questionable characters" were coming his way. When it is remembered that the object of these registers is that foreigners may be easily traced by the police in the event of any harm befalling them, such feeble apologies for humour as the above are unpardonable insults to a highly-civilised and gentle people.

At six the next morning the beating of a drum in the near-by temple woke me. I threw off the thick, comfortable futons, and anxiously peered out at the weather through a tiny hole in the shutters. The sky was perfectly clear, the morning sunny, there was not a breath of wind, and the air was keen with a sharp frost which had coated everything with a thin film of white. Fuji was a poem of beauty in the morning light.

The crest, thickly covered with snow, gleamed against the cobalt sky, and great snow streamers hung down to the mountain's waist, like pendent blooms of white wistaria. Just over the summit a thin line of stratus, which floated like a canopy in the otherwise cloudless heavens, was red with the reflection of the roseate east, and the snow below it was dyed a delicate pink.

The conditions were ideal for the tramp to Shōji, so preparations were hurriedly made, breakfast soon despatched, the coolies harnessed to their burdens, and we were under way. A sharp walk of forty-five minutes brought us to Kawaguchi—the first of the four beautiful lakes which make the district lying at the northern base of Fuji the Westmorland of Japan. As we reached it we found its waters were so swollen that many of the low-lying houses of Funatsu, a village at the eastern end, were flooded half up to their roofs.

On a rocky peninsula stood the inn and a little Shinto temple, both beautifully situated in a grove of pine-trees and surrounded by old stone lanterns. We chartered a sampan and were soon speeding over the limpid depths, past quaint promontories, and pretty bays, and islands all ablaze with autumn tints.

Kawaguchi means "River Mouth"—a somewhat ill-fitting name, seeing that the lake has neither inlet nor outlet. It is four miles long, with an uninterrupted view of Fuji all the way, and it took us an hour and a quarter to reach the western end. We landed at the quaint village of Nagahama, where every path was bordered with streams of water, which raced down from the hills through troughs made of dug-out tree-trunks. Each house was an artist's study, with its heavily-thatched roof and walls completely covered with cobs of yellow corn, drying in the sun, and monster white radishes, half a yard long, called daikon, which are used for pickling. It looked as though the whole community were celebrating a harvest festival.

A steep hill called Torii-zaka, covered with mulberry bushes, divides Kawaguchi from the next lake, Nishi-no-umi.

We traversed this in twenty-five minutes, passing a pretty little temple in a dense clump of cryptomerias on the way. From the top of Torii-zaka—so called because formerly there was a stone torii at the summit—there is a fine panorama of the two lakes: Kawaguchi green as an emerald, and Nishi-no-umi, a deep sapphire blue. We walked the length of Nishi-no-umi, though boats can be had if required. The path rises high above the lake, and for three miles it passes through a real Arcadia. The woods blazed with gold and scarlet, and through the tracery of the silver birches, whose leaves were all shimmering in the soft autumn air, we could see the lake below, flashing and scintillating in the sun.

A high mountain on the south side of the lake concealed Fuji from view; but towards the end of the lake it gradually drops, and first the snow-cap, and then the streamers, re-appeared; and, finally, as we emerged from the wood into Nemba village, there was a superb picture across the lake, with Fuji almost filling the southern heavens.

After leaving Nemba we plunged into another wood—one of the most beautiful I have seen in any part of Japan. We had just left Arcadia, and now we were in Fairyland itself. Beneath the birch and maple trees the ground was thickly overgrown with long, silvery moss, on which the sunbeams lingered caressingly. Pheasants were crowing in the underbrush, and at one place a startled wild boar ran across the glade. I could not help but stop and feast my eyes on the bewildering beauty of the place every few yards—much to the delight of my coolies, who chuckled with pleasure at my admiration—and it was late in the afternoon ere we reached the end of this enchanted wood and Lake Shōji came into view.

We walked for half a mile along its shores, until we came to a spot where the coolies stopped and shouted loudly across the water. Soon there was an answering hail, and a boat appeared in the distance. Whilst waiting for it I could not resist the invitation of the lake, so, quickly stripping, I plunged deep into its clear, refreshing waters, and had a glorious swim—greatly to the amusement of my coolies. Then the

H

boat arrived, and I found Hoshino himself was at the tiller. This was my first meeting with the man whom later I found such an excellent companion and local guide.

Twenty minutes or so served to take us over the beautiful sheet of water to the peninsula of Unosaki, on which the Shōji hotel stands. A winding path led up to the prettily-situated house, and I was soon settled in a comfortable room, then revelling in a stinging-hot bath, and afterwards discussing an excellent dinner.

From my bedroom window there was a lovely view of Fuji through the pine-trees; and as I looked out before retiring, the moon was shining brilliantly over the mountain, and the lake just below me was smooth as a sheet of glass.

Several times since this, my first visit, I have been to Shōji, and every hour I spent there was golden. Shōji is one of the fairest beauty-spots in a land which is one of the beauty spots of the earth. The lake is 3160 feet above sea-level, and from the hotel, which is situated on the southern side of a steep pine-clad promontory, the vistas through the trees are exquisite. There is no place in Japan where one may better study the peerless Fuji, for here one may recline in a comfortable chair and view the sacred mountain at one's leisure. Indeed, it is possible to pay homage more idly still, for all the guest-rooms are on the southern side of the house, and one may lie abed, and on moonlight nights and clear mornings Fuji is the last thing one sees before sleeping and the first on waking. The prospects are, therefore, favourable to dream of the sacred mountain, and to dream of Fuji is, to the Japanese mind, a certain promise of luck to come. Should one, however, dream of it on the first night of January, prosperity and length of days are certain.

The Japanese have a phrase about New Year dreams which runs thus: " Ichi Fuji; ni-taka; san nasubi," meaning, "First Fuji; secondly a falcon; thirdly an egg-plant." These objects are the most lucky to dream of, in the order named. Fuji comes first, because it is the most beautiful natural feature of Japan, and as such it is an emblem of all that is best in

FUJI FROM LAKE SHOJI

everything. The falcon symbolises straightforwardness and honesty, because it can gaze unflinchingly at the sun; it is also a token of clean living, as it never feeds on carrion, but kills and devours its prey whilst the blood is warm. The egg-plant is considered a good omen because of its beautiful colour—the colour of an amethyst, a stone which the Japanese greatly admire.

In order to induce these lucky dreams the superstitious place pictures of the Gods of Luck under their pillows on New Year's Eve. It is, therefore, a common sight to see hawkers going round the towns on the last evenings of the year calling out, "O Takara, O Takara, O Takara!" This means "precious things," and the pictures they sell always represent the seven gods in a boat filled with bags of rice, jewels, gold coins, barrels of wine, farmers' implements, and other good things, and objects emblematical of the earth's bounty.

Though I did not have the good fortune to dream about Fuji, yet it was the last thing I saw before going to sleep, and the first as I opened my eyes the next morning, when the rising sun was tinting it with lovely harmonies of colour.

Every hour of every clear day the mountain was a different picture. There was the Morning Fuji, shaking off the mists of night; the Midday Fuji, with a belt of cumulus cloud floating across its waist; the Sundown Fuji, a symphony of pink and violet; the Moonlight Fuji, hanging like an inverted white fan in the dark sky; and a hundred other phases. The snow-cap is ever changing and never has the same lower outline for more than two or three consecutive days. Wind and sun are constantly at war with it. Sometimes it lies almost in a straight line across the higher slopes; then, as the sun melts it, only the snow lying in the ravines, which straggle down the mountain-side, remains, forming the great streamers which, from a distance, look like pendent white wistaria clusters.

Curiously enough, though fuji is the Japanese word for wistaria, philologists tell us that the mountain does not derive its name from this resemblance: whilst the sound is the same, the written character is quite different. Authorities disagree as to why the mountain was so named, but the Rev. J. Batchelor, who is the leading authority on the Ainu aborigines, claims it is the name of the Ainu Goddess of Fire, and was given to the mountain when these people inhabited this part of Japan, and has ever since been retained.

In winter Fuji is sometimes completely covered with snow, but, lovely as it then is, it is lovelier still when only the upper slopes are white. Then you see the phase that the Japanese worship—the effect that makes this mountain the most beautiful in the world. Having seen Fuji under almost every conceivable aspect, and many other famous mountains of the world also, I know well that all who have seen it under as many conditions will unhesitatingly endorse the claim. There is much about Fuji that cannot be put into words. The subtle charm of its almost perfect symmetry and delicate colouring defy the efforts of the finest artists. I have never seen any painting that did the mountain justice.

However, one does not go to Shōji simply to see Fuji; the lake itself can well hold its own with the most celebrated scenic beauties of Japan. Except on the south, the lake is hemmed in by hills clothed in forest. Nature seems intentionally to have left the south side open so that the entire sweep of the mountain could be seen, down to the spreading skirts which dip into Shōji's waters. That side of the lake is a vast lava-bed, formed by the great streams of molten rock which once descended from Fuji's crater, and flowed until they were arrested by a natural mountain barrier, against which they banked up, walling in great hollows which in time filled with water. Thus the lakes were formed.

Popular belief holds that they are all connected with each other by subterranean watercourses. The fact, however, that they all lie at varying altitudes would seem to dispose of this theory effectually, as the water in the different basins rises and falls concurrently. This would not be the case were they connected; the lowest lake would be always full at the expense of the others. The shrinkage in dry weather is mainly due to the natural processes of evaporation and absorption, which is the cause of the constantly changing water-line.

The Shōji lava moor is covered with stunted trees, and there are sights there which are among the wonders of Japan. At the base of Maruyama, a pine-covered mountain midway between the lake and the lower slopes of Fuji, there are some caves which are well worth visiting. After a severe winter enormous icicles hang from the roof to meet the frozen stalagmites which rise from the floor of ice below, and, meeting them, form into glistening crystal pillars.

One of these caves is like a stage representation of some fairy cavern, and as I made my way, by the light of a flaming torch, under the hanging clusters and among the icy columns, the flickering light cast trembling shadows everywhere, and turned the frozen pillars into jewelled shafts sparkling with every colour, whilst myriads of crystals glittered on the frosted walls. It was all bewilderingly beautiful, and as I crept about, cautiously and quietly—for fear of inviting one of the great frozen spears to fall upon me—in this wondrous underground treasure-chamber, I felt like Aladdin in the genie's cave, and half expected to find great chests of gems lying open, from which I might help myself and live in luxury ever afterwards.

Perhaps the loveliest hour of the day at Shōji is just before the sun disappears behind the hills. Then Fuji is likely to be in complaisant humour and to display its charms without reserve. The breeze, too, often dies away at this hour, and the waters of the lake then become Fuji's looking-glass, and the mountain seems to lean over the edge of the mirror, enamoured of its own reflection.

This charming place has yet another attraction. The bathing is of the best. There are spring-boards, diving-stages, and every convenience for the enjoyment of the swimmer, and one may plunge headlong into deep, crystal-clear water, and swim to one's heart's content amidst some of the loveliest scenery in Japan.

I might devote pages to the pleasure of shooting in this

neighbourhood—for there are wild duck on the lake, and pheasants and wild boars in the forests—but I must hurry on, for whilst Shōji is the base from which to work this district, there is an even fairer sheet of water but five miles away.

Though I have visited Lake Motosu at least a score of times, as many more would not serve to cool my ardour for its beauty. It is the pearl of Japanese lakes, and challenges comparison with the fairest waters of the world.

There are two ways of reaching it from Shōji—by a path which traverses Myōjin-yama, a mountain 1000 feet higher than the lake and on the western side of it; or by a lower road. The former is the finer route, as the views are truly superb, and as one ascends higher and higher, Fuji seems to become higher too.

This path, which zigzags by easy grades up the mountain, was made under Hoshino's personal direction. He never wearied of improving the property he owned, nor of adding to it as he could afford. He therefore bought a large tract of the mountain-side in order to make this path, which enables visitors to gain the summit with ease, and enjoy the lovely panorama that lies map-like at their feet.

It is almost idle to attempt any description of this view. As one slowly ascends, the prospect opens out, and grows ever more beautiful, until a spot is reached, by a short detour from the path, the view from which is so entrancing that language fails to describe the scene. Often, as I have stood there, I have thought how empty must be the soul of, and how poor a thing the precious gift of sight to him who can gaze on such a prospect without a thrill of rapture or a touch of feeling.

What the Gornergrat is to Switzerland, what Le Brevant is to France, what Darjeeling is to India, what Yosemite Point is to California—so is Myōjin-yama to Japan.

When first I saw this glorious prospect, the sudden revelation of so much beauty held me completely spellbound, and entirely speechless. Such moments in a traveller's life are for

APPROACHING STORM ON LAKE MOTOSU

greater things than speech: for thoughts, not words—and perhaps for a silent supplication to one's Maker.

Before me, seeming to touch the arch of heaven, was Fuji, in all the glory of its very loveliest aspect, the upper slopes all shrouded in white, and with a belt of cloud floating across its waist, below which the forest-clad slopes were softly lilac tinted by the haze. To the left, and far below, lay the un-ruffled emerald waters of Shōji lake, reflecting the unbroken image of the sky, and holding up the mirror to the lovely face of Nature that smiled around it. To the right Motosu lake was of that brilliant blue which one sees in mid-Pacific. It was a sapphire set with gold and rubies, for the bordering woods were all ablaze with autumn tints. Away to the north and west, range beyond range of mountains were piled up in the wildest confusion, and, back of all, the snow-capped giants of Kōshu and Shinshu seemed to brush the sky.

When I had absorbed the scene for a while, I turned to Hoshino. His face was beaming, for, Nature-worshipper as he was, there was nothing that pleased him more than to see others appreciate what he himself so dearly loved.

"I thought that would stagger you!" he said; "Now let us have some lunch."

The coolies had preceded us and had lit a fire, so that lunch was already prepared. And what a lunch! At the Shōji hotel they never did such things by halves in Hoshino's day. He knew with what feelings the view would inspire me, and he knew, too, how the inner man would be stimulated by the exercise and invigorating air. He was not going to let my enjoyment be half-hearted, and his wife, who always packed the lunch-basket, knew well what to provide. There were sardines, with tomato and cucumber salad, cold chicken and pheasant, slices of York ham, and a pot of stew that was soon steaming hot. Then there were mince-pies, bread and cheese, and fruit, with a bottle of wine in which to drink the thoughtful little Okusan's health.

This was Hoshino's idea of a lunch whenever I went off for a day in the hills, and who will not admit that enjoyment of even the most glorious of Nature's works may be augmented by an excellent meal?

After a rest we went down by a winding track to the bridle-path which skirts Motosu lake, a few hundred feet above it, and we followed this until we came to Nakano-kura-toge, a mountain ridge at the western end. The view from this place was superb. The great Fuji was all white and lilac, with deep green pine-clad skirts that swept in one magnificent curve into the liquid sapphire of the lake, around which the woods were mellow with the soft colours of a Persian carpet. Snow-white billows floated in the heavens, and silvery kaia-grass, nodding to the breezes, made a foreground for one of the most lovely landscapes I know in any land.

Motosu lake was always wondrously beautiful. When the sun shone brightly, and there was no wind, its waters were no longer sapphire, but the blue of a deeply-coloured turquoise. They changed with every cloud that swept over them. Sometimes they were shot with purple, and where the wind ruffled them and the light caught the ripples, they became streaked with grey; then azure patches would flit across them, and under the shadowing hills they were a bluish green. After sundown, when the heavens began to glow and Fuji's snows were pink, the lake would become opalescent as mother-o'-pearl, and, as darkness gathered, and the burning colours slowly faded away, the waters became chill and grey as steel, and finally blacker than the night.

The encircling hills, too, were changeable as the jewel they embosomed. One minute a mountain-top would be dark, gloomy and forbidding; then, as the heavy cloud which had obscured the light floated from the peak, it would become all golden in the sunshine. On lake and mountain alike the sun was always playing beautiful pranks. Sometimes it would find a tiny hole in a sombre vapoury billow, and, shooting a searchlight ray through it, would single out some mountain-crest and make it gleam like a gilded dome; or, discovering some beautiful spot of colour in the woods, would set it all aglow.

Many happy days I spent with my camera in this lovely

spot; but not until three years later, and after I had tramped
the fourteen miles to Nakano-kura-toge and back more than a
dozen times, and waited patiently for many an hour, was I
able to take the photograph of "Fuji and the Kaia Grass."
Sometimes, when the mountain was clear, there would be
too much wind, and the grass was blown about so violently
as to render the making of the desired picture impossible.
And sometimes the grass would be still, but Fuji obscured by
clouds.   At last, however, the long awaited moment really
came.   The mountain was clear; for a few brief seconds the
grass was still, and during them I secured the coveted picture
—which depicts the mountain in early winter.

The days flew swiftly by at Shōji, and my visits always
came to an end far too soon.   Then the coolies would be
harnessed up again (it always took four of them to carry my
photographic kit and luggage, and there was but a small basket
of the latter), and we would start off to complete the circuit
of the sacred mountain.   There are two ways by which this
can be done—*via* the waterfalls of Kamiide, or by way of the
Fuji river.   Nearly every one chooses the latter route, as it
offers the most novelty.

The Kamiide route is, however, a very fine one, as the
Shira-ito-no-taki, or "White-Thread Waterfalls," are ex-
ceedingly beautiful, and without rival in Japan, for even
Nikko, with all its lovely cascades, has nothing like them.

After leaving Motosu village and traversing a moor for a
dozen miles or so, one comes to some pretty bamboo groves,
in which there are many holes in the earth from which great
streams of water gush forth with a roaring sound.   The water
is crystal-clear, but of a deep blue tint, like the colour of
Motosu lake.   There is little doubt that these holes are the
mouths of a subterranean channel from the lake.   The streams
unite and join the Shiba-kawa, a river which plunges over a
precipice, forming the O-taki, or "Great Waterfall" of Kamiide.

The "White-Thread Falls" are, however, a much finer
sight.   They are composed of a thousand tiny streams which,
percolating through the loose volcanic detritus above the lava

bed, gush out of the face of a cliff, two hundred yards or more in length, and fall in delicate parallel jets that break into mist on the rocks below. This water curtain makes a pretty foreground for Fuji, which towers grandly above in the distance.

One of the wonders of Kamiide is an ancient cherry-tree —the finest in Japan—which is said to have been planted by the first Shogun, Yoritomo, over seven hundred years ago. Its venerable trunk is ten feet in diameter, whilst its branches, supported by many props, extend outwards for fifteen yards all around it.

To complete the circuit of Fuji *via* the Fuji-kawa, one proceeds by the path that skirts Lake Motosu and crosses Nakano-kura-toge; then for the next twelve miles every turning opens out some pretty scene. The path drops tortuously by the side of a limpid rivulet, which dances its way, all sparkling, over gravel and boulder, and under lurid maples and spiky pines, and past persimmon-trees, whose leafless branches in autumn bend low with the harvest of golden ripening fruit they bear. A hundred cascades leap down the mountain-side, through gorgeously-tinted woods, helping to swell the stream which murmurs so merrily on its way to join the great Fuji river; and many a water-wheel squeaks and groans over its task of grinding the yellow corn, which, with rows and festoons of monster radishes, is drying on every fence and on the walls of every cottage. This lovely walk is one to delight the soul of the artist and the lover of Nature.

The way must have been an ill-omened one, however, in the old days, judging by the great number of stone gods one sees. These are carved on stone slabs, and are images of Do-sojin, the protector of wayfarers. Prayers offered up to these images are said to be a certain safeguard against harm. I inquired if the ever-busy saint Kōbō Daishi carved these. To my surprise I was informed that he did not. He was probably taking "a day off" from the strenuous labours of his lifetime!

The way then lay through the village of Kawauchi-Furuseki

FUJI AND THE SHIRA-ITO WATERFALL

—one of the cleanest, prettiest, and neatest I have seen in Japan, where every house was full of rustic charm—and then twisted and turned upwards again, amid scenes of ever-changing beauty, and finally dropped in a long slope till it reached Tambara on the Fuji-kawa, about eighteen miles from Shōji. We arrived at dusk, but, as there was no good inn, we took a boat half a mile down the river to the little town of Yokaichiba, where there is a most excellent Japanese hotel.

At eight o'clock the next morning we started by boat down the river. A galaxy of laughing little neisans came to see us off —each insisting on carrying some small portion of the baggage —and as we pushed off into the current their voices rang out in a chorus of sweet sayonaras. They formed a pretty picture as they stood on the shingly bank, waving their hands to us till we were out of sight, with the quaint houses of Yokaichiba behind them, and the rugged forest-clad mountains towering high in the background.

The boat was about forty feet long, six feet wide, and a yard deep. It was braced by three thwarts, and had a high, pointed, overhanging prow. The crew consisted of three rowers, with short oars; a pilot, who stood in the bow with a pole, and a helmsman, who took up his position on the after thwart and steered with a long sweep. The bottom of the boat was flat, and so pliant that the planks undulated from stem to stern whenever we got into choppy water. It was heavily ballasted with charcoal, which served the purpose of giving the light craft a good bite on the water, instead of letting the swift current slip beneath it. The charcoal also served to keep our feet clear of the water that leaked and splashed in continually. It was done up in neat packages, bound with straw, and was distributed about the boat so as not to interfere with the rowers, who stood up to their work. Thus we started on the forty-five mile journey to Iwabuchi.

The charge for the boat was eight yen (sixteen shillings). This included the wages of the five men. As it takes three days for these men to tow the boat up again, in addition to the half-day spent in going down stream, the net earnings of each man per day, allowing half a day for rest, were less than tenpence (exclusive of the small freight charge which is made on the charcoal). The boats can only be returned empty, and thus the men earn nothing on the return journey.

The amount of excitement to be had from the trip down the rapids is governed entirely by the height of the water. On the occasion here described, the water was not far below the point at which the men decline to take a boat down. In a few hours, however, the water may drop several feet, as the Fuji-kawa is subject to very sudden freshets, which subside as quickly as they gather, and when the water is quite low from start to finish there is not a single thrill. The river-bed in many places is fully 400 yards wide, but the stream seldom occupies more than a small portion of this course; only during periods of most exceptional floods does the water rise to fill the full breadth of the channel.

Shortly after leaving Yokaichiba we passed the village of Itomé, where the Haya-kawa comes rushing down from the Kōshu mountains to join the parent stream. The river, narrowing here, becomes much swifter, and sweeps by a most remarkable cliff called Byobu-iwa, or "Screen Rock," composed of great andesite columns dipping into the river at an angle of 45°.

At 8.30 we passed the first real rapid, but it was only a short one, and we slipped down it at a speed of about fourteen miles an hour. Half an hour later we arrived at Haku, not far from the great Buddhist temple of Minōbu, where the bones of Saint Nichiren are buried. The scenery was now of great beauty. The fertile hills were terraced, and all the lower ground was covered with mulberry bushes—for this is a famous district for silk culture. Lofty cliffs towered skywards on the left bank, and a minute after leaving Haku the boat rushed headlong for the base of a precipice, against which the waters were banked a yard high, as the river made a plunge towards it and was angrily repulsed round a sharp curve. This is one of the few places where the rapids are really thrilling. The pilot sharply struck his pole against the gunwale, to attract the attention of the deity who presided over the destinies of the boat; but for a moment it seemed that the god was unmindful, and that we must inevitably strike and be dashed to pieces. The watchful guardian, however, took heed at the critical instant, and the boat, rising on the bank of water, was swept round the curve with a mere touch of the pilot's pole to swing the high prow clear.

The next hour was steady going, with the current somewhat sluggish. On both sides of the river the rugged mountains were gorgeous with autumn colours, and at the base of the wondrously-terraced foot-hills picturesque villages beaded the banks at every mile. The rhythmic swaying of the standing rowers, whose blades dipped regularly into the water, grew faster and faster, and, perchance inspired by the beauty of the scenery, they broke into a chant, in which the pilot and steersman joined.

Then the river divided. Taking the left channel, which was swifter than a mill-race, we shot down it at exhilarating speed. At the confluence of the two channels the water was broken into great waves. Here, notwithstanding the efforts of the men, the boat got broadside to the stream, and was swayed over till the gunwale was almost level with the water. The heavy load of charcoal ballast served us well here, and kept us from being swamped. Our skilful boatmen quickly had the craft in hand again and then pulled in to the left bank to visit the famous Tsuri-bashi, or "Hanging Bridge," which is suspended over a swift tributary that foams to join the Fuji river between precipitous walls. To cross this bridge—which is sixty yards long, and made of narrow strips of planking laid across eighteen parallel wires, with a narrow board pathway in the middle—is an undertaking which he whose nerves are at all unsteady will be well-advised to attempt warily. As soon as you set foot on it, it begins to shake, and as you proceed, the spring of the bridge causes the floor to seem to rise knee-high at every step. I once saw a visitor get to the middle and become so terror-stricken that he could neither proceed nor retreat, so he lay down, until one of the boatmen went to his assistance. There is a trick about it that requires a little learning, but with perseverance one can master the motion so as to be able to run across.

A most bizarre feature of the landscape here is a modern factory, where timber from the hills is pounded into pulp for the manufacture of paper. This factory supplies most of the newspapers in Japan, but fine-quality papers are manufactured here also, for the mill ranks with the Oji works in Tokyo as a producer of the best paper made in Japan.

After a short stop we pushed off again, and soon a grand scene opened out with Fuji on our left, and the pointed peaks of Ashitaka-yama straight ahead of us. We passed many boats being towed laboriously upstream. The trackers were shod with waraji of a kind peculiar to this river. They were not more than three inches long, and were fastened only to the forepad of the foot, as only the toes need this protection; the body, straining on the ropes, is thrown forward at such an angle that the heel never touches the ground. The work of towing the boats up-stream is most arduous, and if ever labourers earned the price of their hire these Fuji-kawa boatmen are surely they.

There were many curious fish-traps in the river. They were set in artificially dammed-up narrows, and consisted of long, conical, bamboo baskets tied to poles. The fish, bound down-stream, rush headlong into these traps, and being unable to return, or even turn round, are speedily drowned—for it is but a matter of a few minutes to drown a fish held head downwards to a swift current.

Rapid then succeeded rapid in quick succession, and many a time the pilot had to use his pole to ward us off the threatening precipices, as we swept past them with the water swirling and foaming all around us. Near the village of Matsuno the cliffs on the right bank were a palisade of tall, hexagonal basaltic columns standing perfectly upright, and regular in formation as a paling. The river then rippled quietly along, with Fuji now always in view, till we entered the mouth of the Iwabuchi canal, and came to rest in the heart of the town

at one o'clock—the forty-five mile journey having taken just five hours.

We walked to Suzukawa along the Tōkaido—the old post-road that in feudal times connected the Mikado's capital, Kyoto, with the Shogun's capital, Yedo. This is an excellent part of the "beaten track" to study rural Japan, as small villages line the way and everything is picturesque. Outside the cottages the peasants were busily heading rice, or winnowing it by hand, using half the highway to spread the mats on which the grain is dried.

The Tōkaido must have been a beautiful road in the days of Daimyos' caravans; but with the advent of the locomotive it fell into desuetude as the main business artery of Japan, and, in the thirst for modern ideas, fine old pine-trees in the avenue that once lined its entire length were ruthlessly cut down, ugly telegraph poles taking their place. But the Tōkaido still remains, in places, just as it was in the old days, and near Suzukawa one can see it at its best. Hokusai and Hiroshigé made all its sights famous, and even to-day one can see many of the quaint characters, that Hokusai so dearly loved, plodding along, attired just as they were in the days of the great Japanese Cruikshank.

On a summer afternoon, when the cicadas are droning, and the crows cawing in the trees, it is easy to fall into a reverie, as one sits on the grass by the wayside, and conjure up the days of Hiroshigé's "Hundred Views," for here are the very places, and passing you are the very people, that he painted. And there is lovely Fuji too, and one can almost imagine a Daimyo's cortège, with the feudal chief gazing enraptured at the mountain from the window of his norimono, as it is carried by on the shoulders of many bearers—just as one of Hokusai's woodcuts depicted such an incident.

But reveries are apt to be of short duration, for suddenly there comes a piercing whistle, and then a roar, as a railway-train rushes past, not a hundred yards away, and one is brought back with a shock from feudal times to the unpicturesque realities of twentieth-century days.

Late in the afternoon, when I had seen everything settled at the Suzuki inn (which is one of the most extortionate in Japan), I strolled along until I came to the banks of a river from which there was a magnificent view of the sacred mountain.

The setting sun made the waters gleam like molten gold, and in the glowing depths Fuji's inverted cone appeared as in a mirror. The sun sank below the horizon as I watched, and soon all around me was enveloped in the gloom of approaching night. But Fuji still stood out clearly as ever, and I observed the beautiful phenomenon of the shadow of the earth creeping gradually up the mountain-slopes as the sun sank ever deeper below the horizon. Higher and higher it crept, until only the snowy crest was left to hold for a few brief moments the amber light; then, as the shadow left the sacred peak, the sun's rays fell on nothing but the heavens above, slowly tinting them with all the colours of the shells of Enoshima.

CHAPTER IX

AN ASCENT OF FUJI-SAN

FROM the earliest ages Japanese writers have described the beauty of Mount Fuji, and poets have sung its charms. The old landscape painters were so enthralled by the ethereality of the sacred peak that they painted it from almost every conceivable point—and some inconceivable points, too—along its southern base. When nearly eighty years of age, Hokusai, that great immortaliser of the peasant life and character of his day, published a series of no less than a hundred wood-cuts of views of Fuji in colour, from as many different places on the Tōkaido, and with as many distinctive foregrounds. Hiroshigé did the same, and every other artist in the land, famous or infamous, has at some time or other been elevated with the desire to portray one or more of the transitory phases of the matchless peak under the spell of which all have fallen, but which none has ever been able to delineate with justice.

Other mountains may be painted with some degree of truth—even the beautiful Jungfrau. But not so Fuji-san. Its loveliness is so delicate, and its moods so ever-changing and so evanescent, that the most the artist can ever hope to accomplish is to give some idea of the mountain's charm at a particular moment. Every Nature-worshipper visiting Japan has fallen in adoration at the foot of Fuji, and foreign writers and poets have emulated the Japanese in attempting to describe the beauty that has inspired them. Who, that has seen its snow-clad crest floating in the deep blue of the winter sky, will not admit that the mountain is worthy of all the praise that has been bestowed upon it—and more?

It is not only that the physical charms of the mountain

cast so powerful a spell—though they alone would make of
Fuji an object of homage to any lover of the beautiful from
any land on earth—but also that the web of history and legend
spun round the snowy peak is as charming and full of tragedy,
mystery and sentiment as the moods of the beauty are capri-
cious and fitful—a combination that marks Fuji as unique
among the mountains of the earth.

Fuji is a dormant volcano, an isolated cone 12,365 feet
in height—figures easy to remember if one thinks of the months
and days that make a year—tapering from a circumference
of over eighty miles at its base to but two and a half miles at
the summit. It cannot be accounted extinct, for at the north-
east side of the mountain-crest the ground is so hot in places
that in cold weather steam may be seen rising from the ash,
testifying to the presence of fissures leading to subterranean
fires which may at any time burst forth again. Geology shows
that Fuji is but a young volcano which has not yet destroyed
its beauty by bursting its crater rim. Up to the present time
the only sign of degradation in Fuji's shape is a small hump
on the south-eastern slope. This is the crater Hoei-zan; it
opened up during the last eruption, which began in December,
1707, and lasted until 22nd January, 1708.

That was over two hundred years ago; and by most writers
Fuji is now referred to as extinct. But what are two hundred
years in the life of a volcano? What are two centuries in the
cooling of the crust of the earth? In the story of a planet such
an interval is but a passing moment. Vesuvius was dormant
for a much longer period before it laid Herculaneum and
Pompeii in ashes. Indeed, prior to the great cataclysm of A.D.
79 Vesuvius was regarded as an entirely harmless volcano,
and was never looked upon by the inhabitants of the cities at
its base, even to the last moments ere it spread destruction
all around it, as the menace that it ever is to the Naples of
to-day. In Japan—this land of hot-springs, earthquakes, and
solfataras—who, with the terrible calamity which destroyed
the sleeping Bandai-san in 1888 still fresh in memory,
will make so bold as to deny that all volcanoes should be

dreaded? The great Fuji, peaceful as it looks, should yet be viewed with apprehension. The beauty is not dead, but merely slumbers.

Students of history may see, in some of the lurid winter sunsets that dye the snows of Fuji crimson, a reflex of the tragedies in which the mountain has played a part—for on one occasion at least the sacred slopes have been steeped in human blood. Towards the end of the thirteenth century the Mongol Emperor, Kublai Khan, despatched a great fleet, manned by 150,000 men, to Japan, for the purpose of conquering the country and adding it to his own dominions. This undertaking was a disastrous failure; for the Japanese, aided by the fury of the elements, scattered the invading hosts and ships, and many hundreds of the Mongol soldiers were beheaded on the southern side of Fuji.

Thus, alike for the fabric of historical associations and legends with which it is enveloped, and for its symmetry and beauty, does Fuji inspire and appeal to the Japanese—most æsthetic and imaginative of peoples—and thus it is that the peerless mountain has formed so favourite a motive for artists during all the ages since a knowledge of art was first imported into the land.

As I gazed at Fuji, enraptured, in that hour when I first saw Japan, a great desire settled upon me to climb the mountain, to creep foot by foot up that perfect outline which sweeps in one magnificent curve almost from the sea-shore to the sky, and to look far and wide over Japan from the very topmost pinnacle of the Empire. Two years later I gratified that wish, and now the mountain's crest was again my goal.

The train was creeping laboriously up a steep ascent between hills covered with dense undergrowth and capped with crooked old pines—rugged, weather-beaten veterans, all twisted, bent, and straggling—which scorned every law of balance and proportion. From the tops of their red, reticulated trunks a few gnarled branches stretched outwards and downwards, with seemingly no regard for any rules such as govern the growth of well-regulated trees in other lands; and from the extremities of their distorted limbs a few spiky needles stuck out in little tufts, as though bristling with temper, like the hackle of an angry fighting-cock.   By their very defiance of convention these trees were beautiful—and utterly and peculiarly Japanese.

From the pine-clad hills we descended to rice-fields— carpeted like velvet with the verdant spears of tender new-grown shoots—and thence, once more, up into hills covered with feathery bamboos, rustling to the breeze.

The site of every cottage among these hills and dales seemed to have been chosen only after mature and careful consideration with a view to securing the best and most artistic effect.   Each little humble dwelling stood just where it ought; were it moved either to left or right the picture would be marred.   Made of natural-finished woods, bamboo and thatch, and standing in a cane-fenced enclosure, each of these huts was in itself a study.

Before them lay the terraces and network of the rice-fields. No one who has seen the rice-fields and watched the seed mature to ripened ear, will deny that the beauty of the crop, which demands more unceasing toil than any other that the earth produces, is one of the greatest charms of the lands of the East.

Descending again from the terraced hills to more rice-fields, the line bent round to the south, and as the train pulled up at a country station the emerald ocean lay before us.   It was Sagami Bay, flecked with the white wings of a score of sampans.   Long glittering waves were lazily rolling in, foaming as they surged up the pebbly beach, and receding with long-drawn sighs to their appointed limits.

Here, also, by the sea as on the land, everything was typically Japanese.   Near the water's edge there was a rugged bluff with a few straggling pines leaning over the edge.   One of the pines had leant too far, and was in peril of falling into the sea; but some thoughtful soul, seeing the artistic effect of that old tree, bowing to inevitable doom, had placed a firm prop under it, securely founded on the rock, so that for many years there would be no danger of the landscape losing a bold and picturesque feature.

Leaving the placid waters of Sagami Bay behind us, the line bent inwards again, and the great Kōshu range lay ahead —blue, dark, and forbidding under the heavy storm-clouds above it. And now, as the train turned westward, the great Fuji loomed before us, all black and purple in its summer dress. Always splendid, magnificent in all its moods, Fuji on this August evening was grand and awe-inspiring. To the south the sky was clear, but over the great volcano the heavens were filled with great banks and convolutions of clouds—white as snow, and, in places, dark as night—and a bright sunlit mass of vapour behind the mighty peak caused it to stand out black and frowning, towering to the zenith—a spectacle sublime.

As we drew nearer to our destination the prospects for a fair to-morrow grew steadily worse and worse. The snowy billows of cumulus gave way to angry nimbus clouds, deep purple-grey and blue, which filled the western heavens. Once, however, the storm-clouds parted, and the dark brow of Fuji appeared, seeming almost to overhang us, as if threatening with destruction all who should attempt to invade its dizzy solitudes: as if the very goddess of the mountain herself challenged us to dare dispute her right to reign in those altitudes alone and undisturbed.

We reached Gōtemba at 6.30 P.M., and our arrival at the Fuji-ya Inn caused a pleasant diversion for the inhabitants of the town—to judge by the numbers that collected in front of the hotel, awaiting with interest the result of our discussion as to whether it would be better to remain at Gōtemba for the night or push on, as we had intended, and sleep in one of the rest-huts on the mountain-side. We decided to have supper and think it over. The inn, we found, was full of guests— Japanese pilgrims *en route* to do homage to the goddess of the mountain by worshipping at the shrines at the crater's lip.

Mount Fuji is officially "open" only for three months of

the year—July to September. To undertake the ascent at any other period would entail much expense and risk. During the season thousands of pilgrims annually make the ascent, for it can be made in easy stages, as there are rest-huts, called gō-mé, where food and a shake-down for the night may be obtained, at approximately five, six, seven, eight, nine, and ten thousand feet. Some old people, who undertake the pilgrimage as a climax to a life of religious devotion, take a week or ten days to make the ascent, painfully and perseveringly accomplishing a thousand feet or so each day. This being the "open" season, and Gōtemba one of the favourite starting-points for the climb, accounted for the large number of pilgrims at the inn that night. Inquiry of the landlord elicited the information that there were over seventy—as many being crowded into each room as it could be made to hold.

Supper over, any further discussion as to the wisdom or otherwise of starting that night was superfluous, for, through the open window of the room that had been assigned to my Japanese *fidus Achates*, Nakano, and myself, we watched the storm-clouds growing momentarily more threatening, until the skies were black as pitch, though the moon was full. Presently a blinding flash of lightning rent the heavens, and a terrific crash simultaneously accompanied it. The long-gathering storm had burst at last, and even if the cyclopean forces that formed the great volcano had been loosed once more, the spectacle could hardly have been grander than the battle of the elements that we witnessed during the two succeeding hours. The lightning danced, and flickered, and flashed over the whole vault of heaven, and the thunder for an hour was incessant. Many of the pilgrims seemed overcome with fear, and crowded together in the rooms and passages, loudly repeating prayers in whining, sing-song tones. At length the tumult ceased, and we betook ourselves to the futons (padded quilts) to get well-needed rest, preparatory to the tedious tramp of the morrow.

At 3 A.M. the bustle and clatter of the pilgrims, who were preparing for an early start, woke me; I got up to find the sky

FUJI FROM LAKE MOTOSU

clear, and Fuji blocking out a great triangular space in the starry heavens, its whole outline brilliantly illumined by the soft light of the moon. I lay down again, and slept till five, when the little neisan, who had come in to wake us, exhorted me to look at Fuji, which, to my delight, was still in gracious mood, displaying its charms without reserve, and though snowless, save for a few patches, looked lovely, and all pink and violet in the early morning atmosphere.

There was much ado about making the preparations for the ascent, as it was necessary to secure the services of four lusty coolies to carry my photographic apparatus, portable photographic dark-tent, supply of plates, blankets, change of clothing, and food, for I had come prepared to stop a week on the mountain, if necessary, in order to secure the views I coveted from the summit. The food to be got at the rest-huts is of only the coarsest kind; and I hoped my own supply would prove sufficient, so that I might not have occasion to resort to it.

Whilst Nakano was engaging the coolies, I amused myself by inspecting the pendent flags, with which the front of the inn was decorated. These are, strictly speaking, not flags at all but towels. They are often the advertisements of tradesmen, who hang them up at the hotels at which they stay, or by the fountains of Buddhist temples, or near some Shinto shrine. These towels, in addition to having the merchant's name and business described on them, are frequently of very dainty and artistic design. By hanging them up at the temple fountain a double duty is performed. A service is rendered to the temple in the gift, trifling though it be, of a towel, so that those who cleanse their fingers and lips before entering to pray may have the wherewithal to dry them with; and a very excellent advertisement is obtained by placing on the towel an effective design with the donor's name and business description. The inscription cannot escape the attention of the user, as the towel is always suspended by a string and a thin piece of bamboo, so that it hangs straight, and can therefore be easily read. Similar towels are also used as banners by pilgrims,

who donate them to each inn at which they put up, thereby
publishing the enterprise of their own particular club.

Gōtemba is not an interesting town. It is not even picturesque, but is very mean and poor-looking, and lacking in any
single feature except the view of the glorious mountain to
which it owes its existence—for the inhabitants look to make
sufficient earnings during the months the mountain is "open"
to keep them for the remainder of the year. They are as lacking
in interest as the place.

Nakano having secured the services of three brawny
luggage-carriers, called gōriki, on each of whose broad backs
about fifty pounds of luggage was strapped, we left Gōtemba
at 7 A.M. and took to a cinder path through rice and corn fields.
Straight ahead of us the great Fuji towered to the very skies,
and it seemed a hopeless task to expect to reach the summit
that night.

From the rice-fields we tramped over a rising moor, covered
with long grass and studded with stunted pine-trees, where
birds were twittering everywhere in the soft balmy air. Little
bunches of detached cumulus floating in the sky threw patches
of moving shadows on Fuji's slopes, and these clouds, gathering
about the summit, presently obscured it from view.

By ten o'clock we were well up in the forest and undergrowth that clothes the lower slopes. Looking backwards, the
great barrier range of Hakōné was a poem in greens of every
shade, with a belt of silvery clouds floating lazily in from the
west and lightly touching every peak. Sometimes the clouds
above us parted, and we saw thick mists settling in the ravines
which scar the upper heights. These mists were white as
the streaks of snow, so that we could not distinguish where
snow ended and mist began. It was a pretty sight, and
gave the mountain the appearance of having donned its
winter dress.

At eleven we reached Umagaeshi, or "Horse Return."
Formerly, those who came on horseback had to leave their
steeds behind at this point, and make the rest of the ascent
by foot, as above this place the mountain's slopes were held

to be so sacred that no horse's foot might tread them. In former times, women, too, were debarred from ascending the mountain higher than the eighth rest-house. But these old rules have lapsed of recent years. Now, those women who can may ascend to the top with impunity; and hundreds of pilgrims, who do not care to put too great a tax upon the nether limbs, ride on horseback as far as the second rest-house —a good two hours' tramp farther up the mountain.

Indeed, so profaned has Fuji become that in 1906 a Japanese, under the incentive of a wager, rode a horse to the summit —a feat which called forth much protest from the press. Strange to say, however, this protest did not take the form of an outcry against the violation of ancient traditions, but was raised merely on the ground of cruelty to the horse. This was somewhat unreasonable, as there was no climbing to be done by the route taken, and therefore no reason why the horse should not accomplish the journey—which it did, without suffering any ill effects whatever. In the Himalayan passes horses are worked at much greater altitudes than the summit of Fuji. A protest on such grounds was the more remarkable as the Japanese horse is by no means the best treated equine in the world—or even in the East—and is, as any foreigner who has travelled much in Japan can testify, but too often the victim of ill-treatment and abuse.

We reached Tarōbō, 4600 feet above sea-level, at 11.15. This was not such rapid progress as I had hoped to make, but the gōriki complained that they could go no faster, as the loads they carried were so heavy. Tarōbō is an interesting spot, with a large and substantial rest-house, where we had some tea and rice. The place derives its name from a mountain goblin who was formerly worshipped at a shrine near by. One may purchase here, for the sum of ten sen, a staff such as is used by all pilgrims who ascend the mountain. These staves are marked by a burnt impress of the name, Fuji-san, in Chinese, and at the summit the residing priest adds a further impression.

The view below us, as we rested here, was exceedingly

beautiful. The waters of the rice-fields glistened in the sunshine, and the atmosphere was so clear that, with my glass, I could easily pick out every detail of the houses along the old Tōkaido highway. Snowy clouds floating in the azure added greatly to the charm of the scene; and the line of fluffy billows over the Hakōné barrier had lifted, so that between them and the mountain-tops we could see the end of Ashi lake, flashing like a jewel in the sun, and, far beyond it, the blue waters of Sagami Bay, in which a single tiny speck marked the sacred island of Enoshima, distant about forty miles from where we stood.

At Tarōbō we left the pleasant green and shade of the woods behind, and emerged suddenly on to the desolate waste of ashes up which we must toil for over seven thousand feet of height, and along a zigzag path of more than fifteen miles in length. It was indeed a dreary prospect. Yet it was a wondrous sight which burst upon the vision as we left the grateful woodland. A vast expanse of cinders stretched before us, slowly merging from black at our feet to purple-grey, where, miles and miles away, it lost itself in cloudland. It was a burnt-up wilderness, covered with ridges and hillocks of pumice and scoriæ, in which the torrential rains that deluge the mountain-slopes had torn great clefts and deep ravines. From this point to the top, the mountain sweeps in one beautiful unbroken curve—a curve so perfect and even that it reminded me of the wire rope, bending of its own weight, down which loads of fire-wood are sent across the Nekko river in Kōshu, to Furuseki from the mountains on the opposite shore.

As we struck out on to this barren waste the heat absorbed by the black cinders was terrific, and with the hot August sun scorching down on our backs the ascent of even so easy a mountain as Fuji became no joke. That toilsome journey to the top of Europe is not more laborious than the weary tramp over these interminable ashes; and the two mountains offer strange and striking contrasts. Mont Blanc is white— a colossal pile of ice, held by the highest *aiguilles* of the Alps. Fuji is black—an isolated, stupendous heap of cinders. One

FUJI AND THE PINE TREES

may sit on the hotel verandas at Chamonix and through telescopes observe, occasionally, a few black specks—like a little string of ants—creeping slowly, almost imperceptibly, up the virgin snows of Mont Blanc. As we left all vegetation behind us, and set out on the now desert slopes of Fuji, the mountain ants were here too, only there were many more of them, and they were white ants instead of black ones, and crept amongst sombre ashes instead of stainless snows.

Tradition says that Fuji rose from a plain in a single night, when a great depression appeared in the earth, a hundred and fifty miles away, which is now filled by the waters of Lake Biwa. That a volcano may have been formed here in a single night is likely enough. Who can say? But that it arose from a plain is clearly a myth, for a mile to the right of the second rest-hut there is a deep rift disclosing solid masses of rock, quite different from any found elsewhere on the mountain. These rocks appear to mark the summit of some lesser peak which this mass of ashes has overwhelmed—and a chain of hills running from the south-east to this spot seems to confirm the theory.

The heat—which had been getting almost intolerable, for there was scarcely a breath of wind—was now gratefully tempered by clouds which came between us and the sun, and our progress at once became more rapid. We reached the ni-gō-mé, or second rest-hut, at one o'clock, and rested for twenty minutes. On starting again we plunged into mists which came swirling down the mountain from every point of the compass, formed by some rapid barometric change that caused a cool, refreshing wind to blow. For this we were all very thankful, as it was a great relief after the sun's demonstration of how painfully wearisome he could make the journey up these soft heat-absorbing slopes.

The trail up the mountain was well bestrewn with waraji, those cheap and serviceable straw sandals which every native of Japan uses when travelling in country districts, and of which I had come provided with a good supply, of a size sufficiently large to affix to the soles of my boots. They not only afford a good grip on the loose cinders, but give very necessary protection to the leather, which would otherwise speedily be torn to pieces by the sharp, rough clinkers. Even with the protection afforded by waraji, Fuji is "good" (?) for one pair of boots, and I would advise all who follow in my footsteps not to wear boots by which they set any store, as after the descent they will be of little further use. The right footgear for a trip up Fuji is a good, comfortable pair of old boots and several pairs of waraji. Two pairs of the latter may be reckoned on for the ascent, and about four pairs for the descent. Leather leggings are better than stockings, as they prevent the small cinders—in which, on the descent, one's feet are intermittently buried—from entering the boots. The Japanese never use boots for mountain excursions. They wear blue cloth socks, with a separate compartment for the big toe, and waraji tied to them.

At 3.45 we reached the fifth gō-mé (8659 feet), with over 3500 feet to go. I was glad enough to stop here and have a cup of hot cocoa, as the mists that had enveloped us were damp and chilly. Owing to the altitude and heavy going, and to the fact that we could not leave the gōriki behind, as they seemed intent on loafing, we had not been able to proceed fast enough to keep warm. I had started out in summer clothing, suitable to the heat of the plains, and now, being quite insufficiently clad for these raw, driving mists, was shivering with cold. Whilst the gōriki rested I got out some thick woollens and clothed myself more suitably for the great change in temperature.

As we were leaving the fifth hut the mists parted, disclosing Lake Yamanaka bathed in sunshine and reflecting the clouds above it. The clouds overhead also melted for a few moments, and there was Fuji's crest, as far off as ever it was a good three hours ago, when we had last had a glimpse of it. Surely we had not moved an inch, or else the mountain was ascending too!

A band of descending pilgrims—laughing, shouting, and singing, in high spirits at having accomplished their mission

—came running and leaping and glissading down the straight path of the descent. [The ascending path is zigzag, the descending one is straight.]

Nearly an hour earlier, as we met another descending band, I had shouted in Japanese, "How far is it to the top?"

"Three ri," one of them replied.

Now again I put the question as the merry pilgrims passed me. "How far to the top?"

"Three ri," came the answer.

I knew it! The summit was as far off as ever, and looked it! Without doubt, the mountain was getting higher as fast as we were scaling it. At this rate we should never reach the top. Thank heavens, we were at least keeping pace with it!

By half-past four the clouds had cleared away, and the whole upper Fuji was visible. We were well above the waist —in the middle of the great sweeping curve from the mountain-top to Tarōbō. From a distance this curve is not very perceptible, but from where we now stood we could see how great was the deviation from the straight line. Away to the west the mountain outline was much steeper, and perfectly straight —a stupendous incline which leapt up at a dizzy angle into space.

How weary this interminable zigzag was getting! Mile after mile there was no variation to the monotony of turning its everlasting corners. Several times I tried to relieve the tedium by making short cuts, straight up; but as soon as I left the beaten track the cinders slipped under my feet, and progress was slower than ever. At 5 P.M. we were at the sixth gō-mé, 9317 feet above sea-level. We had scarcely ascended 700 feet in three-quarters of an hour. It sounds slow, and would have been so if the others had been as unhampered as I; but each gōriki's load was a third of his own weight, and our pace was that of the slowest member of the party.

Some rollicking students from Tokyo University were making the mountain ring with their songs, and a number of pilgrims, too, had settled in the rest-hut for the night. These pilgrims, who flock from all over the land to Fuji in summer, are mostly of the rustic class. They are very poor, and are assisted on their mission by funds furnished by village clubs to which they belong. The members pay trifling annual sub-scriptions, and each year lots are drawn to decide who of their number shall visit certain holy places. Most of the pilgrims are dressed in white, with broad-brimmed hats, shaped like Fuji, made of straw. Each carries a staff, bought at Tarōbō —which, when the mission is over, will become an heirloom in the family—and a large piece of matting tied to his back. This projects at each side, and as it flaps about in the wind gives him a most droll appearance—like a young chick trying to fly. This mat serves as a waterproof coat; as a shield to keep the sun off the back; and, at times, as a bed—if, as is often the case, the owner finds the available supply of futons already engaged on his arrival at the rest-hut. Each pilgrim has also a tiny bell tied to his girdle. Thus, when the mountain is "open" and the weather favourable, its slopes on the Gō-temba and Subashiri sides—for Fuji may be ascended with safety only on certain well-kept routes—are all a-tinkling with these little sweet-toned bells. As the pilgrims slowly wend their way upwards they continually sing out, in sharp, staccato accents, the Shinto words "Rokkon-Shōjō, Rokkon-Shōjō!"—a formula signifying the emptiness of life, and conveying the exhortation to keep the body pure.

"Rokkon-Shōjō" is an abbreviation of the formula "Rokkon-Shōjō O Yama Kaisei," which means, "May our six senses be pure, and the weather on the honourable mountain fine." Professor Chamberlain says that the pilgrims "repeat the invocation, for the most part, without understanding it, as most of the words are Chinese." When the full formula is used, it is chanted antiphonally, sometimes between bands of pilgrims a mile or more apart, as sound carries a long way on the mountain-side. It is usually abbreviated, however, to the first line.

At 6 o'clock we reached the seventh rest-hut, and found

it closed. The panorama from this place was a dream of beauty. Fleecy tufts of cloud floated above the landscape far below us, as if great bales of cotton had been torn to pieces and scattered o'er the earth. The sun, long since gone over the mountain, and now nearing the horizon, was turning the fleece into golden foam, and Yamanaka lake, steeped in shadow, peeped between the foaming wavelets, grey and smooth as steel. Far beneath us, and now many miles away, the forests on the lower slopes of the mountain looked sleek as velvet, and above, Fuji's crest was blue and violet against a turquoise sky.

The trail of the ascent is intersected at the seventh gō-mé by a path called "Chudo Meguri," which encircles the mountain. Many Japanese Nature-worshippers make the circuit of Fuji by this path. It is about twenty miles round, and the journey takes about eight hours. If one desires to see scenic effects only, there is no object in ascending higher, as from the summit everything appears more dwarfed, and is liable to be obscured by haze.

Above the sixth rest-hut the ascent becomes rapidly steeper, and the mountain is bestrewn with great blocks of lava. I would fain have made more rapid progress, but my gōriki were evidently not moved by the enthusiasm that urged me on, and kept up the steady plodding gait which they knew by experience is the pace that lasts.

Those who have spent holidays in the Alps, and have slowly fought their way up some icy peak, will know the steady mechanical pace set from the outset by the Swiss guides. Probably, before they knew better, they wanted, as I did, to go faster, much faster, but were kept in check by the men to whom this is no pastime but the business of their lives. It is the only way to scale a mountain—to adopt a slow and steady pace and keep it up like a machine; and it is marvellous what that slow, steady gait will accomplish. Hour after hour you plod on, slowly and surely, yet, almost imperceptible as your progress seems, eminence after eminence is gradually gained in the silence of deadly earnest, broken only by the crunching of your boots and the squeaking of your ice-axe, as, using it for a staff, at each step you plunge its point into the snow. The light of the moon that helped you on your midnight start now pales, the sky becomes grey, and the grey gives way to pink and amber as the sun rises; but still you plod on, stepping in the footprints of the guide in front. At last, almost before you realise it, the struggle is over. Your pulse beats quick and strong, and your whole body glows—not only from the effects of the exertion, but with the joy of knowing that you have achieved your ambition. You have gained, for the time being, the height of your desire; and, from the topmost pinnacle of that icy finger which beckoned to you from the skies, you can revel in joy undreamed of by those who have never sought the solitude of the mountains, and the joy which they can bestow on those who love them.

So it is with Fuji too—steady perseverance tells, and only by its exercise can the crest be won. My gōriki knew this, and could not be urged to change the pace which had become to them a habit. Moreover, to them the ascent had no incentive of novelty. These men were mountain porters for three months of the year, carrying supplies to the rest-huts. Between the four of them they could aggregate over thirty ascents that year to the top, besides a greater number of journeys to the lower stations, although the rest-huts had scarcely been open a month. Small wonder was it, then, that they were not to be carried away by enthusiasm.

How wearisome this plodding was becoming! How steep the mountain was getting! I was beginning to feel tired, too, and marvelled how those fellows could do all this with those heavy packs. They must have sinews strong as wire. The path was now very steep, and care had to be exercised not to disturb the stones, otherwise they might roll down the slope, to the danger of some one below. My feet were getting very heavy, and my thighs beginning to feel sore at the un-wonted tax upon the muscles. The clinkers were rougher and sharper at every step. Should we never reach that eighth gō-mé?

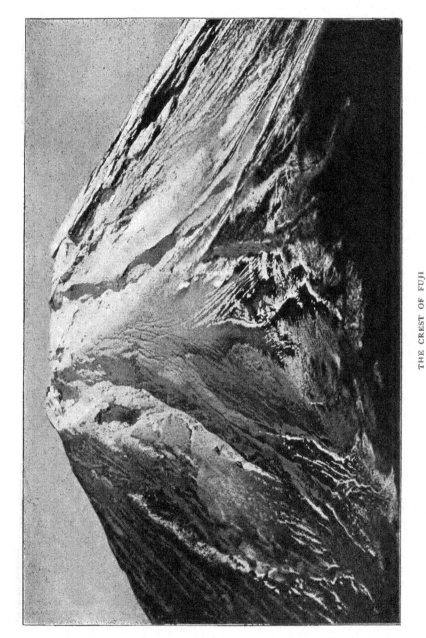

THE CREST OF FUJI

A TELEPHOTOGRAPH FROM SHOJI (15 MILES)

The gōriki were tiring too, for they had been going very slowly and were now stopping to have a smoke. I began to suspect them. Were they conspiring to try to induce me to stop for the night at No. 8? I knew very well that they were used to transporting greater loads than this from Gōtemba to the top in a day, so I determined to reach the top that night; I would not be cajoled out of it. I dared not stop to admire the view. That would be fatal. I must not waver till No. 8 was reached, or they would suspect me of being as tired as I was. These thoughts spurred me on to renewed efforts, and at last I reached the hut, ordered some tea, and refrained from sitting down for fully five minutes—an act of self-denial which called for all the will-power I possessed—in order to deceive the gōriki, whom I knew were closely watching me, as to the real state of my muscles. I lit a cigarette and walked outside to smoke it, scarcely thinking I had it in me to dissemble thus.

The eighth hut is 10,693 feet above the sea, and about 1500 feet from the summit rest-house, which is in a hollow on the mountain-top, some 200 feet below the highest point. The sun had long since set behind the mountain. The turquoise sky had turned to coral and amber, and Japan below was growing dark and being enveloped by the mists of night, which were spreading lightly over the earth, like a *robe de nuit*. It was only a thin stratum, however, and through it rose the peaks of Ashitaka-yama, O-yama, the Hakōné range, and many others, seeming to float like romantic isles in a mystic sea of legend. The daylight died rapidly as I watched, and a radiance over the "Maiden's Pass" in Hakōné foreshowed the rising of the moon. Darkness was gathering fast, and faintly shimmering stars began to stud the opalescent heavens. The luminous east turned silver, and, whilst yet the after-glow was burning in the zenith, the moon peeped over the ocean's edge and threw a dancing shaft of light across Sagami's waters to the rugged coasts of Izu. Only to have seen this glorious sight had been more than worth the journey. A hundred times had I gazed on such scenes depicted in golden lacquer, and marvelled at

K

their beauty. Now for the first time I saw the reality that inspired them.

As I anticipated, the gōriki, who had arrived during my contemplation of these wonders, complained of fatigue, and said they could go no farther that night; but I put on a firm front at once and declined to consider breaking the journey. I was really anxious to reach the top and record a few impressions before turning in, so I offered them each 50 sen extra if we were on the summit by nine o'clock. As we started off from No. 8 my suspicions that they were merely "playing possum" proved to be well founded, for such was now their desire to reach the top as soon as possible that I was hard put to it to keep ahead of them. The incentive of an extra shilling each had worked marvels in dispelling their fatigue.

By this time the moon was shining brilliantly, and near by the trail one of the snow-patches, which had seemed but a mere speck from Gōtemba, was a quarter of a mile in length, and had a ghostly glimmer amidst the surrounding blackness. Above and all around us were great masses of slag and lava. Weird and unearthly-looking was this holocaust of hideous shapes—this vomit cast up by the mountain in the throes of its agony and fever. The path was much harder and firmer now, but exceedingly steep; and every step amongst the eerie shadows was bringing us visibly nearer to the crater-lip above. My heart was beating fast and my head ached badly, the result of the elevation and rarefaction of the air. We slowly passed a great gully, looking black and bottomless—a yawning chasm which from the world below was but one of those creases that serrate the mountain's crest. Then the sky-line appeared just above us. Another moment's scramble—one last and final pull—and I stood on Fuji's crest!

It was 8.40 P.M. The rest-house was scarcely a hundred yards away, and the gōriki with their loads went unconcernedly on, without once looking behind them. As for me, I was content to sit awhile where I was, and survey the scene about me. It was freezing hard, but not a breath of wind was astir, and the heavens were scintillating with glittering diamonds. For every star I ever saw before there were now a thousand, all glimmering in the firmament and adding soft radiance to the rays with which the moon strove to pierce the blue-black void below. There was no *robe de nuit* over the earth now. It had dissolved away, leaving nothing but inky blackness, parted by one great streak of silver where the rapid Fujikawa raced onwards to the sea.

Around me was naught but distorted shapes, and space, and silence. Though I strained every faculty to catch some faint murmur from the world below, naught but silence absolute and supreme fell upon my ears—a silence broken only by the pulsations of my heart, which seemed to make great resonant thuds. It was awe-inspiring, sublime, this vast, tremendous hush that could be almost felt. It was the infinite calm of great altitudes, and of the deep.

Shivering with cold I went into the rest-house, and soon a meal was ready and steaming hot. Afterwards, I was glad enough to take to my rugs and futons and get to sleep.

From this point I quote from my diary written during my stay on the mountain top:

August 3.—I told the hut-keeper last night to be sure and call me well before sunrise if the weather were fine, but when I awake it has long been daylight, and I have a racking headache. The wind is whistling round the hut, which is in a sheltered hollow, and hail is pelting on the roof. I get up, and we all crowd round the charcoal fire and have breakfast. There is another fire where wood is burnt for cooking. Both fires are near the door of the hut, which is wide open, on the most sheltered side of the building. Outside nothing can be seen but swirling mists and driving snow and hailstones.

August 3, Noon.—As hour after hour passes, the storm increases. Fortunately I have a good supply of canned provisions, and bread sufficient for several days. Nakano is lying down, wrapped up in futons, overcome with mountain sickness. The gōriki are all huddled up in a corner of the hut, completely covered, heads and all, with futons.

August 3, 2 P.M.—The storm is worse. I am evidently

destined to incarceration here for a day or two at least, so I may as well record my impressions of my haven from the storm. The house is not comfortable, but it is strong and weather-proof. It is constructed of blocks of lava, each block being chiselled so as to fit exactly to its neighbours without mortar to bind it. The walls at the base are three feet thick, sloping on the outside to a width of one foot at the top. The interior is tightly lined with boards, and a solid framework of wood, braced with iron, supports the roof, which is the least substantial part of the structure, being made of one-inch planks covered with tin from kerosene-oil cans. Plainly it is only the solidity and number of the supports that enable the roof to carry the weight of snow it must have to bear in winter. A portion of the building is taken up by a large pile of snow, which constitutes the water supply. The floor is of crushed cinders, and a raised dais—made of boards, and covered with tatami (padded mats) on which visitors wrap themselves in blankets and futons, to sleep—runs the whole length of the building. There is no chimney, and the smoke from the burning pinewood diffuses itself most effectually into every corner of the structure.

August 3, 4 P.M.—Twice during the afternoon I ventured outside the rock-walled compound enclosing the hut, but had to beat a hasty retreat, for icy winds were raging over the mountain, and I could scarcely stand. I venture a third time when the wind has subsided a little, and find the building has two wings, the central portion being occupied by an old Shinto priest who sits and waits for the pilgrims who, in fine weather, are continually straggling in to have their staves and garments impressed with the outline of Fuji's top—the hall-mark so envied by the pilgrim element of Japan. The postcard craze has penetrated even here. I buy some postcards from the old priest, direct them to friends, and have them stamped with the impress which he places on the pilgrim's garments. The first carrier going down will take them.

The gōriki haven't moved all day except to unearth themselves from their futons once to eat. I don't suppose they care how long the storm lasts. They are paid by the day, and are having an easy time of it. It is quite evident they are not worrying about the weather. Why should they? They are probably dreaming about their accumulating wages. Nakano, however, is very unhappy. Poor fellow, he is suffering greatly with headache and sickness from the altitude and smoke. He has lent me Lafcadio Hearn's book *Kwaidan*, which he fortunately brought with him. It is a collection of tales of Japanese superstitions and imagination, and thus the hours pass delightfully. The weird tales possess an added interest as I read them on the highest part of Japan, from which so much legend and fable emanates.

August 3, 8 P.M.—With darkness the storm increases again. Two pilgrims have come in during the afternoon, having struggled up from No. 8 in five hours, and are stopping here to-night. They have, of course, no alternative. There are less expensive huts on the north-east side of the crater, but it would be as much as life is worth to try to reach them.

The chronicles of Fuji show that about sixty years ago a number of pilgrims were caught in dense clouds on the mountain-top and lost their way. The clouds were the precursors of a blizzard, which broke suddenly and with terrific violence. When it abated, and the weather cleared, the frozen bodies of the pilgrims, to the number of over fifty, were found closely packed together, showing that they had kept united to the last for warmth and companionship in that dread hour. This is but one instance of the many sacrifices that Sengen Sama, the goddess of the mountain, has demanded of the faithful. The place where they died is now called Sai-no-Kawara, or the "River-Bed of Souls." It is covered with hundreds of stone cairns, raised to the memory of these martyrs by those who follow more fortunately in their footsteps.

It occurs to me to offer—for the benefit of those who aspire to undertake this expedition—a few words of advice. When you ascend Fuji be sure to provide yourselves with several large sheets of Japanese oil-paper, and do not forget

your gun and powder. I do not mean by this to imply that
you should bring a muzzle-loader, nor yet that you may
expect any shooting. The weapon I refer to is what is known
as an "insect-powder gun," and the powder I mean is
"Keating's"; the former is an ingenious little contrivance
for sprinkling the latter effectively. These precautions are to
be directed against the onslaught of stalwart, energetic fleas
which is certain to ensue the moment you lie down in any of
the rest-huts.

The Fuji fleas are famous; they have a well-deserved
reputation for activity and attention to business. They are
borne to the mountain in the clothes of pilgrims. In the
rest-huts they meet and mate, and bring forth a strain that
must perforce endure the rigours of the altitude, or perish.
Only the most robust survive, and these make life a burden
to those who come unprovided with means to repel their
onset. Well sprinkling the mats around me, therefore, and
spreading a huge sheet of oil-paper on them, I make my
bed, and for the second night lie down to sleep, drawing
another oil-sheet over me as an additional protection. Thus
only can I rest with any degree of comfort.

August 4, 7 A.M.—The storm is now a hurricane. For
hours I have scarcely slept a wink, and have a splitting headache—due to the rarefied air. It is 7 A.M., and every one is
buried deep in futons. The rising and falling cadences of the
wind have been dismal enough, but they have now become an
almost incessant shriek. Now and then there is a moment's
lull, but it is only the storm-fiends drawing back to make a
fiercer, more determined effort. Gathering all their strength,
the winds rush upon the structure, and smite it terrific blows.
But the solid, well-braced walls resist the fiercest onslaughts;
there is scarcely even a tremor, and the baulked furies go
tearing past, screaming and howling in impotent rage. I would
not have missed this for a good deal. I may never have such
an experience again, nor do I wish to; but to be on Fuji's
crest when the mountain is in the angriest of its moods is
something to remember. When the wind woke me, and I lay

A SHRINE AT THE CRATER'S EDGE

in the futons, listening to its onsets growing momentarily fiercer, I was somewhat ill at ease; but now all anxiety is gone, and my confidence in the staunchness of the hut grows stronger as each fresh assault is baffled.

August 4, 9 A.M.—We all get up and breakfast. The wind seems to be lessening. I have finished *Kwaidan,* and must read it through again. I have nothing else but Murray's *Handbook*—best of all guide-books on any land—but I know much of it almost by heart. Nakano is still suffering greatly, and says if it were only possible to descend, he would have to go down. Mountain-sickness is a very painful thing. I have had it on Mont Blanc and know what it means. One of the pilgrims who came in yesterday had a dreadful cold. He was sneezing almost incessantly, and thought he was going to die. I took him in hand and gave him a strong glass of whisky and hot water and ten grains of quinine. I had great difficulty in getting him to take the whisky, but he didn't mind the quinine pills. This morning the cold and fever have left him, and he thanked me with brimming eyes. He said he knew I had been sent by the gods to save his life!

Our host is the very model of patience, apathy, and taciturnity. All day long he sits and smokes, and smokes and sits, and thinks. I have come to the conclusion he is on the verge of Buddha-hood, for he appears to be practising austerity. Every one else in the hut is covered up with futons, but he sits right in front of the open door, through which the icy fog is sweeping. There he squats, with the full force of the back-draughts of the wind blowing on him, and sometimes I, who am at the farthest end of the room, shivering in my overcoat and thick futons, can scarcely see him for mist. He is surely attaining much store of merit. His gaze is riveted, hour after hour, on the swirling clouds; but he moves only to fill his pipe, and light it, and tap out the ashes, and then begin the process over again. Smoking appears to be his only vice. A man who can sit in his ordinary clothes in a temperature like this must be impervious to the elements, and dead to all carnal desires. The marvel to me is that he even smokes. He should certainly renounce the habit.   Then he would perhaps attain Nirvana.

Three times he has relieved the monotony of his penance —I suppose it must be a penance—by taking a piece of paper and doing some figuring.   I begin to suspect his meditations may be baser than I thought.   Perhaps he is cogitating how much of a bill I will stand to compensate him for the loss of patronage of transient callers, who, in fine weather, would drop in continually, night and day.   The arrival of a foreigner, with a Japanese and four gōriki, must have been a very opportune incident for him, as otherwise his hut would have been all but deserted.   He has a servant to assist him in the duties of the household.   The servant's office chiefly consists in attending to the fires, which need almost constant watchfulness to keep them going—the effect of insufficient oxygen in the rarefied air.   Thus the dreary, dismal day passes, the storm all the while steadily abating.   As night approaches, the winds have almost ceased.   For the third time I make up my bed, and bury myself in futons, evil-smelling oil-paper, and Keating's.

August 5.—For the third time I wake up with a racking headache.   The storm has completely subsided, but a cold drizzling rain is falling, and chilly mists enshroud the mountain-top.   Towards noon the weather brightens, and later the clouds begin to break.   At two o'clock—oh, joyous sight!—a ray of sunshine makes the wet rocks sparkle, and a great tinkling of bells announces the arrival of a band of some thirty pilgrims, all in white, with dangling saké bottles at their girdles.   They have been immured for two days in the huts on the Subashiri side, and are now making the circuit of the crater.

I started out for a walk round the crater's lip, and met an old and wrinkled woman slowly making her way amongst the ruthless clinkers.   After exchanging greetings with me, the Obã-san (old woman) told me she was over seventy years of age, and had taken seven days to climb the mountain.   Like us, she had been a prisoner during the last two days' storm, but had experienced no ill effects.   She had been on pilgrimages to many of the Holy Places of Japan, but this was her first ascent of Fuji.   Like all Japanese country people she was respectful and gentle of speech.   She had started with a band of comrades, but she had been unable to keep up with them, and they went ahead, leaving her to make the ascent by easy stages alone.   She had met them coming down four days before she reached the top.   As we parted I noticed that, notwithstanding her age, which for a Japanese was great, she went her way slowly, but with steady, unfaltering steps, nothing daunted by the trials she had undergone, and unshaken in her resolution to accomplish the mission on which she had set her heart, unless death met her on the road.

There was something infinitely pathetic about that lone, aged figure, slowly and tediously wending her way amongst the cruel crags; and I sent one of my gōriki to assist her, and see her safely round the crater and to the various points that it was her desire to visit.   This incident gave me food for reflection for some time, and often afterwards.   Truly that wrinkled body was but the earthly covering of a noble, indomitable soul.   She had undertaken this arduous journey for a devout purpose—to lay up for herself greater store of merit with the gods—and I thought of other religions, and the women of other lands, where the Japanese are looked upon as heathens, and I wondered how many of those other women, with but half her measure of years, would embark on such a task for such an object.

August 5, 3 P.M.—The mountain-top is now quite clear, and appears to float in a sea of clouds which are driving past a thousand feet below the summit.   This gives rise to a curious illusion—that it is the mountain which is moving, whilst the clouds are still.   We seem to be on an island forging through an ocean of foam.   It is a most beautiful hallucination, but makes me dizzy as I watch it.

The summit of Fuji, which looks so flat and smooth from the plains below, is covered with enormous crags burnt to every colour of the spectrum.   In places great cliffs of slag tower a hundred feet above the rim of the crater, which is five hundred feet or more in depth, and about a third of a mile across. There are two separate craters—a smaller one beside the large one—but the wall between them is broken down. Both are choked with the detritus which is constantly falling from the walls, and one may walk at will over the entire crater floor. On the south and west sides, where the slope is sheltered from the sun by the surrounding peaks of slag, there is a snow glissade to the crater bottom; this is the only semblance to a glacier that Fuji can boast.

Not only is Fuji sacred, but it is the most venerated of many sacred peaks in Japan. At the crater's eastern lip, near the rest-hut, there is a Shinto shrine, consecrated to the worship of Sengen Sama (otherwise known as Ko-no-Hana-Saku-ya-Himé-no-Mikoto —"Princess who makes the Blossoms of the Trees to Flower"), which ranks high among the holiest of Holy Places of the Empire. There are several other shrines, and the great pit is a gigantic shrine itself. As we stood on the brink of the crater, a band of enthusiasts, intent on consummating what they had come so far to do, had descended to the bottom of the abyss, and were making a myriad echoes awake as they clapped their hands to invoke the attention of the deity, and chanted to the kaleidoscopic walls. On the verge of the steep, near by, others were making their supplications with equal manifestations of zeal to the yawning gulf before them, and the whole mountain-top was ringing with the clapping of hands and prayer.

Shortly before sunset I went alone to Ken-ga-miné, the highest point of Fuji, on its western side. Here there is a little stone hut clinging to the edge of the mountain, which, on this side, is so steep that a mass of lava, which I managed to urge over the edge, struck the ground but twice, and then, with a great bound, leapt far out into the sea of clouds and disappeared. This hut was built for the reception of a Japanese meteorologist named Nonaka, and his wife, who essayed to spend the winter of 1895-6 in it, for the purpose of making scientific observations. The couple took up their abode here in September, but before Christmas, owing to the terrific

weather which prevailed that winter, apprehensions were felt for their safety, and a relief expedition was organised to reach them and bring them down. Notwithstanding the severity of the weather, and the great difficulty of ascending the mountain when covered with snow and ice, the expedition was successful, and reached the hut in safety. Nonaka and his wife were found nearly frozen to death. It is said that they both refused to leave, preferring death to failure in their effort. Their entreaties to be allowed to remain were, of course, disregarded, and they were carried down. For many days afterwards their lives were despaired of, but ultimately they both recovered.

As I stood near this hut, on the utmost pinnacle of Japan, the sea of clouds was rising slowly higher—borne upwards in heaving billows by some under-current—whilst the wind was filling the crater behind me with scudding wrack. My pinnacle was soon surrounded, and no other part of the mountain was visible. I stood alone on a tiny island of rock in that cosmic ocean, seemingly the only human being in the universe. Soon the illusion of being carried rapidly along in the cloud sea was so real that I had to sit, for fear of falling with dizziness.

When the sun sank to the level of the surging vapours, flooding their waves and hollows with ever-changing contrasts of light and shade, the scene was of indescribable beauty. I have never seen a spectacle so replete with awesome majesty as the sunset I witnessed that evening from the topmost cubic foot of Fuji. A few moments only the glory lasted. Then the sun sank into the vapoury ocean, the snowy billows turned leaden grey, and darkness immediately began to fall.

As the last spark of the orb of day disappeared into the foaming breakers there was a rush of wind across the crater, due to the instant change of temperature, and in a moment the mountain-top was in a tumult. The great abyss became a cauldron of boiling mists, and icy blasts moaned and whistled among the crags which loomed like ominous moving phantoms in the turbulent vapours and dying light. It was a wondrous, almost preternatural spectacle, like a vision of Dante's dream. I was Dante, and the gaping crater before me was the steaming mouth of hell.

Riveted to the spot with the fascination of the scene, I did not realise my predicament till the mists suddenly enveloped me. Then conviction flashed upon me that I was half a mile from the rest-hut, and had not the remotest idea which way to turn. Groping my way among the rocks, I found the well-worn path, made by the pilgrims, which encircles the mountain-top; and following it, by feeling with my stick, as a blind man finds his way, I soon brought up against the wall of Nonaka's hut. This gave me my bearings, and I started off in the opposite direction; but it was slow work, and several times I lost the trail. Soon the dense fog and darkness baffled me, and, losing the trail again, I found myself on the brink of a precipice. A stone that I pushed over, to test the height, took three seconds to reach the bottom. I could go neither backwards nor forwards, as to do so was to run the risk of falling into the crater or over some cliff at the mountain's edge.

For a long time I shouted as loud as I could, hoping some one in the rest-hut would hear me, and at last I heard an answering shout from one of my gōriki, who, becoming alarmed at my long absence, had come out to look for me. Without a light I dared not move a foot, and with the enforced inaction I was chilled through, as I crouched under a rock for shelter.

I waited nearly an hour more after hearing the first answering shout. It seems that the man, being unable to locate my calls, started off in the opposite direction, for in heavy fog all sounds are very misleading. At length, however, guided by my shouts, he reached me, but so thick was the fog that not until he was within a few yards of me did I see the welcome glow cast by his lantern on the mist.

I had had no wish to be a sacrifice on Sengen Sama's altar, and when I was once more deep in warm rugs and futons in the rest-hut it seemed a veritable paradise of comfort after the chilly experience I had just been through.

August 6.—What was my joy when one of the gōriki awoke me, bidding me get up quickly, as it was clear weather and an hour before sunrise! We soon had a hasty breakfast, and I write these lines on the eastern side of the mountain's edge, where we have come to witness the pageantry of the heavens at the break of day.

A number of pilgrims are waiting to salute the sun. The blue-black heavens are turning grey and the myriad stars are dimmed. The grey becomes a more beautiful grey, soft and opalescent—like pearl. A timid blush comes over the pearl, rose-tinting it. The blush suffuses slowly into delicate pink. The pink deepens and becomes momentarily more vivid, flushing the arch of heaven, whilst golden shafts radiate from the east to the zenith and the poles. The clouds, which lie close-wrapped about the earth two miles below, are a fiery sea, with purple shadows, and waves whose crests change from silver to scarlet and vermilion, and then the whole slowly metamorphoses into a crucible of molten gold. It is a spectacle of sublime magnificence.

Breathlessly and with throbbing hearts the pilgrims drink in the glorious phenomena of this climax of their lives. They will tell of it to their children, and their children's children, and their names will ever be deeper reverenced for the Mecca they have seen. The skies have gone through every colour of the prism. Suddenly a spark! a flame! and then a dazzling burst of fire! and the rosy morning is awake once more on Fuji's pearly crest, whilst Japan below is yet enveloped in the filmy mists of night. The pilgrims bow their heads to the ground in adoration, and, with much rubbing of rosaries, the plaintive cadence of their prayers rises, like a lamentation, to the heavens above.

At Benares, the sacred city of India, as the sun rises each morning across the holy Ganges, the prayers of the multitude, assembled on the ghauts and bathing in the river, are as the roaring of the sea. But even this—one of the greatest and most stirring religious spectacles of the world—is not more picturesque than that little band of pilgrims, 'twixt heaven

and earth, high up in the blue profound, on the very top of
Japan, kneeling in praise before the great orb that is the
emblem of their Empire.   In truth, not to see sunrise from
the summit of Fuji-san is to miss the most magnificent spectacle
of Japan.

As the morning grows, the clouds, lying shroud-like over
the earth, dissemble into little cotton-tufts once more. Amongst
them blue lakes appear. Yamanaka, nearest of them all—two
miles below us, and fifteen miles away as an arrow speeds its
flight—mirrors the azure heavens and the clouds that float
above it; whilst in Kawaguchi's limpid depths—whose
placid beauty one has but to see to love—the surrounding
mountains seem to gaze, enchanted with the scenes reflected
there.   The panorama on every side is exquisite. Japan lies
below us, like a huge map in relief.   Great mountains are but
mole-hills, and ranges are mere ridges, over which we can
look, and every range beyond them, to the horizon, which,
from this altitude, seems half way up the sky.   The waters of
Suruga Bay are bordered with a line of white—big breakers,
the baffled pursuers of the recent storm. As we circle the
mountain's vertex other lakes come into view: Nishi-no-umi,
Shōji, and Motosu, most enchanting lake in all the land; and
then the earth is riven by the flashing Fujikawa speeding
onward to the sea, divided at its mouth into a delta of many
streams.   The forests clothing the lower slopes are sun-kissed
lawns, but seamed with many a wrinkle—great gullies torn by
the torrents of water which the mountain sheds in the heavy
summer rains. Fifty miles westwards the slumbering giants of
Shinano, forming an impregnable barrier across the centre of
Japan, are a mass of colossal peaks whose tops are lost in
cloudland.   In the midst of all this loveliness Sengen Sama's
altar, on which we stand, bathed in warm sunshine, and
caressed with gentle zephyrs, strives to touch the sky.

The circuit of the crest of Fuji is replete with points of
interest.   Near Ken-ga-miné there is a precipice called Oya
shirazu, Ko shirazu, which Professor Chamberlain translates
"Heedless of Parent or Child,"—"from the notion that people

in danger of falling over the edge of the crater would not heed even their nearest relatives if sharers of the peril." The mountain slope near here is reft by a huge lava gorge known as Osawa ("Great Ravine"). This chasm scores the mountain as far as the eye can reach, seemingly to its foot. The path then enters a region bearing graphic testimony to the fierceness of the furnace which formerly raged in Fuji's crater. Enormous cliffs of lava, fire-streaked and stained to every imaginable hue—some a hundred feet or more in height—lean over the mountain's brow, momentarily threatening to descend upon the praying pilgrims far below them. These lava crags bear such names as "Thunder Rock," "The Rock Cleft by Buddha," "Sakya Muni's Peak" (the second highest point of Fuji), etc., names that reflect something of the direful grandeur of the place. This is where a great lava stream once poured out from the crater, and flowed for nearly twenty miles till it reached the Kōshu mountains, and dammed up the hollows now filled by the waters of the chain of lakes at Fuji's foot. The well-worn path then passes round the smaller crater; the spring of "Famous Golden Water"; a row of pilgrims' huts, and a precipitous cliff called "The Peak of the Goddess of Mercy," near which steam rises from the loose pumice and scoriæ, showing that Fuji's heart still glows. One cannot bear the hand longer than a few seconds in the ash, and eggs can be cooked in it in ten minutes.

On the eastern side is Sai-no-Kawara, or "The River-Bed of Souls," before alluded to. I was about to make a photograph of Lake Yamanaka from near this place, when the inevitable cloud, which so frequently appears when I produce my camera, floated up the mountain-slope, blotting the prospect from view. For fully an hour I waited, and then jocularly said to one of the gōriki: "Go and pray to Sengen Sama to send the cloud away." The man took me at my word. He ran over to the crater's edge, summoned the deity as he would a serving-maid by loudly clapping his hands, and prayed. Curiously enough, the cloud passed by immediately. He came running back, chuckling with glee at the speedy manner in which his petition had been so favourably answered, and I took the photograph which faces this page. Long before evening the cloud - sea had closed about the mountain again, and at sunset I was able to record with my camera one of the most remarkable and beautiful phenomena I have seen in any land.

I had been four days on the summit of Fuji—for the greater part of the time in no little discomfort—but the lovely views and wonderful phenomena of those days come vividly back to me as I pen these lines, and I feel that the price I paid was little enough for the never-to-be-forgotten glories of Nature that had been revealed to me.

The next morning, when I came to pay the reckoning at the rest-house, prior to descending, I found that I had done its keeper a deep injustice by my suspicions. The bill was exceedingly moderate, so much so that I marvelled at the meagreness of its total. I had been charged but one yen (two shillings) per day for lodging, very reasonable rates for such food as had been consumed by the gōriki, and but fifty sen (one shilling) each for their beds per day. Thus, though I had had a somewhat rough time on Fuji's crest, I left the mountain-top without a grudge against it.

On the occasion that is here chronicled the descent was devoid of any particular interest; but after another ascent of the mountain I had a somewhat unpleasant experience.

One September I ascended Fuji from Gōtemba with three gōriki in ten hours, in fine weather; and the next day, which was also fine, having exposed a large number of photographic plates, we started down the Yōshida side at 10.45 A.M. As we went over the mountain's edge I determined to see how rapidly I could get down to the base. Fuji is exceedingly steep on this side, much more so than the Gōtemba side, which is the easiest and longest route to make the ascent. A young Japanese artist of Tokyo was with me.

After leaving the great lava precipices at the crater's lip, we got on to the glissade of the descending track. We started down this slope as fast as we could run, and found we could

take the most prodigious strides. At every step our feet sank deep into the loose pumice and cinders, but I outstripped my companion, who had repeatedly to stop to take off and shake out his boots, as my leather leggings rendered me proof against this trouble. I wore out four pairs of waraji, however, as they were rapidly cut to pieces.

For nearly an hour we sped on thus, running, leaping, and bounding down the steep glissade—at times gathering such impetus that we could not stop, until some ridge in the gradient enabled us to check our speed. Every bound took us a dozen feet or so down the slope, and as our feet struck the loose ash we slid on a couple of feet more. The reader must not infer that this is the usual gait to come down the sacred mountain. More reverent and sober spirits take the descent at a much more dignified pace. We, however, were bent on record-breaking.

At a quarter to twelve I reached the half-way rest-house just above the forest line, my friend arriving fifteen minutes later. I had descended 5000 feet and come about eight miles down the mountain in an hour. At one o'clock the gōriki arrived.

So far all had been simple enough, but from here onwards trouble began. As we rested for a further half-hour whilst the gōriki had a meal, Yamanaka Lake, a mile below us, and nine miles away, looked so beautiful that I decided to change my plans about going down to Yōshida, and to proceed to the lake instead. Yamanaka Lake is called by the Japanese Mika-dzuki Kosui, or "Three-Days'-Moon Lake," from the similarity of its shape to the moon at that period of its phases.

The rest-house keeper and the gōriki at once said that they never heard of a descent being made at that point, and that it would be quite a dangerous thing to attempt it, as there was no track. But if there was no track, I thought we would find our way easily enough, as I had a compass and we had only to keep going eastwards and downwards. It looked simple enough. There was the lake below; we had only to

L

go along the mountain-side a mile or two and then descend straight to it.

Leaving the hut at 1.30 P.M., we therefore went along the Chudo Meguri path for about two miles until we reached a deep depression. This, we decided, would be a suitable place to descend, as the depression would develop into a gully which would go straight to the plains. It all looked so easy that I ventured the opinion we should be at the lake by five o'clock. The gōriki were of a different mind, however, saying that when we reached the forest it would be exceedingly difficult work to penetrate it.

The depression gradually became deeper, and soon there was no longer loose scoriæ under foot, but rough lava from which the ash had been washed away, and the going was very slow. The depression became a gully, the gully a ravine, and the ravine, in an hour, was a cañon, with walls a hundred feet or more in height. Few people have any conception how the erosion of ages has torn the sides of this mountain, which looks so smooth and unbroken when seen from the beaten track many miles away. The bed of the cañon became rougher and rougher, and progress slower each minute, till we came to a precipice, fully sixty feet high, which there was neither any way of descending nor of circumventing. In the rains this place is doubtless the site of a fine waterfall. There was nothing to do but retrace our steps some distance and climb to the top of the gorge. This was exceedingly difficult, and by the time we had got up, with all the impedimenta, it was five o'clock—the hour at which I had expected to reach the lake.

We were now in a thick forest, but by keeping along the edge of the gorge we made some headway, until the underbrush became so dense that it was no longer possible to follow it. We then struck off into the forest, and progress was painfully slow—as the gōriki had prophesied it would be. Alas, for the misery of the next three hours! Rain began to fall, and before we reached the edge of the forest it was eight o'clock, and we had miles of Yamanaka moor still before us. We had to proceed by lantern light—fortunately we had three oil-paper chōchins with us, such as are used by rikisha-runners.

The skies were black with heavy clouds, and we soon found that the moor was worse than the forest, for it was clothed with a dense mass of brambles and small apple-bushes, with long thorns which tore our clothes and scratched us all over. As if this were not bad enough, the underbrush was full of hidden lumps of lava thrown out from the volcano, and against these we were continually hurting our legs. "It never rains but it pours," and so, to add to our difficulties, a thunderstorm of tropical severity broke.

We were soon wet to the skin, but my cameras, plates, etc., were all well wrapped up in oil-paper and waterproof. Struggling through the brush I stumbled on a rough clinker and fell, twisting my ankle severely. Every step now gave me a good deal of pain, and I could only proceed by limping on one foot with the help of the gōriki and my pilgrim's staff.

Although the moon was nearly full, the heavy thunderclouds obscured its light completely, and without the lanterns we should have been in a sorry plight, as we could scarcely see a yard ahead. Every now and then a flash of lightning lit up the moor and the lake ahead, making the darkness that followed blacker than ever. For three hours we struggled along thus, and when we finally reached the Yōshida road it was eleven o'clock. I was too done up to go another step. For ten hours, although putting forth great exertion, we had found no water to drink, and my strained ankle was giving me a good deal of pain. Wrapping myself up in oil-paper, I lay down on the grass by the roadside, telling the others to go on to Yamanaka for a horse. They went off, and in half an hour I heard the rumble of a basha, which they had fortunately been able to engage. We all got in, and by midnight were comfortably installed at a Yōshida inn.

Our arrival caused the whole household to turn out of bed, and the gōriki all talked at once, relating the story of our adventures to the host, his family, and several guests, who all

listened with wide-open eyes and mouths, and many inter-
jections of "Naruhodo!" [1]

The innkeeper then delivered a long and fatherly oration,
telling us he had lived in Yōshida for over fifty years, but had
never heard of any one attempting to descend the mountain
at that place. I believe he doubted my sanity for having insisted
on such a crazy undertaking. As I sat there, with the good-wife
carefully massaging my swollen ankle, and thought of our woes
of the last few hours, there was no one in the room who agreed
with the old man more heartily than I; and I vowed that if
ever I ascended Fuji again I would descend the mountain
by one of the established routes, and that nothing should ever
induce me to wander from the beaten track.

[1] I have noticed that when a Japanese is spinning a yarn his victim
chimes in with a " Naruhodo " at every point the raconteur makes.   This
word may be rendered into English by such phrases as " Well, I never ! "
" You don't say so ! "   " Who'd have thought it ! "   " Indeed ! "   " Good
gracious ! "—according to the inflection of the voice.

A SHOWER IN THE WOODS

CHAPTER X

NIKKO AND CHUZENJI

NIKKO, where the greatest of Japan's old-time rulers was buried, does not rank among the "Three Principal Sights" of the land. It ranks above them. It stands in a special class, alone. It is the climax of Japanese wonders. It is the goal of every traveller to the East, and the name betokens, to the Japanese mind, the standard by which the claims to scenic fame of all other places are measured.

The scenery of Nikko is deservedly renowned throughout the world, for it is unrivalled in all Japan, and the air is soft and sweetly scented, and stimulating as rare old wine. It is here, in the midst of the "Mountains of the Sun's Brightness," that all the Japanese sprites, and elves, and brownies live. And it is no wonder that Nikko is the Japanese Fairyland, for surely never was there anywhere a place with so many things that such little people love. The plashing of silvery cascades, the murmur of rippling rills, and the roar of foaming rivers fill the air with fairy music, and the grand old forests are just the very place for fairies to play their rings of roses; whilst as for the wondrous temples, they are simply fairy palaces of beauty.

Just below the garden of the Kanaya hotel runs the torrent whose music "fills the sky-roofed temple of the eternal hills," and across it are the magnificent forests, deep in the brown-green heart of which the temples are buried. The river is spanned by a vermilion bridge, which leaps across it in one beautiful curve. This bridge is for the especial use of the Emperor whenever His Majesty comes this way. But how did the bridge get there? One of Nikko's prettiest legends explains.

151

Nearly twelve hundred years ago the Buddhist saint Shōdō Shōnin, in his search for the holy mountain of his dreams, Nantai-zan, arrived at Nikko, and found his farther progress barred by the waters of the swift Daiya-gawa. As he stood on the bank, revolving in his mind whether he should turn back or endeavour to find a ford to the river higher up, a snake appeared in the grass. Now it so happened that the practice of extreme austerity for many years had enabled the saint to understand much that it is not given to ordinary mortals to comprehend. Amongst other things he had learnt the language of animals; when, therefore, the snake spoke, Shōdō Shōnin at once understood the words it uttered.

"What are you thinking of?" it asked. "Do you wish to cross the river?"

"Yes," answered the saint, "I desire to reach that high peak yonder, which I believe is the holy mountain of my dreams."

"Have faith in me, and I will help you," said the snake. "Lay yourself on my back and I will carry you across."

Shōnin did as requested, and the snake then stretched and stretched itself out across the foaming torrent, and as it stretched, it became a great red dragon, whose head reached easily to the opposite shore. The priest alighted safely, and as he turned round to thank his benefactor, what was his surprise to find that the great dragon had disappeared!

That was the origin of the first Red Bridge of Nikko, and the present structure stands in the place where Shōdō Shōnin crossed the river.

Every American writer on Japan has told how, when General Grant visited Nikko, the local authorities opened the Red Bridge for him to pass across, but he declined to break the old tradition. The small boys of the place, however, have no such compunction in treading the sacred planks, and there are few youngsters in Nikko who have not stolen across it after dark. A young Japanese, with whom I once visited this district, made no bones whatever about leaping over the gate

THE CRYPTOMERIAS AVENUE AT NIKKO

and crossing the royal footway, and then invited me to do the same. But following the famous American example, I declined the proffered honour, as there is another bridge for ordinary mortals fifty yards lower down the stream.

When the great Shogun Iyéyasu, first of the Tokugawa line, died in 1616, his son, Hidétada, who succeeded him, began at once to carry out his father's dying wish that his remains should be interred in a mausoleum eclipsing in gorgeous splendour anything hitherto seen in Japan. The body was therefore buried on the heights of Kuno-zan, over-looking the beautiful Suruga Bay, amidst temples of great magnificence.

Later, it was considered that a still more worthy resting-place could be found among the Nikko mountains, and the building of a much finer shrine was at once embarked upon. For this purpose vast contributions of money and material poured in from all the various Daimyos. One Daimyo, however, was too poor to give a sum of money befitting one in his position, or an expensive gift of timber; so instead he offered to plant two rows of cryptomeria-trees from Utsonomiya to the shrine, a distance of twenty-seven miles. In course of time these trees grew into an avenue exceeding in grandeur any other in Japan, and for two hundred years and more this avenue has been one of Nikko's most famous sights. Though storm and tempest have made many gaps in it, it stands to-day a beautiful aisle of grand old trunks and redolent foliage nearly ten leagues long.

Nikko village has grown up since the old days, and the avenue does not now reach to Iyéyasu's shrine, but breaks off abruptly at the lower end of the village's single mile-long street. When entering the avenue from this end it is truly grand. In the midst of the sunlit fields the twin files of veteran trees, whose branches almost meet overhead, make one long bower of greenery. They do not begin, or straggle off, with weaklings; two stalwart giants head the lines, and behind them stand other giants just as sturdy. Under the canopy of the grand old trees the afternoon sun throws bars of deep shadow from the bulky trunks across the ancient highway, and between them

> The sunshine darting through
> Spreads a vapour soft and blue
> In long and sloping lines.

Now the road lies on a level with, now deep below, the bordering farm-lands, and the roots of the trees entwine themselves and form a broad rampart on either side. The beauty of the avenue is marred by ugly telephone poles, which interpose themselves on the view at every hundred yards. These could just as well have been placed outside the avenue as inside it, but consideration for scenic effect is no more a part of the electrical engineer's education in Japan than in any other land.

Nikko is the name of the whole of the mountain district hereabouts, but to the foreign mind it denotes the villages of Hachi-ishi and Iri-machi. The former stands at the head of the avenue; the latter lies half a mile away on the opposite bank of the river.

Hachi-ishi is one long street of curio-shops, and shops for the sale of local products—skins, carved furniture, and lacquer boxes. As one walks up this street one is pressed by sweet-voiced little maids to enter every doorway, and it is hard to run the gauntlet of so many smiling sirens without loading oneself up with another box or some quaint curio. Near the end of the street is the beautifully-appointed Kanaya Hotel, commanding a wondrous panorama of scenery from its verandahs, and at night, when weary with sight-seeing one is lulled to sleep by the murmur of the Daiya river below its windows.

Across the bridge there are a few more shops, and no one ever passed that way without making the acquaintance of Mme. Onuki, the owner of one of them. This little lady was formerly a geisha, and has all the arts and blandishments of the cleverest of her kind. She waylays every visitor to the temples, and few can resist her greeting and entreaty to "Please

come and see my shop." The man who hesitates here is lost,
for of all the wheedlers and coaxers in Nikko she is the most
adroit. "You are very nice gentleman," she purrs, as she
shows some lacquered box. "I see you very well understand.
Every one cannot understand like you, because every one have
not so good taste." Her flattering tongue never ceases its
"blarney" the whole time she has a possible customer in the
shop, and no human fly ever extricated himself from this little
spider's web but was lighter in pocket and richer by some
dainty piece of native workmanship.

A hundred yards away a broad path strikes up the hillside
from the main road, and plunges at once into magnificent
cryptomeria groves, where only a few stray rays from the
noonday sun ever penetrate. A broad and beautifully-kept
gravel walk leads to the temple gates. It is flanked by deep
stone culverts, and down the middle of the way there is a
broader culvert still. Dancing, rippling, gurgling, and flashing
in these granite beds, crystal streams hurry from the hills
to join the noisy river in the ravine below. The soft, religious
silence of the place is broken only by the murmur of these
limpid rills, the occasional croak of a hoarse old crow, or
the shrill squeal of a lazily-soaring hawk. The great sweeping curves of Buddhist roofs peep from the groves by
the wayside.

The largest of these buildings is the "Hall of Three Buddhas," beautifully situated in a landscape garden with a lotus
pond—a meet place to tarry awhile in meditation should the
sacred flowers be blooming. There is a curious "evil-averting
pillar" in the grounds, and near it is a belfry, in which hangs
a bell that is probably the greatest triumph of the bell-founder's
art in Japan. Others there are that are larger, larger by far,
but greater bulk of metal has only served to produce a deeper,
more sonorous sound—a mellow *basso profondo*—whereas the
Nikko bell is the very sweetest and purest tenor. At every
hour from dawn to sunset a priest comes from a neighbouring
building and strikes the time by means of a light, suspended
log. Immediately after the last stroke he sounds one lighter,

softer note—a mere touch of the swinging bole—as a sort of punctuation mark to apprise all hearers that the final blow has been struck.

The Irai-no-kané, or "Sundown Bell," was to me always the sweetest—coming at that quiet, subtle hour when day was giving way to night; when the skies were turning golden; when the redolent woods were giving off the most fragrant of their perfumes, and everything in this tranquil spot seemed to breathe of centuries of hallowed peace. I used to wait for its note, and listen to the silvery sound with keenest pleasure.

At the top of the gravelled slope is a granite torii of noble lines and grand proportions, with majestic cryptomerias all around it. Beyond, are a spacious terrace, with footways flagged with granite, and the finest pagoda in Japan. Its five blood-red stories are all agleam with gold, and bright with brass and green old copper. Bronze bells hang from every corner of its multiple roofs, and flowers and curious animals, and the crest of the Tokugawa family, are carved and worked in gilt all over it. Facing the torii is the Ni-Ō-mon, or "Gate of the Deva Kings"; but the terrible figures of the guardian giants have been removed to the temple where the bones of Iémitsu, Iyéyasu's grandson, rest. In their place now stand a pair of the Heavenly Dogs.[1] This is the main gate to the long series of courtyards and temple buildings that stand in memory of the great warrior who founded the Tokugawa line of Shoguns.

To describe these temples in detail is not within the scope of this book, for no description that I might offer could convey any adequate conception of their beauty. A mere sketch must suffice. As one passes through the paved courtyards, and by superb pavilions, gorgeously painted in coloured lacquer and gold, one marvels at the manner in which each separate part is made subject to the idea that is the nucleus of the whole. The most renowned wood-carvers of the time adorned the buildings. Each gallery and pavilion is richly carved. On one of them is the famous monkey trio, with hands to eyes, mouth, and ears, conveying the exhortation not to see, hear,

[1] See page 217.

THE YOMEI GATE AT NIKKO

or speak any evil.   In addition to this masterpiece Hidari
Jingoro is represented by several other examples of his skill.
In the courtyards there are torii, drum-towers, bell-towers,
and wonderfully-carved bronze lanterns; and a stone fountain,
the brim of which is levelled with such precision that the
over-flowing water falls in a perfectly even sheet all round it
without a bubble or ripple.   To all appearance the bowl is
surrounded by a plate-glass wall.   This fountain is one of the
greatest wonders of all this wonderful place—it is, indeed,
one of the most remarkable works in bronze I have seen in
any land.

From time to time the complete restoration of Nikko's
temple buildings is undertaken.   The work, I was told, occupies
about five years.   Those of the buildings already restored when
I last visited Nikko were gorgeous in vermilion, black, and
gold; but their splendour was marred by no tawdriness.

So cleverly has Nature been made to serve as the handmaid
of Art at Nikko that one feels that the temples and the forests
are one—part and parcel of the great master-work, as indeed
they are; for the buildings were designed to accord with their
surroundings, and every spot of the rich colouring and gleaming gold is in perfect harmony with the deep greens of the
forests that tower over all, giving the sense of height in which
the buildings are lacking.

One of the gateways, the Yomei-mon, was considered by
its builder to be a work of such perfection that he feared to
complete it, lest it should invoke the envy of the gods and
bring ruin upon the house of Tokugawa.   A main pillar, therefore, was turned upside-down, and thus impending evil was
averted.   This surpassingly ornate structure—more like a
casket for gems than a building—is deeply sculptured with
an almost incredible wealth of embellishment.   The heads of
gilded dragons, with gaping mouths and scarlet throats, and
of unicorns and the mythical kirin, glower at the end of every
beam, and floral arabesques adorn every possible space, whilst
the balustrade running round a projecting balcony is richly
carved with high relievos of children at play.   A medallion on

one of the central pillars is a curio such as the Japanese love. It represents a pair of playful tigers — the natural grain of the wood combining perfectly to form the hair in their coats.

Beyond this gate is another, smaller, but almost equally beautiful—the Kara-mon, or "Chinese Gate." It is inlaid with designs of plum-trees, dragons, and bamboo, and is richly carved with figures of Chinese sages. This is the entrance to the oratory, the interior of which is ablaze with gold and coloured lacquer.

In the court between these two gates is a building for the performance of the sacred kagura dance. A priestess, wearing a white surplice over a scarlet skirt, with a nun's bonnet on her head, goes through the motions of the dance; but it is not artistic, and consists merely of a few steps to and fro, a few shakes of a rattle, and a few passes with a fan.

Iyéyasu's tomb lies at the top of a long, winding stairway on the cryptomeria-clad hillside. The stone steps and massive balustrade are all green and grey with moss and lichens, and the soft mossy carpet under the stately old trees is inches thick from the damp of centuries.

After all the grandeur and splendid elaboration of colour of the buildings, this old stairway amidst the stately trees subdues the exhilaration that every visitor feels until this spot is reached, and any sound from human lips seems almost sacrilegious in the hush of these silent shades. That the awe of the great Shogun's presence should be felt in death was the central idea in the building of the shrine. The pomp and majesty of his life is shown by the magnificence of all that has gone before; now one is made to feel the greater majesty of the death of one who was supreme among his fellow men— whose spirit seems to haunt his shrine, though three centuries have passed since his mortal clay was laid to rest.

The tomb is a large pagoda-shaped casket of bronze, standing within a stone-balustraded enclosure with heavy bronze gates—the metal of both gates and tomb being so heavily impregnated with gold that it is of a rich light brown.

MEDITATION

A Study at Gamman-ga-Fuchi, Nikko

The extreme grandeur of its environment and the peaceful solemnity encompassing the shrine cannot be described. It is Japan's grandest triumph, and a glorious tribute to the memory of the greatest name in the long list of her rulers.

Iémitsu, third of the Tokugawa Shoguns, was buried on a hill half a mile distant. The shrine and pavilions are somewhat similar to, but less magnificent than, those of the last resting-place of his grandfather, Iyéyasu.

One does not go to Nikko, however, only to see these splendid temples. Kindly Nature, when she made this lovely land, surpassed all her other efforts in the glorious profusion with which she scattered feathery woods and sombre forests, gauzy cascades and white-robed waterfalls with either hand; and for each day of a month one can find some new and yet more beautiful walk to explore. Rambling about the deserted bridle-paths in the silent forests, one is ever discovering some moss-overgrown old stairway; a few stone lanterns; a lone, but not neglected, little temple; or some tiny shrine bedecked with a few paper prayers, offered by the patient pilgrims who scent such places of communion from afar, and pass by none of them without a supplication or simple oblation. Everything is green and hoary with age, for there were monasteries in these secluded wilds, and monks and abbots were laid to rest in ancient graveyards here for centuries before Iyéyasu saw the light. There are other "God's acres" too, where

> Each in his narrow cell for ever laid,
> The rude forefathers of the hamlet sleep.

Grand old trees have wept over their graves for hundreds of years, and out of these tears thick moss has sprung and covered the pock-marked tombs with a velvety garment.

From the gravelled avenues centuries-old, stone-paved pathways lead, and entice one to wander under the proud cryptomerias high up the hillsides to find temples which are poets' dreams of picturesque beauty, with lilting cascades all round them; and every crevice in the hills is filled with some purling stream, and every break in every wooded cañon flashes with some rainbowed waterfall. The "Pitch-dark Cascade," so called because of its sombre surroundings; the "Back-View Cascade," which leaps out so far from a cliff that one may walk behind and under the falling torrent; the "Mist-falling Cascade," which slides down hundreds of feet of the mountain-side over slippery beds of rock—are but a few of them; but there are scores more, and there are mountain views without end which are famous throughout the land.

Nikko children are nothing if not lovers of nature. One day as I was going over the hills to the "Mist-falling Cascade" I passed a pond by the wayside, and two farmer's youngsters, whose combined ages could not have amounted to more than ten years, stood beside it uttering ejaculations of admiration at the simple beauty of a dewdrop nestling in the cup of a lotus-leaf, and shining in the brilliant sunshine like a gem. During another ramble I came across a group of little ones greatly delighted over a spider's web spun among some bamboo branches. The strands of the web were thickly covered with dew, and as the sun shone through the thousand tiny crystal globules it turned them into many-coloured opals. When rustic children of tender years take pleasure in such pretty glimpses of nature, one ceases to marvel longer at the dainty turn of Japanese art and design.

Paradise of peace and restfulness as Nikko is to the traveller, he penetrates deeper yet into the mountains to find a summer resort such as European and American visitors love.

Lake Chuzenji is eight miles from Nikko, and more than two thousand feet higher in the hills. The way lies by the river-bank for half the distance; then it rises far above it and creeps up the abrupt hillsides by a zig-zag pony path. The scenery along the route is some of the loveliest and most interesting in Japan. For the first few miles the road is broad and well-metalled, with a narrow-gauge tramway at one side. Once every day a train of flat cars, each drawn by a broad-backed ox, comes down the line, bearing heavy ingots of copper. The track is the property of the Ashio Mining Co., and is used for no other purpose than the transport of copper to the railroad, and of supplies to the mine, which is a day's journey further up in the mountains.

In the mossy shade of the cryptomeria-clad hillside, by a cataract which rages madly down the river bed between enormous polished boulders, a company of ancient Buddhas sit. Carved in stone, they are mottled with the lichens of centuries and, rapt in contemplation, they gaze into the troubled waters as though in meditation on life and its afflictions. Formerly these images were so many that no two persons could ever agree as to their number, but of late years time has dealt roughly with them. Only a dozen or two of the once uncountable idols now remain, the others having been swept away by the maddened torrent during the storms which of late years have ravaged this district.

The higher one ascends and the nearer one gets to Chuzenji the more magnificent are the views. The road is well beaded with tea-houses and tateba, or look-outs, at every point of vantage. As each traveller or pilgrim appears, bright-eyed, rosy mountain maids run to place a cushion on some rustic seat, or on the edge of the tea-house floor, and bring tea and dainty cakes, and a delicious peppermint sweetmeat—a speciality of this district—to stimulate the tissues for further effort, whilst enchanting views of distant waterfalls and lovely vistas of the gorges far below are a feast of beauty to the eyes.

Through my glass I have seen many monkeys on the cliffs hereabouts, and once as I was coming down the road there was a loud crashing in the trees, and three great apes came swinging from bough to bough overhead. The Japanese saru is a pink-cheeked, comical-looking fellow, and is dearly beloved by native artists; but, like the Japanese cat, he has no tail.

As the top of the pass is reached, the road plunges into an undulating forest, where the booming of a near-by cataract is heard. It is Kegon-no-taki, Chuzenji's overflow, a chute of water which leaps over a precipice nearly a hundred yards in height.

There are tea-houses and more tateba, with charming

peeps of the fall through the maple trees, and a path leads down almost to its foot, amidst bewitching woodland scenery. In places the track burrows deep under dripping overhanging cliffs, and once when I came this way in the depths of winter, when the snow lay a yard deep on the ground, these cliffs were fringed with colossal icicles and we had to make our way warily over the slippery path for fear of being precipitated into the gorge below.   It was worth the arduous journey in the snow to see those icicles, but I made the trip in the hope of seeing this fine cascade locked in the arms of the frost king. In this I was disappointed, for there was only an insignificant cluster of icicles at the top of the precipice, and no other evidence that a great waterfall ever existed here.

In spring, however, Kegon is a glorious sight.   The cliff is a break in a bed of laminated lava strata, and the water, as it falls, sends up a mist which spreads wide in the breezes, and, catching the rays of the sun, forms brilliant rainbows to bridge the gorge with glowing arcs of colour.

Near by are the "White Cloud Falls," where a hundred jets of water gush out of the middle of a still higher cliff to form perhaps the most curious cascade in Japan.

Kegon is an ill-omened waterfall. Some years ago a youth inscribed a despairing poem on a tree and then cast himself into the vortex. This novel and spectacular method of departure for the Land of Shadows won for the suicide great notoriety, and such was the admiration of the students of Japan for his act that several hypersentimental youths quickly followed his example. It was found necessary to establish a police guard in order to discourage the vogue for this new fashion in self-destruction.

The Lakeside Hotel, charmingly situated at the south end of the lake, near the Kegon fall, is one of the favourite foreign resident resorts of Japan.   There are beautiful views from its gardens and verandas; and boating, picnic, and fishing parties sally out with well-filled lunch-baskets every morning to spend the day on the lovely sheet of water, or to explore the equally lovely woods—and the Chuzenji woods are among

NANTAI-ZAN AND LAKE CHUZENJI

the most enchanting in all Japan. The cool blue lake, lying mirror-like among the mountains, is bordered with forests reaching to the loftiest heights; and the trees are all festooned with moss, and in spring are draped with purple wistaria clusters.

Chuzenji's season is the hot months, but the maples in late October make a wonderful display of colour, and in May every hillside is scarlet with the azaleas which blaze amidst the forests. Few have seen Chuzenji in winter, for the hotels are closed and there is little comfort to be found, and the journey up the steep road in the snow is very arduous; but when I came here once in January, the woodland—thickly carpeted with white, with every branch of every tree filigreed against the winter sky, as if in silver, with the hoar frost —was every bit as beautiful, if less gorgeous than in its autumn garb.

But even Chuzenji is not the last word of Nature in this district. The palm for subtle loveliness must be given to Lake Yumoto. Effort is asked of no one in these Nikko mountains without the promise of reward rich beyond one's hopes; and those who tramp eight miles higher and deeper into them will find the way bestrewn with scenic gems, and at the journey's end one of the most beautiful little lakes imaginable.

For the first half-hour of the walk the road skirts Chuzenji's waters under a bower of birch and maple branches; then it turns away to the "Dragon's Head Cascade," where, from a tateba under the pine-trees, one may feast one's eyes on as pretty a waterfall as Japan has to show. For wellnigh a quarter of a mile a mountain torrent, on its way to join the near-by "River of Hell," tumbles down a series of rocky ledges, half-covered with moss, and the trees leaning over the foaming stream are moss-grown too, and in places meet to form sylvan arches overhead.

A vast solitude, the "Moor of the Battlefield"—so called because of a conflict that took place here in feudal times— must then be crossed. Great mountains tower above the forests which hedge the barren waste on every side. On the

M

right Nantai-zan reflects its image in the waters of a swamp, and, far over the western peaks, the volcano Shirané-san, queen of all, in height as well as beauty, lacks but seventy yards of nine thousand feet of altitude. Miles away the forest is divided by a thin white line. It is Yu-no-tani, a fine waterfall which slides, a chute of snowy foam, down a smooth bed of rock at an angle of 60° for over two hundred feet of perpendicular height.

The road winds up the face of a steep hill to the head of the fall, and as the brow is reached Yumoto lake bursts into view in all its bewitching beauty. Small, and of an exquisite colour, the polished emerald of its unruffled waters mirrors every twig of every bordering tree, and every cranny of the sheltering peaks that guard this liquid jewel is reflected in its surface. Blue-green pines—mossy, mouldy, and splintered with age—lean over the water at every possible angle; and fat salmon-trout glide about in the limpid depths.

Along the road skirting the bights and bays of its uneven shores are grand vistas of the ever-steaming Shirané-san and other encircling peaks. In July the banks are bordered in many places with a fringe of irises, and when I came this way one autumn, lake and mountains alike were splashed with all the colours of a painter's palette. At the far end, which after all is not so very far, is Yumoto village.

The water here is all steaming and discoloured from the numerous hot-springs which flow into it, or rise, bubbling, out of its bed. It is strange that in a lake so largely impregnated with sulphur, fish should be so plentiful. I have even seen them leaping amongst the vapours in the "milky" water at the northern end.

Yumoto village is the resort of numbers of pilgrims who swarm to this district in the summer months to do the round of the sacred heights—adding a little to their balance of merit with the gods for each fresh holy peak they conquer. The pretty hamlet is all hotels and inns, and tea- and lodging-houses, and the whole place is malodorous with sulphurous fumes.

The Yumoto air and hot-springs are very beneficial for skin and blood; and the visitors, being apparently unable to permeate themselves sufficiently by breathing sulphuretted hydrogen into their lungs all day, must needs also spend many hours soaking in the sulphur waters. For this purpose every inn has its dependent bath-house, and the guests adjourn their conversation on the balconies only to continue it in these public tubs.

The bathing arrangements are managed with an ingenuous-ness as natural as at villages much more remote from the beaten track; and men, women, and children throng the bath-houses all day long. Slipping off their garments, the bathers drop into the water and soak a while; then they emerge, and, sitting on the edge, cleanse themselves with bran-bags preparatory to another immersion.

This process is sometimes continued for an hour or more, and twice or thrice each day; and as the bathers soak, and scrub themselves and each other's backs, they chat with the casual strollers-by who pause to gossip at the open doorways.

There are grand excursions to be made into the surrounding mountain fastnesses, with magnificent scenery everywhere. The ascent of Shirané-san is the finest, but it is a roughish climb, and should not be attempted without a competent guide.

Nantai-zan, the holy mountain of Shōdō Shōnin's vision, which is so prominent a feature of every landscape in this district, is seen at its best from Chuzenji. From the eastern shore of the lake it rises to a height of 8150 feet, and from this point it is almost as perfectly shaped a cone, and as richly wooded to its summit, as is beautiful Merapi, one of the queenly volcanic peaks of Java.

Nantai-zan ranks high among the sacred mountains of Japan, and pilgrims swarm up its steep slopes by thousands every summer. Formerly a picturesque old Shinto temple at the lake-side marked the beginning of the ascent. Passing under the great torii, the pilgrims made their contributions at the temple threshold, prayed for strength to brace their muscles, received the blessing of the priests and the temple stamp upon their garments, and then slowly ascended the long flights of interminable steps leading to the crest of the defunct volcano and the goal of their desire.

But the year 1902 brought dire disaster to Chuzenji, as it brought unprecedented ruin to Nikko. Rain fell for many days, without ceasing, that autumn, and the mighty Nantai-zan—a vast pyramid of loose ash and volcanic tuff—became so sodden with water that an avalanche broke loose well up towards the summit, and, gathering in volume as it fell, swept a wide path through the forest and bore straight down upon the ancient Shinto temple. The priests at prayer heard the roar of the coming doom, but so swiftly did it fall that they had no time to fly to safety. They no more than reached the doors when the landslide was upon them, and temple, priests, and all were swept bodily into the lake, and buried in its limpid depths beneath thousands of tons of the holy mountain-side.

This enormous mass falling suddenly into the water caused a huge wave to sweep the surface of the lake. Over the Kegon precipice leapt the flood, and then went raging down the valley of the Daiya-gawa, destroying all in its path, tearing the Red Bridge from its massive foundations, and carrying houses and great trees on its crest to scatter them along the river's bank, as driftwood, for a hundred miles or more.

A few days after the first anniversary of this catastrophe I walked from Nikko to Chuzenji. The rain, which was falling as we started, became steadily heavier as we proceeded, and on reaching a little tea-house nearly half-way along the road, drenched through to the skin, we tarried awhile for some hot tea and saké. I noticed that the house was perfectly new, and that only an old woman and a little boy were in charge. On my remarking about the unusual severity of the storm the beldame burst into tears, and told me of that other dreadful tempest just a year before, when she and her daughter and her two grandchildren, a boy and a girl, were living here together. A peasant came along, on his way to Chuzenji, and tarried for a cup of tea and to purchase a pair of waraji. Her daughter was in the house preparing the refreshment, and her little grand-daughter was tying the waraji to the old man's feet. She herself and her small grandson had gone a little way up the hillside to fetch some firewood. Suddenly the boy called her attention to a terrible and quite unusual sound that filled the air. It was like an angry growl, growing momentarily louder, and seemed to come from up the valley. Looking in that direction, she saw a vast wall of water sweep round a bend in the river, uprooting trees and sweeping rocks before it as though they were but weeds and pebbles.

Before she could even shout to warn her dear ones of the peril, the wave was upon her house. She saw the water smite it, and the frail structure rise like a match-box on to the breast of the flood; in a moment more it was crushed and crumpled like an egg-shell, and her daughter and granddaughter, and the old peasant at whose knees the little girl was kneeling, together with everything the house contained—all she had and loved in the world except her little grandson—were swept away before her eyes. All was over in an instant. The water rose and passed on like a horrible dream, and when it had gone its way she rubbed her eyes to be sure she was not dreaming. But it was all, alas! too true. In that passing moment her little home had gone for ever. Kind friends, it seems, came to her assistance and enabled her to have a new house built, on the spot where the old one stood; for she could not find the heart to leave the place where she had lived so long and so happily, yet where in one awful moment she had been bereaved of all.

Sad at heart at the old woman's recital of this tragedy— to which my coolies had listened with tears—we started out again in the blinding rain to climb the slippery road. Every minute the storm grew fiercer, and when we reached Chuzenji it had become almost a cloudburst. We put up at a native hotel within a hundred yards of the scene of the landslide of a year ago.

All that night the storm continued unabated. There was not a moment's diminution of the deluge. The very heavens seemed to have opened. Neither I nor a Japanese friend who

was with me could sleep. We sat up all night, as also did the
entire hotel staff, discussing the possibility of another landslide.

The whole of the next day the storm never ceased for a
moment, and the ensuing night it was even severer still; our
fears lest another disaster might happen caused us a further
sleepless night; indeed, sleep was out of the question for the
rattle and roaring of the storm. And when the morning dawned
and the skies began to clear, all of us felt greater relief than we
cared to tell.

The next morning Kegon was a marvellous sight. An
enormous volume of water shot out over the top of the cliff
and fell fully fifty feet clear of its base. The Daiya-gawa was
a raging cataract, and when, a day later, we returned to Nikko,
we found that irreparable damage had again been done. The
road for a mile or more had been completely washed away,
and the Ashio copper-mine track was a tangled mass of iron
in the centre of the river. It was only possible to reach Nikko
by taking a detour high along the hillside, and already nearly
a thousand workmen from the mine were busy endeavouring
to make a new route for the tramway.

What the previous storm had left of the beautiful Dainichi-
dō gardens was now but a shapeless morass, with a forlorn
stone lantern or miniature pagoda still standing here and
there; whilst the river had cut for itself an entirely new channel
at one place—a hundred yards away from its original course.

Such are the storms which sometimes devastate this lovely
mountain district.

KEGON-NO-TAKI

CHAPTER XI

MATSUSHIMA AND YEZO

MATSUSHIMA ranks in native estimation as one of the San Kei, or "Three Principal Sights" of Japan; but not every foreigner sees it with Japanese eyes, and the charm of the famous bay near Sendai is completely lost on those who go there for an hour or two, and rush away. Matsushima is one of those places which must be studied leisurely and in detail, and seen in this way it fully deserves its renown.

As the name implies, it is an archipelago of pine-clad islands—on the east coast about two hundred miles north of Tokyo. It is said that there are no less than eight hundred and eight islands, all composed of soft volcanic rock which the erosive action of the waves has worn into most fantastic shapes. Each island is named; one, for instance, being designated "Buddha's Entry into Nirvana," whilst a little bunch of a dozen is called "The Twelve Imperial Consorts."

I arrived at Matsushima station one August morning, and took a rikisha for the village, distant about a couple of miles. As we passed a cutting between two hills my kurumaya suggested that I should walk to the top of one of them and see the view. I did so, and am glad that I first saw this beautiful place from so favourable a view-point. First impressions have a lasting effect, and though, in after years, I saw the island-studded bay under less favourable conditions, Matsushima always remains in my memory as I saw it on that August day.

It was only a few minutes' walk to the top of the eminence, from which the view is famous as one of the fairest seascapes in Japan. The neat village lay close below, and a precipitous

little island, with sides as steep as the wall of a house, rose out
of the sea not ten yards from the shore, to which it was connected by a rustic bridge. From among the pine-trees that
covered it a temple peeped, and a line of sampans were anchored
at the near-by quay. Scattered about the bay, in every direction,
were other islands, seemingly painted on a mirror, for the
surface of the sea was unruffled by a breath of air. Billows
of cumulus clouds filled the skies, and here and there a boat
sent long widening ripples across the water to prove that the
scene was real. The summer chorus of the cicadas about me
was a deafening pandemonium. *Wee-wee-wee-wee-wee-wee-wee-
weeeeeeea!* shrilled a thousand of them in the pine-trees, till
my ear-drums seemed to whistle with the sound. Yet I love
these noisy insects, for their song is always merriest when
the weather is warmest and brightest, and Japan in bright
weather is Arcadia itself.

A Japanese dearly loves to see a foreigner appreciate the
beauty of the land. He takes it as a personal compliment to
himself. My kurumaya, who had come to the hill-top with
me, chuckled with delight at my comments on the scene, and
there were even tears in the old fellow's eyes. (I do not know
any people so easily touched by a few appreciative words as
the Japanese.) When we returned to the road, he had to
recite all my remarks to his companion (who was waiting with
the luggage), to the equal pleasure of the latter; and when
we arrived at the inn my appreciation was reported by the pair
of them to the landlord (with, doubtless, copious amplifications,
judging by the time it took to tell), and the landlord retailed
the story to the servants in a longer version still—so that I
was *persona grata* with the lot of them just because of my
favourable impressions of the place.

I wasted no time in chartering a sampan, and we were soon
under way to see the principal sights. For the whole of that
day and the next we cruised about the calm waters of a smooth
shining sea, visiting island after island, each more grotesque
than the last, and exploring caves and natural arches and every
whimsical freak that the sea could carve in stone. Each island

is crowned with a few pine-trees, even to the very smallest, which are but a few yards in area. How the pines grow is a mystery. Many of them appear to find subsistence in the solid rock, and every crevice is occupied by one or more. They grow at every angle, as often as not leaning down to the water, or horizontally over it.

Some of the islands have tea- and summer-houses on them; some are carved with Buddhas; one has long rustic bridges connecting it with the near-by shore; but the finest sight of all is the view from Tomi-yama. From this place on a clear day the prospect is one of the most famous in Japan. The sea bristles with islands and promontories, and the surface of the water is streaked with currents and tide-rips that change in colour with every hour of the day, whilst every cloud that floats over the bay alters the composition of the picture. The largest of the islands is the holy Kinkwa-zan, which has been a Mecca to pious pilgrims for centuries; but the day I had planned to visit it was wet and stormy, and, though I waited for two days more, the storm only increased in violence, and I was reluctantly obliged to give up the trip, as I was bound still farther northwards—to the island of Yezo.

As I crossed the sapphire Tsugaru Strait one hot, sunny September day, and saw the tiled-roofed, wood-and-paper houses of Hakodaté nestling at the foot of the great Gibraltar-like rock known as The Peak, I decided that no other port in Japan was fairer or more inviting, not even the far-famed Nagasaki.

The town was clean and neat, and business seemed to be in a thriving and prosperous condition; coolies were every-where, bustling about with bundles of cured fish, bags of rice, bales of dried seaweed, and other merchandise; and the bay was full of shipping. My entry into the Katsuta Inn confirmed the good impression already formed. It was immaculate in its cleanliness. My window looked out on to the harbour, which is a miniature Hong-Kong of activity; and if anything were needed to complete the fitness of the simile, the mountain towering above the town filled the blank, for it is but a small edition of Victoria Peak, which dominates Britain's South-China colony.

It is well to drink in such beauty as one finds in the situation of Hakodaté. The farther one penetrates into the island the more one becomes impressed with the fact that Yezo is an untidy country—as inferior to the mainland as it possibly could be.

Though the Tsugaru Strait is not more than ten miles wide at the narrowest part, it is exceedingly deep, and has severed the island of Yezo from Hondo, the Japanese mainland, for untold ages—if indeed these lands were ever joined at all. North of the Strait the fauna and flora are as different from those found south of it as if they belonged to widely-separated countries. We are told that there are no monkeys in Yezo, nor any pheasants; and that even the bears are of an entirely different species from those of the mainland.

The singing birds are numerous and varied—a most remarkable thing, for the more temperate mainland can boast of only nightingales and skylarks—which latter are plentiful on all Japanese moors.

My object in coming to this little-visited part of Japan was to see the Ainu, that strange, hairy race who were the aborigines of the land before the Japanese arrived and took it from them. The nearest Ainu settlements, however, are a hundred miles or so up the east coast, and this necessitated our embarking again on a small steamer for the port of Muroran—a place of little interest, which is reached in about nine hours.

There are many places on the east coast near Muroran where colonies of Ainu are to be found, the largest of these being at Shikyu and Shiraoi. I was accompanied thither by a Japanese interpreter. On the way we turned aside for a day or two to visit the great solfataras of Nobori-betsu, which are among the most interesting natural phenomena of Japan. The large and comfortable hotel at which we put up was thronged with Japanese visitors, who come here to enjoy the curative properties of the mineral hot-springs. The water is piped to a long series of public baths, ranging in temperature from

AT MATSUSHIMA

about 105° F. downwards. These baths are very interesting.
Here, at any hour of the day, one can study Japanese humanity
of both sexes in a state of nature. The baths are the meeting-
place for guests at the hotels, and a convenient rendezvous
for the villagers. All meet on a common footing, man and
woman, youth and maid, young and old, rich and poor—and
I was going to say dirty and clean; but the Japanese are never
dirty—unless one include the Ainu, who are a separate race
and type.

Comfortably immersed to the neck, the sexes mingle
together, and laugh and talk as freely and unrestrainedly,
and with equal courtesy and etiquette, as in their own, or
each other's homes.

It is some two miles to the solfataras, which are the crater
floors of an exceedingly old, double-vented volcano, with
towering precipitous walls, whose jagged, serrated ridges—
burnt brilliant red—frame with weird grandeur and beauty
the awful abomination of desolation of the sulphur-beds
below. In all Japan one cannot find a more interesting example
of a volcano which has destroyed itself than these solfataras
of Nobori-betsu. The vividly-coloured walls are a striking
object-lesson in geology. The lower lava bed is covered with
several hundred feet of black ash and red pumice, which were
ejected by the volcano for ages after the foundation of lava
was formed. When later the heavy lava rose once more into
the great cup, and filled it up to the brim, this unstable pile of
loose tuff was broken down, and a terrible cataclysm must
have occurred when the vast rent in the crater's western wall,
over half a mile in length, was made.

This self-destruction is in the end the destiny of most
really old volcanoes. I use the word "old" in the geological
sense. Fuji, for instance, is but a baby as volcanoes go, and,
though called extinct, is merely dormant, as the steaming
fissures on the lip would seem to testify. Fuji has not yet
marred its beauty by bursting its crater's rim.

On the north, south, and east sides of the Nobori-betsu
volcano the abrupt, inflamed walls stand in a great half-circle

round the sulphur-mounds and the lakes of boiling sulphurous water, which now cover the bed of what was originally a crater floor. The whole of this huge solfatara is honeycombed with great yawning cavities, some of which emit fearful sounds from the seething cauldron below, and belch forth vast columns of steam at terrific pressure.

There are pools of soft, sticky, bubbling, sputtering mud, and cauldrons of boiling water as clear as glass; and there are fountains of boiling liquid mud, and geysers of boiling water of crystalline purity, spouting with equal ferocity but a few feet apart. There are great cavernous apertures, twenty feet or more in diameter, encrusted with lovely sulphur crystals —fragile as foam—and little holes, not an inch across, each adding, according to its powers, to the general pandemonium, and imparting its tribute to the boiling, sulphur-tainted river which springs from the crater's heart, and flows hissing, seething, and steaming over the treacherous surface as though the eternal fires were but a few feet below.

The noises of the place are as varied as the phenomena. Some of the holes emit a muffled murmur; others almost scream; whilst others again give out sounds of such fierce boiling as are truly harrowing to listen to. As we cautiously wended our way amongst these safety-valves, over hills of flower-of-sulphur, and pumice, and vermilion ash, carefully poking the ground with long sticks before venturing each step—for to break through the crust would have meant a hasty end—we came at length to a great hole which gave forth a most blood-curdling sound. As we approached, it breathed a deep sigh, and then sent out a wailing shriek, as if some subterranean demon were in agony. For a few moments both I and my Japanese friend stood rooted to the ground in consternation. To run would have been to court destruction by stepping on some weak spot in the treacherous crust. We did not know what was coming next. For my part I fully expected the ground to open and engulf us, or a boiling geyser of mud and sulphur to overwhelm us; and not till some minutes after the wail had died away into a sigh and silence, did we realise that this was only another of the harmless, intermittent noises of this diabolical place.

Curiosity would not be satisfied, however, till we had taken a look into the great hole from which this terrifying sound had come. We went to the edge, and as we stood by the gaping cavity it gave forth deep and regular sighs, as of some cyclopean creature breathing. Indeed, if we shut our eyes and listened, we could almost imagine there *must* be some great subterranean monster near at hand. It was a positive relief to open them again.

We waited, fascinated, near the spot, and in half an hour the sound began again. More horrible than ever it was, as we now stood on the actual brink of the hole; but long before the scream had reached its climax, we had retreated as fast as the necessity of carefully choosing our footsteps would permit. We felt that this hole was not to be trusted. I have seen many volcanoes and solfataras in several lands, but never any other that emitted such truly horrible sounds as Nobori-betsu.

According to the Ainu creed the world is governed by a Goddess of Fire. It is certainly not surprising that such simple, ignorant people—living in a land where there are such appalling manifestations of the devastating power pent up in the earth, and where such terrifying sounds issue from the ground amidst boiling mud and sulphur streams—should have had the fear of fire instilled into their hearts, and have formed the belief that the world is ruled by a deity whose abode is in such places.

As evening drew nigh, swallows circled and twittered in thousands about the bastioned, blazing precipices, which glowed with every colour in the rays of the setting sun; and as we traced our steps homewards the tumult of the place lingered in our ears for a mile, like the roar of a rock-bound coast beaten by the angry waves of the sea.

The next morning we left for our objective point, the Ainu settlement, and the nearer we approached it the more slovenly became the methods of the farmers and the condition of their millet crops. Although the fields are owned and worked by

Japanese, they bear little semblance to the trim and beautifully-kept farms of the mainland.

We arrived at Shikyu at nine, and put up at the most miserable apology for an inn that it has ever been my lot to stay at in any part of Japan. Yet it was the best the place afforded. Our arrival at this inn was the signal for the greater part of the inhabitants of the village to come and satisfy their curiosity by staring at us. This stare of the Yezo Japanese is something which must be experienced to be appreciated. A man would place his face a couple of feet from mine, and glare into my features with as much assurance and self-possession as if he were regarding a poster on a wall. Apparently foreigners were not often met with in these parts, judging by the intensity of the scrutiny to which I was subjected.

It seemed that much difficulty was likely to be experienced in persuading the natives of the Ainu settlement, which we were about to visit, to be photographed. A coolie had been found to carry the apparatus, but it appeared that the man would not come unless his wife was engaged too. As they knew the Ainu well we took them both. The man unchivalrously proceeded to load his wife up with the heaviest packages, whilst he contented himself with a little case weighing about five pounds. I protested against this division of labour, but he declared that his wife was much stronger than he—though she was obviously a fragile little woman and he was as lusty a fellow as I ever employed. But I insisted on a more fair division of the loads.

Then there was a further hitch, and my interpreter said, indicating the innkeeper: "I have decided it is necessary to contract with this gentleman also; the Ainu are so spontaneous and will rebel to submit to the picture. He is the owner of this house." The last sentence was accompanied with a dramatic gesture. I cannot say that this commendation carried the weight with me that it was evidently expected to, and I inwardly breathed a prayer to the weather-god that he would not entail upon me the necessity of accepting the gentleman's hospitality longer than was necessary.

I soon found, however, how indispensable this man's services really were. I am firmly convinced that without his help it might have taken many days to secure a single photograph of these timid folk, for the Ainu prejudice against the "evil eye" of the camera is deep-rooted, and cannot be overcome except by the judicious admixture of gifts and diplomacy —the one as necessary as the other.

This man proved to be a most valuable assistant. For two days he was indefatigable in my interests, and when the time came to pay the reckoning I was quite unable to persuade him to accept anything for his services. Only with great difficulty, indeed, could I induce him to receive payment of our board bill. He maintained that it had been an honour to lend his assistance to any one who came for the purpose of learning about his country. I have met few like him. Humble as was his abode, and evil-smelling from the quantities of dried fish stored in it, yet he had a proud and generous spirit, and I doubt not sprang from stock that had seen more prosperous days.

We then proceeded to the large Ainu village at Shiraoi, a few miles distant. My olfactory nerves were the first to apprise me that our destination was near at hand; the great distinguishing characteristic of an Ainu settlement is the stench of dried and rotting fish with which everything in it, and about it, is permeated.

Three women were the first of the Ainu to put in an appearance. We met them just outside the town, carrying large bundles on their backs. They were young and good-looking, with rosy faces, and hair hanging round their heads to the shoulders; but their features were badly disfigured by broad moustaches tattooed on their upper lips—reaching almost to the ears. This is the prevalent custom amongst almost all Ainu women. The hair which grows so luxuriantly on the face of the Ainu man is lacking on that of the woman, so to supplement this deficiency the upper lip is tattooed. Some Ainu women are not content with submitting merely the lip to this disfiguring treatment, but have thick lines tattooed on their forehead and arms, and ugly patterns on the backs of their hands. These marks are considered by the Ainu greatly to enhance their beauty.

After a consultation with the chief of the village—a fine-looking old man, whose long beard and shaggy locks were turning grey—we were conducted to the house of a prominent member of the community who lay on a bed on the floor, sick unto death. An old grey-bearded man, whose face was almost hidden with thick hair, knelt beside him, reciting prayers for his recovery, whilst many relatives sat round him on the earthen floor of the rude thatched hut. The dim light was just sufficient to show the anxious expression on the faces of the silent figures, who indicated so plainly, by their quiet, gentle manners, the deep concern they felt. It was a sad initiation into the home life of these poor people, and respect for their feelings made me take a hasty leave, for I felt that the intrusion of a stranger at such a time was quite unwarrantable. The few moments, however, that I tarried in the hut, and saw this little group of gentle, yet ignorant, uncivilised figures—gathered together in the sombre interior of a structure which in some lands would be thought scarcely fit for cattle —waiting for the approach of the Reaper whose harvest lies in every land and at every season, left a deep impression in my mind. My feeling turned from disgust at the animal-like condition in which these people live, to pity that any human creatures, dwelling amongst a highly-civilised race, should know nothing better than mere existence in such a state of degradation. Bare existence and sustenance seem to be the whole ambition of the Ainu, who are held in utter contempt by the clever, enlightened Japanese, and are left to work out their own salvation. The Japanese name for the Ainu is Aino, the literal meaning of which is mongrel. This arises from a Japanese tradition that the Ainu are the descendants of a race of creatures half man, half dog. Little consideration, therefore, can these humble people expect from their masterly conquerors.

The huts in which the Ainu live are of coarse kaia-grass,

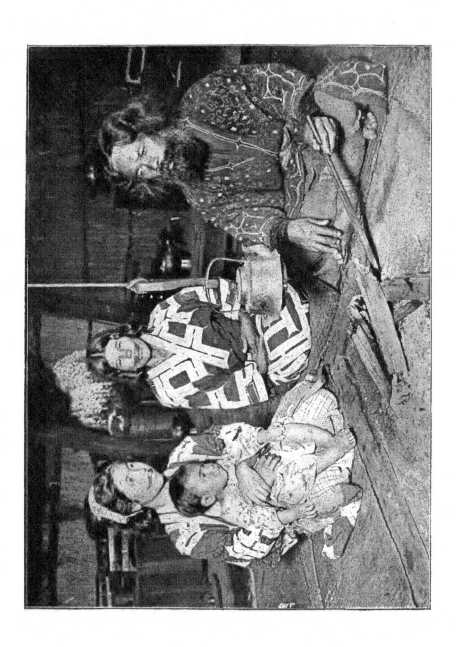

thatched with reeds. Each hut has two small windows—one on the east side, one on the south. The east window is sacred, and outside it are placed offerings to the gods. At the west end is the door, and over it a hole in the roof is provided for the escape of the smoke from the fire, which is made on the ground near the centre of the hut.

All Ainu dwellings are constructed in this manner. There are no neat wooden houses, such as the Japanese live in, for Ainu custom forbids any departure from traditional methods. Their huts are primitive, uncomfortable, dirty places, reeking with the odour of dried and rotting fish, which are hung in the roof. Nor are the people who inhabit them any cleaner, for they have none of that love of hot water which makes the Japanese, as a nation, the cleanest people in the world.

Formerly the Ainu dressed in garments of wood-fibre, and many do to the present day; but Japanese cotton goods now largely supplant the native cloth. Men and women dress much alike, except that the patterns woven into the fabrics are quite distinctive in character for each sex. No man would ever wear the patterns used by women. When old, the women closely resemble the men in feature, saving for the lack of beard. With middle age comes ugliness, but many of the young girls are very comely. Men and women alike wear their hair about their shoulders in a thick, bushy, unkempt mass.

The lot of the Ainu woman is not a happy one. Dirty, slovenly, barefooted, miserably clad, and disfigured by tattoo-marks, she subsists, a wretched drudge, to whom life holds out none of the pleasures and diversions known to the women of other parts of Japan. To her, life means naught but work from morn till night. Not only must she attend to all the household duties, but she must clean, smoke, and dry the fish; cut and pound out the millet; cut and carry from the forest the winter's supply of wood; dig up the fields and sow the crops; and such time as she can find to spare must be given to helping her lord and master, to whom she is little more than a slave. She has none of the little graces which distinguish other women of the East; the Ainu woman is a poor untutored

N

savage, unlearned even in the instinctive arts of Eve. But in common with her sex the world over, she loves jewellery. Cheapest of metal though they be, she loves to adorn her scanty attractions with rings, sometimes on her fingers, sometimes in her ears. And yet she has charms—that I had almost overlooked: she is gentle and submissive as a child, and her voice is low and musical.

The Ainu men are sturdy and well-built, averaging about five feet four inches in height. Their long, shaggy hair and bushy beards give them a patriarchal and even distinguished appearance. The hairiness of the Ainu has been grossly exaggerated by travellers. Only the faces of the men bear any excessive hirsute growth. In comparison with the sparingly moustached Japanese, they are, of course, a hairy race; but they are not more so than many Europeans. They are grave and taciturn, and laughter is almost unknown to them; though perhaps this is not strange, seeing that their mode of life offers little inducement to merriment.

Drink is the great Ainu vice. Their appetite for the Japanese rice-distilled beverage saké is insatiable. "They will not submit to the picture without provision for the saké feast. They are so spontaneous," said my interpreter. With the Japanese fondness for long and ambiguous words, "spontaneous" appeared to be his adjective for expressing their shy and retiring nature.

I therefore made provision for the feast, which consisted in purchasing a large tub of saké. In consideration of this present a selected number of the head-men of the village were prevailed upon to permit me to photograph them and their households as I pleased. When this was over, the feast began.

Drunkenness being considered among the greatest of virtues, libations of saké are accompanied by the observance of much etiquette. The feast was held in the house of the chief of the colony, and three chiefs from neighbouring settlements were invited. Each wore a crown of seaweed, shavings, and flowers. Guests of lesser rank did not wear these, and women were not invited. As each took his place and squatted on the matting spread on the floor, he saluted each of the others in turn by stroking his hair and beard. Host and guests sat in a circle, and it was a picturesque spectacle, not without a touch of pathos—that group of patriarchal, shaggy-locked figures, squatting in the dim light of the hut, waving their hands and stroking their hair and beards before each bowl of saké was imbibed.

The hut speedily became insufferable to me on account of the smoke from the fire, the stench of the fish in the roof, and the smell of the numerous people partaking of the feast or watching the feasters. Just over the fire—which burnt on a bare patch of ground, about three feet square, in the centre of the hut—there hung a wood canopy, the purpose of which seemed to be to distribute the smoke to all parts of the structure —which it did most effectively. The combined effect of the smoke and stench was so sickening that, though my nostrils had become fairly well accustomed to evil smells in the East, I was glad enough to forgo the pleasure of witnessing the end of the feast and to regain the open air.

Hanging from a beam near the fireplace, so that plenty of warmth might reach it, was a cradle, and in the cradle was a baby, which steadily screamed throughout the time we were in the hut. How it managed to scream as it did was inexplicable to me. Any other but an Ainu child would have perished from suffocation by the smoke. No one soothed it, or paid it any attention whatever; nor did the guests show that they were conscious of its screaming. Seemingly it was allowed to cry itself to exhaustion and silence. This, my Japanese friend told me, is the Ainu custom. To permit a child to cry itself to sleep is to discipline it, and teach it the futility of such behaviour.

Though I did not wait or desire to see the end of the feast, I heard that all who participated in the orgie were intoxicated to the point of insensibility.

The interior of Yezo is largely virgin forest, where few but the Ainu ever penetrate. These wilds are the haunt of wild bears, which are becoming scarce. There is no meat the

Ainu prize more than bear flesh. Among the feasters was a fisherman named Happu Konno, whom I learnt was also one of the most famous bear-hunters in Yezo. So striking in appearance was this man—so long, and thick, and shaggy his hair and beard—that I prevailed upon him to strip, that I might secure a photograph of him. His body showed no superfluity of hair beyond that on many Europeans; nor was he of the muscular development of the Japanese; but he was firmly built and athletic, as he needs must be to pursue his perilous calling. Whatever may be the shortcomings of the Ainu, lack of courage in a bear hunt is not one of them. I heard from this man's own lips, through two interpreters, his method of attack.

The killing of a bear is looked upon by the Ainu as the greatest of all possible feats. The only weapons are a knife, and a bow with poisoned arrows. With these the hunter is prepared, if necessary, to engage the bear single-handed in its lair. If he fails to induce it to come out by his cries, so that he may shoot it with an arrow, he clothes his body with a skin, and creeping into the bear's retreat, armed with his knife, he rushes upon the brute, and as it rises to embrace him, he endeavours to stab it to the heart. This, however, is an exceedingly dangerous proceeding; so, if he sees an opportunity, as the surprised bear rises to fight he dodges under its forepaws and attacks it from the rear. This manœuvre has the effect of inducing the bear to seek safety in flight, and as it emerges from the den, an assistant hunter discharges an arrow or two into its body. It is only a question of a few minutes till the poison does its work and Bruin is dead. If the flesh round the arrows be immediately cut out, the poison does not affect the rest of the meat. There are many hunters in Yezo who will attack a bear in this manner, but such men are renowned for their courage. The use of poisoned arrows is now illegal, I was told, but nevertheless they are still used surreptitiously.

The rivers of Yezo abound in salmon, especially in the season when they seek the fresh water to spawn. The Ainu

H.G.P.

HAPPUKONNO, THE HUNTER (IN CENTRE), AND TWO AINU FISHERMEN

catch them by means of hand-nets, and by spearing from dug-out canoes. One man stands in the rear to propel the canoe, whilst another stands at the bow, harpoon in hand. It is paddled down stream or kept stationary, and as a salmon approaches, the harpoon is let go, usually with unerring aim, and the fish is impaled. Harpoon fishing is also carried on at night. A torch is used to attract the fish, and as they are attracted to the unaccustomed glare, they fall easy victims to the spear.

Although the Ainu have neither priests nor temples, yet, so says the Rev. John Batchelor, who has probably spent more time among them than any other foreigner, "they are an exceedingly religious race. They see the hand of God in everything. Their great religious exercises take place on the occasion of a bear feast, removing into a new house, death and burial."

Their religious nature is not patent to any casual visitor, but it needs little observation to reveal the deep superstition which governs all their actions. Their gods, of whom there are many, must be propitiated by offerings; these are to be seen everywhere, and consist of willow sticks, with the bark whittled into shavings, which hang in clusters. A number of these are placed outside the east end of each hut, and prayers are made to them each day. They are called inao, and may be seen by the seashore, or on the banks of rivers, and in other localities to which it is desirable that the deities who preside over such places should be petitioned to bestow special attention. The inao ensures this. Offerings of deer and bear skulls, placed on sticks, are also looked upon with much favour by the gods. Hence those who have been fortunate in the chase make such an altar, and place it at the east end of the house. The willow wands may also be seen inside the house; and in case of sickness—if they are newly made, and stuck in the floor near the fireplace—they will ensure all possible aid from the Fire-goddess. This is about the extent of the assistance that the sufferer receives — the offering of inao, and the chanting of prayers.

The Ainu have no arts or crafts, literature or ambition, and appear to have fewer claims to anything more than animal instinct than any other race in the East. Their numbers, it is said, are becoming less each year, and it is estimated that there are now not 15,000 remaining.

If they should in course of time become extinct, their place will be taken by a race to whom humanity in general owes a greater debt.

CHAPTER XII

THE BAY OF ENŌURA

THERE is a village on the shores of the bay of Enōura—which lies between the Izu peninsula and the town of Numazu—that is very little known to foreigners.

I do not believe a globe-trotter has ever turned aside to visit this place, which is less than an hour's journey by rikisha from the main line of the Tōkaido. Certainly no tourist accompanied by a guide ever went there. No Japanese cicerone would ever dream of piloting his employer to such a place, for there are no curio-shops. Indeed, there are no shops of any kind at all; and how dull the evening hours would be to Guide San if he missed that feeling of prosperity born of pondering on commissions earned from the merchants and curio-dealers whose establishments he has visited with his Danna San during the day!

No, the tourist will never hear of Shizu-ura, and Guide San will never turn a hair between Kodzu and Shizuoka to show that there is anything of interest on the sea side of the train. He will tell all sorts of things about Fuji on the north —and of praise he could not say too much—but he will not mention Shizu-ura, or Ushibusé, or Mito—not because he does not know about these places, but because he considers it better his master should not know, lest he might want to go there.

As I have already said, Ushibusé can be reached in less than an hour from the Tōkaido railway—from Numazu station, to be exact—but a far more interesting way is to go there, as I once did, by a detour into the Izu peninsula. A branch line runs from Mishima junction, on the Tōkaido, to Ohito, where we took a basha for Shuzenji. A basha is a small one-horse omnibus, and this particular one was the cheapest method of travel I have ever found in Japan or elsewhere. It was a forty-minutes drive, yet I engaged the whole vehicle for 45 sen (about tenpence). This was the regular tariff, and is a good instance of how prices shrink as soon as one gets off the tourist track. Near Fuji at least treble this price would have been demanded. We had just come from the east side of Fuji, where Yamanaka plain was two feet deep with snow; yet here—but thirty miles away as the crow flies—the weather was so warm that the visitors were basking in the sunshine in summer attire on the hotel verandas.

The Izu peninsula is the Riviera of Japan, and Shuzenji is its most sheltered and popular winter resort. I put up at a delightful native inn, the Araiya, where everything was in Japanese style. My room, which overlooked the Katsura-gawa, which flows through the town, was of the most immaculate cleanliness. Its sliding doors were beautifully painted with a pair of flying peacocks, and the ornament in the place of honour was a piece of fossil wood resembling the mountains the old Chinese artists painted. It was curiously carved to represent a band of samurai attacking a fierce dragon which was issuing from a cavern near the top.

From my windows a scene of constant interest could be observed in the river below—from early morn till midnight. A fine hot-spring rises in a rocky basin in the centre of the torrent, and an open bath-house is built around it—connected with the banks by narrow bridges. In this spring men and women bathe promiscuously.

As I was having my lunch, shortly after arrival, two dainty little women stepped from the spring, where they had been bathing in the company of several of the sterner sex. They walked out on to the bridge, with their beauty innocent of any concealment, dried themselves in the sunshine, and then donned their clothes before the eyes of all the town —only no eyes in the town but mine were looking; for in Japan "the nude is seen, but never noticed," as Professor Chamberlain puts it.

THE PINES OF SHIZU-URA

In Japan, what custom sanctions the conventions approve; and in remote country districts, even in these modern days, modesty is no higher a virtue than cleanliness, and any exposure of the person for this necessary purpose is both pertinent and proper.   Indeed, a few days before, at Kamiidé, I saw a young man and a young woman, strangers to each other, and both guests at the same hotel at which I was staying, bathing together in a tub which was not more than two feet square and a yard high, and into which, after the man had entered first, it was barely possible for the girl to squeeze. The weather was so severe that any water splashed over on to the stone floor froze instantly; but they parboiled themselves and chatted and joked with each other for twenty minutes or more—whilst I was having a lonely bath at the other side of the room immersed to the chin in a two-foot tub of my own. When the lady had finished her ablutions she emerged, and sweetly bowing to what she could see of me above water, returned to her apartment, clad in nothing but her chastity—a somewhat scanty garment for so frigid a day.

There is nothing of any particular interest at Shuzenji except the hot-springs, so next day I started out for Mito in a basha. The distance is about five miles, and the scenery is worthy of no particular comment until the end of the journey is reached. Indeed, the most interesting object on this journey was the basha-driver himself. He was one of the most extraordinary "characters" I met in all Japan. He positively oozed good nature from every pore. His questions, and comments, and sallies of wit never ceased until the journey's end, except for the moments when he drew a few whiffs from his pipe, which he did frequently. Each time he refilled it he knocked the hard fire-ball of ash, which remains in the pipe when Japanese tobacco is smoked, into the hollow of his palm, lit the fresh fill from that, smoked it out in three or four puffs, and then repeated the process. How he could hold a ball of glowing fire in his hand puzzled me. I tried it myself, but had to drop it in a twinkling, much to his delight, and he rolled about on the box so much with laughter that he nearly tumbled off, and the horse, taking fright, bolted down a hill and landed us all in a ditch. But there was no harm done, fortunately, and we soon had the light vehicle out again, and in due course arrived at Mito, where I paid him off. I was sorry indeed to see the last of him, for my heart warmed to this simple, happy, contented soul; but at Mito we had to take to the sea.

Mito is a fishing village on the shore of a little sheltered bay, with rugged precipitous cliffs almost surrounding it. A wonderful island stands like a guardian sentinel at the mouth of the bay, as pine-clad as the isles of Matsushima; and white-winged sampans sailed on either side of it, whilst many others lay alongside the stone jetty, or were beached on the sandy shore. In all Japan I have seen no prettier little fishing port than Mito.

Mito Bay is an arm of Enōura Bay, which in turn is part of Suruga Bay—the eastern part, lying between the Izu peninsula and the mouth of the Kano-gawa, a river which runs into the sea just beyond Ushibusé. The whole of this coast-line is weirdly beautiful, and its charms have been perpetuated in every form of art.

We engaged a sampan to take us round to Shizu-ura. It was a stout, seaworthy craft, made out of natural-finished wood, in which not a single nail was used—the planks being fastened together with wooden pins—yet the sendo assured us that it would weather the roughest storms the wind could blow. The crew consisted of an old man and his son, splendid specimens of hardy humanity both, and typical members of the class from which the Japanese tars are recruited. They were gentle and kindly of manner and courteous of speech, as becomes men who might well be the reverse, seeing that their life is a constant battle with the elements. Danger is but too often the portion of the fishermen on these seas, where a cloud no bigger than a man's hand may be but the precursor of a typhoon, which, long before their craft can make land, breaks and scatters death and destruction in its wake. More than once I have read in the papers in Japan, after a sudden storm, that an entire fleet of fishing-craft had been lost, and their crews drowned to a man.

There is no more interesting class in Japan than the fisher-folk. Their customs and methods differ from place to place round the coasts as widely as though they belonged to different countries. They are the first inhabitants one sees on visiting the land, and the last on leaving it; and, if the coast-line be followed much, they are continually in evidence during one's stay. Like most seafaring people, the world over, they are superstitious, and the legend connected with their craft is voluminous.

Offerings of old parts of vessels are freely made by them to the sea-gods, as such things are very propitiatory, and in return the gods send fine weather and direct the fish into their nets. Fishermen who have had the misfortune to be wrecked hang tablets in the temples, and offer the gods such relics of the ship as have escaped destruction.

Worship at a Shinto temple before setting out is very advisable, and aids in securing a good catch; but should a Buddhist priest be met with on the way, bad luck is likely, as the bonzes do not eat fish. At least they are not supposed to, but they do!

No worse-omened incident can befall a fishing-craft than that a bucket should fall from it into the sea and sink, for sooner or later the evil spirits that live in the ocean depths will use the bucket to pour water into the vessel and founder it. A cat must invariably be carried on a deep-sea fishing junk, as cats have the power to repel these spirits. Should the cat be spotted or piebald, the greater is its virtue; and the more colours there are in the cat's coat, and the wider the contrast in these colours, the higher is its value as a mascot.

I have spent many an interesting day studying the fisher-folk and their curious methods. On one occasion, attracted by a group on the shore, I found that two large tubs of white-bait had just been brought in from a junk. The fish were very small and uniform in size, being little over an inch in length. The master of the junk stood by, his hands drawn up into the

capacious sleeves of his kimono. Around him were four or
five individuals who plunged their arms deep into the tubs
and then stood for a moment or two with brows knitted in
thought. Each, in turn, then put his two hands up the junk-
owner's sleeves; but the face of the latter was blank, and gave
no indication of what this pantomime meant. No words were
spoken, but I quickly guessed the meaning of it all. Each was
a buyer making a bid for the fish, of a sum unknown to his
competitors, by placing in the owner's hands as many fingers
as he was willing to pay yen for the lot. When all the bids were
in, the highest offer was accepted, and the tubfuls changed
hands for the sum of eight yen (sixteen shillings).

Our old boatman's granddaughter—a little brown-eyed
lass of nine—came down to see us off, with her baby brother
on her back. They were the children of the younger
man and father and son alike were delighted when I
made a hasty photograph of the little maid and told them
I would show the picture to some of my small friends
in England and America.

As we sailed out of the harbour I noticed that the eminences
of the cliffs had bamboo platforms built in the highest branches
of the trees. These are called uomi, or "fish outlooks." When
a school of magaro, or bonito, enters the bay, a watchman takes
up his position in each of them. From these vantage-points
he can see a long way off, and also down into the clear water,
and observe the movements of the fish. At a distance the
location of the fish is known by the colour of the water; they
come in shoals which make dark patches in the sea. By signals
the look-out men then direct the movements of the fishermen,
who have proceeded out into the bay to surround the shoal
with nets. The nets for this work are of great length and
made of rope, for the magaro sometimes runs to several hundred
pounds in weight, and would easily tear its way through
anything lighter. Directed by the look-out men, the fishermen
then draw the nets gradually closer to the shoal until the fish
are driven into the narrowest portion of the bay, across the
entrance of which the nets are fixed, and the quarry imprisoned.

A FISHERMAN'S CHILDREN

They are then caught, and shipped to Tokyo and other cities as the market demands.

The magaro is immensely esteemed by the Japanese. It is a tunny-fish, not unlike a monster mackerel, and is cut in the thinnest of slices and eaten raw. The coarse red flesh of the magaro is full of small parasitic worms, but this appears to be no objection to the native palate. I have never been able to face this dish myself, nor have I ever met any foreigner who could; but some of the daintier fish that are served raw in Japan are really very nice. The magaro season is from March to August, and during these months the Enōura fisher-folk subsist entirely by this traffic.

We sailed slowly along over the waters of the bay, as the wind was very light, and it finally dropped altogether as we drew near Shizu-ura. Then the boatmen took to the yulos and swung us along at a splendid pace. This method of propelling a boat is productive of astonishing speed. The craft was large enough to hold twenty people comfortably, yet two men sped it onwards at a good four miles an hour or more. As they yuloed they sang a monotonous chant. Japanese boatmen are always able to put much more "back" into their work when they accompany it with the elementary rhythm of such simple chants.

When the wind dropped the water became perfectly calm, and so crystal clear was it that we could see objects on the bottom, ten or fifteen feet below us, without being conscious of any water intervening at all. We seemed to be floating on air.

Huge shell-fish, called awabi, are found in the bay. They are easily discovered in water thirty or forty feet deep by means of glass-bottomed tubs, through which the sea-bed can be minutely scrutinised. When an awabi is located, it is dislodged by means of a long bamboo with an iron hook at the end. This mollusc has immense muscular power, and it is by no means a simple matter to capture it, even when found; it is a univalve, and clings with incredible tenacity to the rock.

Shizu-ura is the name of the long stretch of sandy beach which bends like a bow from a promontory on Enōura Bay round to the village of Ushibusé. A forest of weather-beaten pines straggles almost to the water's edge, their tortured trunks clutching the ground like great claws, as they lean shorewards, strained to impossible angles by the sea winds which blow the sand from their roots.

As our boat was beached, stern first, on this lovely strand, there were reasons enough apparent all round us why its enchantment should have been sung by every Japanese poet. The very tiniest of wavelets lapped the silver sands, and in the golden sunshine each crystal ripple, as it broke, became a row of rainbow opals. Little children in gay kimonos—the children of the rich—were playing at the water's edge, and in the distance the snowy crest of Fuji hung from the blue sky over the deeper blue of the ocean.

Cheery little maids came running down the beach to greet us, and carried my packages up to the hotel embosomed in the pine-trees—the Hōyō-kwan, one of the finest and best-appointed native houses I have ever stayed at in Japan. As soon as I was settled in my room the host and hostess came to pay their respects. As they entered, they bowed their heads with much ceremony to the mats, for the most scrupulous etiquette is observed in this favourite resort of the aristocracy of Tokyo. There was none of that free-and-easy manner which characterises one's reception at Japanese hotels in "foreign style." They sat and talked to me in the most respectful honorifics, whilst I sipped a cup of yellow tea and nibbled at the cakes which are always brought immediately to the room as soon as a guest arrives. When I told them that my mission was to illustrate and write of the scenery and customs of the country, they expressed their pleasure in phrases of delight, and begged leave to bring and present to me some of the other guests who were staying there. So that evening I entertained a number of visitors by showing them photographs I had made of various countries. None, however, interested them so much as those of Japan.

Nothing pleases a Japanese more than to find that a foreigner can appreciate and love this beautiful land as much as he does himself.

Near the hotel the Crown Prince has a palatial residence, with spacious walled-in grounds deep in the heart of the pine woods, to which he retires each summer from the heat and cares of state of the capital. It would be difficult indeed to find a more secluded, restful spot, or one more replete with sea-girt beauty.

This Ushibushé pine grove is far finer than the famous Mio-no-matsu-bara, twenty miles across the bay. Among the weather-beaten old trees—all bent and twisted by the winds that blow—the peasants, with bamboo rakes, scour the ground for the needles which are always dropping from the branches; these they take home to be used as fuel to start their charcoal fires. The sun by day, and the moon by night, play strange shadow-pranks amidst the tortured trunks, and the breezes murmur softly in the branches to the accompaniment of the waves beating on the near-by shore.

Shizu-ura's beauty is mutable as the weather's moods, and one day—when I was out in a boat, peering down into the depths trying to catch awabi—I found that the sea was all alive with pretty nymphs. The sunlight, glinting through each surface ripple, was decomposed as by a prism, and the rays that pierced downward through the crystal water turned the ocean bed into a garden of Nereus, in which the rainbow colours, that danced among its plants and rockeries, were the Nereides, the Sea-god's daughters.

My old sendo was as delighted as I with the sight, for my pleasure warmed anew his interest in a spectacle with which long familiarity had bred unconcern. He searched out beautiful and still more beautiful spots, till he came to a rugged little island. Here he bade me step ashore, and, beckoning me to a crevice in the face of the rock, said, "Honourably glancing deign, sir master."

I followed, and found a peep-hole, worn by the erosion of the waves. Through it there was an exquisite vista of Fuji and the pine-clad strand, framed roughly by the rock—a view made classic by Hiroshigé half a century ago.

"It is the 'Shizu-ura Fuji,' sir master," said the old man, and the pride glowing in his face told me that in native estimation this was the climax of Enōura's wonders.

GREETINGS IN THE OLD GARDEN AT KINKAKUJI

CHAPTER XIII

THE TEMPLES OF KYOTO

In no other city of Japan have Nature and Art scattered their favours with such lavish hands as in the old-time capital, Kyoto. After years of travel in many lands, I look back upon Kyoto as one of the most picturesque and fascinating cities I have seen.

Many are the happy weeks I have spent roaming amongst its grey old temples; exploring the surrounding woods; rambling over the hills that half encircle the old city; searching its innumerable pottery- and curio-shops; shooting the rapids of the lovely Katsura river; visiting the homes of famous artist-craftsmen; viewing seas of cherry-blossoms or gorgeously coloured maple-trees—and in a hundred other ways storing up memories that have left this enchanting old city dearer than any other to my heart.

Many a time, too, I have seen old-time religious and feudal processions pass along its quaint old-fashioned streets, taking one back in spirit to the days, not half a century gone, when Japan had as yet made no endeavour to fall in line with even the least of the Powers of the world.

My first impressions of Kyoto were not reassuring, for the station is in an uninteresting part of the town, and the houses seemed devoid of interest as I passed them on the way to the Miyako Hotel. But as my kurumaya drew me farther along, the feeling of disappointment gave way to interest, and then to pleasure, as he entered a street in which every house seemed to be a curio-shop, and where the crowd was so thick that he could scarcely make his way. A great matsuri was being held—the yearly festival of a near-by temple. Stalls lined the thoroughfare for the sale of every kind of article, and scores

of vendors had not set up stalls at all, but had merely laid
their wares upon the ground.

The street blazed with the light of innumerable paper
lanterns and oil lamps; and by their coloured glare I could
see silks, pottery, bronzes, brasses, beautiful boxes, and a
thousand other dainty things and curios peeping out from a
perfect forest of dwarf trees. There were tiny maples, and
pines, and wistarias, and peach- and plum-trees, and many
others; but the bulk of these Lilliputian arboreal wonders
were cherry-trees, whose branches, pink with blossoms,
drooped over the pots, in which the trunks from which they
sprang were gnarled and grizzled as veterans of the orchard,
and, though scarcely a foot in height, were often more than
two-score years of age. Among this pretty scene of lanterns
and flowers the gay kimono of many a geisha was a dash of
colour in the crowd, and the whole street was full of holiday-
makers, seemingly without a trouble in the world.

It is characteristic of the gentleness of the nation that all
these dainty, delicate things could be displayed by the owners
in the open street, and even on the ground, amongst a throng
of people and passing vehicles.

I learnt later that my kurumaya, spotting me as a new
visitor, had specially gone a little out of his way and sought
that crowded street for the sole purpose of giving a new-comer
the pleasure of a pretty spectacle. Innumerable little acts of
thoughtfulness such as this, during my three years of travel
in Japan, come back to mind, and help to deepen my affection
for that charming country.

The Miyako Hotel is situated high on the slopes of Higashiyama, "The Eastern Mountain," and a lovely panorama lies
before it. Far below are the tiled roofs of the city. It is the
Awata district, one of the most famous centres of the world
for high-class pottery and enamel. To the south, standing out
in brilliant red amidst the grey house-tops, are the main gate
and wing turrets of Tai-kyoku-den—most modern of Japanese
temples. Directly in front there is a thickly-wooded hill, with
the beautiful buildings of the ancient Kurodani monastery

H.G.P

INTERIOR OF A BUDDHIST TEMPLE

peeping between the pines; and northwards, Nanzenji temple struggles to show itself from the dense foliage surrounding it.

All round the valley there are forest-clad hills, and as the sun sets over Arashiyama, "The Storm Mountain,"—the beauty of which has been sung by poets for ages—the deep note of a mighty bell breaks on the air. It is the voice of the Chio-in temple colossus proclaiming to all that the sun has run its course, and that the day is done. Softly for a moment the vibrations tremble in the air, and then come swelling out in volume through the trees. Quivering waves of sound go surging over the town, and the hills catch up the booming note and throw it to each other, until valley and mountain are all throbbing and echoing with the sound. It seems to come from everywhere. It is in the air above and in the earth beneath, and a full minute or more lapses ere the undulations tremble away to silence, seeming to bear a message to all corners of the land from the ponderous lip of bronze.

This bell is one of the largest in the world, and hangs in a belfry in the grounds of the Chio-in temple, a grand old monastery of the Jodo Buddhists on Higashiyama. The broad and spacious approaches of the temple are gravelled avenues, with pine and cherry-trees spreading their branches wide overhead; and a vast terrace lies in front, from which a flight of stone steps leads to the great two-storied entrance gate— one of the finest in Japan. It is a typical piece of the purest old Buddhist architecture, over eighty feet in height, with beams, ceilings, cornices and cross-beams all deeply carved with dragons and mythical creatures, and decorated with arabesques in colours. Again, long flights of steps lead higher up the wooded hillsides to the plateau where the temple buildings stand.

As the top is reached, great flowing lines appear—the splendid curves of heavily-tiled roofs, sweeping upwards far above the massive pillars that support them, and the surrounding tree-tops. Great halls and little halls and pavilions meet the eye everywhere. At the threshold of the main building streams of pure water flow over the scalloped edge of a

Brobdingnagian lotus-bloom of bronze into a granite trough, at which the worshippers cleanse all impurities from their lips and fingers before entering the sanctuary. Inside the massive doorway a priest sits all day long, from dawn till dark, and from dark till dawn, mechanically tapping a drum; and every few hours the automaton is relieved and another takes his place. These drum-tappers are very old, with heads shaven as clean as the parchment of the drum they beat.

A forest of pillars, polished like bronze, raise their tops high to support the massive beams and rafters, and the chancel is all aglow with gold and rich embroidery. At the hour of Mass a hundred Buddhist priests, clad in flowing vestments of silk and rich brocades of every colour, file in and settle on the padded mats before their lacquered sutra-boxes. Gong-beats punctuate their chants, and incense fills the air as the smoke curls upwards from the altar censers, and the whole scene is of bewildering beauty—a kaleidoscope of colour.

Chio-in's fine old buildings are rich in works of art. Iémitsu, most peace-loving of the Shoguns, built the priests' apartments; and the sliding screens that form the walls are embellished with masterpieces from the brushes of many famous artists of the Kano school. Among the best examples are the fusuma, or sliding doors, of a little room of eight mats, decorated by Naonobu with plum and bamboo branches. In the next room Nobumasa painted some sparrows "so lifelike that they took wing, leaving only a faint impression behind"; and a pair of doors, painted with pine-trees by Tan-yu, were such faithful reflections of nature that resin exuded from their trunks.

A curious feature of Chio-in is the floors of its verandas and corridors. They are made of keyaki wood, the boards being loosely nailed down, so that, as one walks over them, they move slightly, and in rubbing against each other emit a gentle creaking sound. The sound is very pleasing, and so soft and musical as to suggest the twittering of birds. These floors are called by this most poetical of people, uguisu-bari, or "nightingale floors," and they certainly add greatly to the fascination of the temple.

H.G.P.

THE GREAT BELL AT CHIO-IN TEMPLE

A pavilion in the courtyard contains the great bell. It was cast in 1633; it is ten feet eight inches high, with a diameter of nine feet, and weighs seventy-four tons. For exactly a century this monster sound-maker was peerless among the bells of the world, till in 1733 the "Czar Korokol," the "Great Bell of Moscow," was cast. This bell, however, is said never to have been hung, and stands in the Kremlin grounds useless, with a large piece broken from its side—a disaster which occurred in a fire a few years after it was made, and not, as is generally supposed, during the burning of Moscow in 1812. The Chio-in bell can now only claim second place among Japanese bells, as in 1903 a bell was cast at the Tennōji temple at Osaka which weighs over two hundred tons; it is twenty-four feet high and sixteen feet in diameter.

Others of the great bells of the world are that at the Daibutsu temple in Kyoto, which is fourteen feet high and weighs sixty-three tons; and the bell at Nara, a dozen miles away, is thirteen feet and six inches high, and weighs thirty-seven tons. The "Great Bell of Mingoon," Burma, is conical-shaped, twelve feet high, and sixteen feet in diameter at the lip. It is reported to weigh eighty tons, but the impression I gained was that this was an exaggeration. The next in order are the Ta-chung-tsu bell at Peking, which hangs in a temple outside the Tartar Wall, and another of equal size which is suspended in the Bell Tower in the centre of the Tartar City. These bells are two out of five—each eighteen feet high and ten feet in diameter—which were cast about the year 1420, by order of the Emperor Yung Loh. They are said each to weigh about fifty-four tons. Two more of the bells are in other temples near Peking, while the fifth is at the Imperial Palace. Another monster which holds a foremost place among the bells of the world hangs in a pavilion in the centre of the city of Seoul, the capital of Korea. These Oriental bells are never sounded by a tongue, but by means of a suspended tree-trunk, which is swung and brought sharply into contact with the lip.

The sounding of Chio-in's great basso is accompanied by some picturesque ceremony. The chains that hold the heavy

log are unlocked, and a gang of some dozen coolies man the
hand-ropes hanging from the suspended beam, and commence
a chant in unison as they set it a-swinging. When a certain
line is reached, they strain upon the ropes, and bring the bole
against the chrysanthemum crest on the bell with all the
strength that they can muster. A muffled roar springs from
the monster as the burred edge of this battering ram opens its
lips, but the roar quickly turns to soft, musical reverberations
that go singing over the city, and slowly purr away to silence.
The beam is checked ere it can strike again from the rebound,
and the chant continues for some minutes before another
booming note is sent forth to awake the echoes in the hills
and dales.

Higashiyama's slopes are densely wooded with pine and
maple-trees, and in spring-time the greenery of the forests is
everywhere the ground-work for an embroidery of cherry-
blossoms. From these lovely woods at least a dozen temples
peep. Chio-in is the grandest, and Kiyomizu-dera the most
picturesque.

To Kiyomizu, one must pass along Gojo-zaka, a narrow
street that is a bazaar of toy and pottery shops, and shops
whose whole fronts are curtained with long strings of dangling
saké-bottles, made from gourds; and there are curio and wood-
work shops, and shops where only knives and blades are sold.
One may purchase here a cherry walking-stick, with a blade
concealed in it that will cut through half a dozen copper coins
without dulling its edge, and the old shopman—the very
incarnation of Hokusai's sketches—will apply the test before
he accepts the small sum he courteously demands. Gojo-zaka
is the centre of the porcelain-maker's art. At Seifu's, Nishida's,
Kanzan's, or a dozen other shops, one may see exquisite
specimens of the beautiful blue-and-white porcelain of Kyoto,
known as Kiyomizu ware, offered at prices so wholly inadequate
for the art with which they are embellished, that few visitors
passing along this street ever reach the temple till long after
the hour they have planned for.

Along this fascinating thoroughfare the stream of humanity

which flows to the popular old temple ceases only for the still
night-hours, and the ancient capital offers no better opportunities for leisurely studying human nature than on this
interesting street.

The hillside is very steep, so steep indeed that many of
the buildings of the sanctuary—so ancient that its origin is
lost in legend—do not rest on the ground, but are supported
on a scaffolding of massive beams and piles. Amongst its halls
and colonnades, turreted pavilions and pagodas, one can find
fresh beauty at every visit; and each balcony discloses new
and lovelier vistas of the old-time capital below.

The temple is one of the "Thirty-Three Places" (Saikoku
San-ju-san Sho) sacred to Kwannon, Goddess of Mercy, in
the provinces near Kyoto. These are all numbered, and
Kiyomizu is the sixteenth on the list. The shrine of the goddess
is opened but once in thirty-three years—so the chances are
somewhat against the casual visitor having the privilege of
paying respect to the deity. Her "Twenty-Eight Followers,"
personifying the twenty-eight constellations known to the
ancient astronomers of the East, stand on either side of the
shrine; and at each end of the dais are two of the four
"Heavenly Kings," or Shi-Tenno, who guard the world
against attacks of evil. They are Tamon, Kōmōku, Jikoku,
and Zōchō, and they defend respectively the North, South,
East, and West.

One of the lesser sights of Kiyomizu, but a truly pathetic
one, is a shrine to Jizo—the guardian god of Japanese children.
It is a mere shed containing some hundred stone images
decked with babies' bibs—relics of their little dead which
mothers bring as offerings. Women are always to be seen
before this shrine praying earnestly for the souls of their little
ones. It is a sad, depressing spot, and I always turned away
from it heavy-hearted at the spectacle of those bereaved mothers
and their silent grief.

Outside of the hondo, or main temple, there is a dilapidated
old idol sitting on a stool. He is a queer old fellow, with
features defaced and almost obliterated with much rubbing.

His name is Binzuru, and his history is interesting, for he is a deity with a "past." He was originally one of the Ju-roku Rakan, or "Sixteen Disciples of Buddha," and had the power to relieve all the ills of the flesh. The mantle of his holy state did not, it seems, subdue his human nature; for one day he gave his nearest companion a dig in the ribs and remarked on the beauty of a woman passing by. For this imprudence the susceptible saint was expelled from the fraternity; so Binzuru's image is always seen outside the sanctum, whilst his brother disciples are placed inside it. He is, however, exceedingly popular with the lower classes, who believe that by rubbing any portion of his image they will obtain relief from ailments afflicting the corresponding portion of their own persons. Hence his face and limbs are polished smooth, and almost worn away in places by centuries of such friction.

Many an evening I went to the old temple at sunset to admire the beauty of the view. The flaming vermilion pillars and sweeping eaves of the main gate frame a lovely picture at that hour. A long flight of granite steps leads to the street of dangling saké-bottles, which in turn leads straight to the old Yasaka pagoda, standing like some grey old guardian spirit watching over the town below. Here and there, among the houses of the city, the great curved roof of some Buddhist temple looms gigantic in the evening haze; and westwards over Arashiyama the sun sinks in a blaze of yellow glory, which turns the pillars and turrets of venerable Kiyomizu into some wondrous vision of fable.

But Kiyomizu by moonlight is even lovelier still. Once I prevailed upon a Japanese friend and his little daughter to accompany me to the temple when the moon was full. The Japanese do not like such places at night, for among this highly imaginative and superstitious people belief in the supernatural is rampant; and temples and other such gloomy places are haunted by the ghosts of those who have lived in them. A great silence, therefore, hung over the deserted buildings.

At the threshold of the second gate, where a scowling dragon sends a stream of crystal water gushing from his brazen

throat, my friend made furtive attempts to prevail upon me to stop and admire the beauty of the moon, instead of going farther; and little O Kimi San, finding her father's hand insufficient security, came between us, taking mine as well. I pressed on, however, resolved to see it all. As we entered the dark portal, the creaking floors awoke a myriad echoes among the walls and ceilings, and O Kimi San, walking on tiptoe with trepidation, her little Japanese brain busy with all the ghost and fairy-tales she knew, peered into the gloomy shadows, seeing "spooks" in every corner and lurking goblins by every post. Old Binzuru's leprous head looked fearful in the moonlight, and O Kimi, her face hidden in her father's kimono, clung to us both for protection.

In the shadowy corridors we all involuntarily glanced back more than once, thinking some one followed behind; no one was there, however, the fancied follower being naught but our own foot-falls reflected by the whispering walls. At the Oku-no-in a voice rang out in challenge. It was one of the resident priests, who, finding we were only harmless sightseers paying a nocturnal visit to the temple, courteously offered to conduct us, much to O Kimi's relief.

As we stood on one of the verandas, far above the trees, watching the twinkling lights of the old city, the moon was braiding the clouds with silver, and shedding soft radiance and fitful shades on the balustrades and heavily-thatched gabled roofs about us. Not a sound broke "the soft silence of the listening night" save the gentle murmur of a little cascade below us, and the chirruping of the crickets, until a nightingale burst into song in one of the tree-tops below us. It was a pretty climax to our ramble, and as rare as delightful, for the uguisu is seldom heard so far south, though I have heard them nightly in summer at Ikao and Karuizawa.

Higashiyama's lower slopes are labyrinths of pine avenues, paved with broad stone flags, and are all a-whispering with the streamlets that course in deep culverts on either side. The grounds of temples and monasteries abut each other everywhere, and one discovers some fresh carved gate or old stairway among their shady groves at every turning. Near the Yasaka pagoda there is one of the finest bamboo groves in Japan, where a small forest of tall, slender shoots bow to every breeze, and mingle their feathery tips full fifty feet overhead. I studied it well before attempting to photograph it. In a high wind it cannot be successfully done, nor in bright sunlight can its full beauty be shown. One day, however, the sun, being very weak, gave just the light I wanted. I hurried to the avenue, and was fortunate enough to induce some women to pose for me in their rikishas. In order that I should not be interrupted I told one of my kurumaya to stop at each end of the grove and prevent anybody from passing. Having some difficulty in arranging the picture, a good deal of time passed, and just as I secured it, two dapper policemen came up and demanded to know why I was obstructing the road; and with them came some scores of people whom the zealous kurumaya had been keeping back. My explanations were of no avail, though they were courteously received. My name and address, and the names of all the kurumaya and of the girls, were with much ado taken down, and I was notified that fines would be imposed upon all of us. The picture did not, however, prove so expensive as might be supposed, for when the bill for the aggregate fines was presented to me the same evening, I found it amounted to three yen, or about six shillings.

At Higashiyama's base there is a curious temple, called San-ju-san-gen-do, the "Hall of Thirty-Three Spaces"— the spaces being those into which it is divided by a single row of thirty-two pillars. The place is as different from Kiyomizu as it well could be. More like a great barn than a religious edifice, it is yet very interesting, and although not resembling it architecturally, nor possessing any of its beauty, it reminded me of the "Thousand Buddha Temple" at Peking. The two temples have one feature in common: that at Peking boasts one thousand images of Buddha; San-ju-san-gen-do possesses one thousand and one effigies of Kwannon, Goddess of Mercy. These effigies are covered with smaller ones on their foreheads, halos, and hands, until it is said the grand total of 33,333 is

A BAMBOO AVENUE AT KYOTO

reached—a statement which I accepted without attempting to verify its accuracy.

They are a tawdry, motley company, these tiers of gilded goddesses, whose serried ranks, a hundred yards long and a full battalion strong, fill the vast building from end to end. The images, many of which are of great age, are continually being restored. In a workshop behind the vast stage an old wood-carver sits, his life occupation being the carving and mending of hands and arms, which are constantly dropping off, like branches, from the forest of divine trunks—for Kwannon is a many-limbed deity, and few of the images have less than a dozen arms. Rats scuttled over the floors and hid in the host of idols as we made our way round them; and at the back of the building we were stopped by an old priest, who sat at the receipt of custom and demanded a contribution from every visitor.

One day, as I suddenly turned a corner in this temple, I saw a tourist, who supposed no one was looking, deliberately break a hand off one of the gilded figures and put it in his pocket. It is strange to what acts of vandalism the mania for collecting useless relics leads some people. Once in Kyoto I was invited by two travellers, whom I had just met, to come to their room, where they were busy packing, prior to leaving for home. I noticed some beautiful specimens of hikité—inlaid ornamental bronze plates used as finger-grips on sliding doors—lying on the floor. I picked them up and admired them, asking where they had bought them, as a glance showed me they were very good ones. To my amazement they told me they had ripped them from the doors of a Japanese hotel at which they stayed, and were now discarding them because they could "not be bothered with them any longer."

When such acts as these are committed in a land where one is often on one's honour with regard to some dainty work of art in the simple furnishing or decoration of one's room, the wonder is that foreigners are not viewed with real distrust. It will certainly take many years to undo the evil left by that act in that hotel-keeper's mind. And these young fellows were the sons of wealthy New Yorkers, and appeared to have unlimited money to spend!

In summer Higashiyama's woods ring with the shrill chirping of a myriad cicadas, called seimi; and small boys, with long bamboo poles tipped with birdlime, swarm from the town to hunt the festive insect. Many a time, as my kurumaya ran past these seimi-hunters, I have had to dash their bamboo points away from my face, and have so often seen others narrowly escape injury from these dangerous playthings, that it is not surprising to learn that much of the blindness seen in Japan is due to the careless handling of sticks by Japanese children.

The captured seimi are sold for a trifling sum to an entomological dealer, who imprisons them in tiny bamboo cages which are often specimens of delicate and beautiful workmanship; and his wayside stall is all a-twitter with the cries of scores of singing insects. There are many different species, but the children class all cicadas under the generic name of seimi. From some of the little cages the intermittent lights of a dozen fireflies flash; in others as many glow-worms shed a feeble glimmer, and the insect-merchant's stall is always the centre of a group of admiring children.

The sounds emitted by some of the cicadas are very pleasing and sweet, whilst others have a shrill metallic note that hammers one's brain to distraction. The vibrating song of the seimi marks the arrival of summer. From end to end of Japan their cries increase in volume as the season advances, until the drowsy hum of the woods at times becomes a fortissimo of one continuous scream. In places they gather in such prodigious numbers that their song becomes a veritable pandemonium, and the air quivers with their unceasing clamour from morning till night. From August on this woodland music becomes a gradual diminuendo, which ceases altogether in November.

I love the song of the seimi, and always listened for its first lone call as in England I used to look for the first swallow or listened for the cuckoo; only the sweet chirp of the Japanese

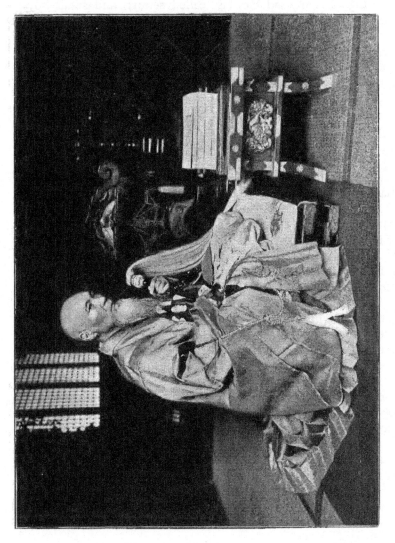

A BUDDHIST ABBOT

insect gave me even greater pleasure.   I love the Japanese summer, too, and the seimi's voice, proclaiming that summer was at hand, always filled me with gladness.   More than once, as I have listened to the happy little singer in the autumn, it has fallen lifeless from the tree.   To the very last the muscular power, which enabled it to produce by friction its joyous song, had escaped the dread disease that fed upon its vitals, and it died as it had lived, a merry-maker and joy-giver, happy and giving happiness to the end—fulfilling to the final moment of its life the service entrusted to it by its Creator.   Thus the woods have their tragedies to those who love them.

And every autumn there came a day when I found an indefinable something missing in my woodland rambles. Suddenly I would come upon the tiny body of what was once a joyous seimi, lying in my path.   Then I knew what it was that the woodland lacked.   It was the gladsome song of summer: the chorus of the seimi, which, whilst the woods slowly turned from green to gold, and brown, and scarlet, had become gradually hushed, until now every voice of that chorus was stilled in death.

Higashiyama is the home of other, and less pleasant, members of the insect-world.   Mosquitoes, which breed in swarms in the rice-fields, seek the shelter of these woods, and make life a burden to those who have to pass the summer in them.   After dark no place is secure from this pest, and even the mosquito-curtains over one's bed must be carefully searched each night to ensure that no crafty, enterprising intruder is lurking in ambush for its victim in their folds.

Most Japanese Buddhist temples of any note, if not framed by Nature's graces, have beautiful gardens.   Some of them are veritable paradises of peaceful beauty, for the priests are past-masters in the art of landscape gardening.

In Kyoto one of the finest is that at Kinkakuji, where natural and artificial beauty are combined so skilfully that there is little but what appears to be the unhampered handi-work of Nature.   It is the lovely grounds that foreign visitors go to see rather than the old temple buildings—though these contain many famous masterpieces. Many Kyoto temples shelter a feast of art on their walls, but no other temple in Japan can show such grounds as Kinkakuji. They have been the inspiration of many a famous garden, though few others can equal their tranquil beauty.

The temple was built by the Shogun Yoshimitsu in 1397 —as a country villa to which he could retire from the cares of the world. He founded the adjacent monastery, became a monk, and ended his days there.

Kinkakuji means "Golden Pavilion," from the fact that formerly the upper story of the building was entirely covered with gold. Few traces of its pristine splendour now remain, but it makes a charming picture as it stands overlooking the lake, and is a favourite motive for artists, and for craftsmen working in every kind of material.

As one approaches the old pavilion a shoal of carp appear at the water's edge, begging for some of the popped corn which the watchman sells. Whilst I was feeding them my attention was distracted by a youthful acolyte—whose shaven head was polished to the lustre of a billiard-ball—who was acting as cicerone to a party of Japanese country visitors. They followed in single file, as the boy, in monotonous, high-pitched tones, described the paintings on the doors and walls, and then, leading them out into the garden, commented on each spot and stone of note, never once lifting his eyes from the ground the while. He had it all by rote, and his thoughts were obviously busy with other matters; but his charges listened respectfully, now and again sibilantly sucking the breath between the teeth when famous names were mentioned. Presently one of the visitors, of a more inquiring turn of mind than the rest, craved further information, and interrupted with a question. After vainly trying to answer it, there was much rubbing and scratching of his bald pate before the cicerone could regain the run of his discourse.

The lake, which in summer is almost covered with a flowering plant, is surrounded by shady walks beneath pines and maple-trees, and little islets and ornamental stones break

H.G.P.

THE PINE-TREE JUNK AT KINKAKUJI

up its surface. In autumn the groves are ablaze with colour; and in winter, when the pines and temple roofs bear, as they sometimes do, a thin coating of snow, the old garden is more beautiful than ever.

In the monastery court there is a wonderful example of the tree-trainer's art which has taken a couple of centuries to produce. It is a full-grown pine representing a junk under sail—hull, mast, sails, and all—the branches being restrained by careful trimming and training on bamboo frames, until the result attained constitutes the most famous arboricultural effort in Japan.

Kinkakuji stands outside the city at its north-western corner. At the north-eastern corner is Ginkakuji, whither Yoshimasa, eighth of the Ashikaga Shoguns, retired in 1479 upon his abdication of the Shogunate. Japanese society owes much to Yoshimasa, for during his meditations in this lovely secluded spot, he, with Sōami, the artist who designed the garden, and the Buddhist abbots Shuko and Shinno, his favourites, "practised the tea-ceremonies, which their patronage elevated almost to the rank of a fine art." [1]

The road to Ginkakuji lies through terraced fields, which are planted out to rice as soon as the barley crop is harvested. The roofs of half a score of grand old temples appeared amidst magnificent cryptomeria groves and bamboo coppices as we sped through this bounteous farmland; and when at length we pulled up at Ginkakuji's gate, a Lilliputian priest, with shaven head and polished crown—the counterpart of the little cicerone at Kinkakuji—acted as our guide.

He conducted us by winding paths round a pretty lake, over the "Bridge of the Pillar of the Immortals" that spans a stream called the "Moon-Washing Fountain"; chanted out the story of the "Stone of Ecstatic Contemplation"—a tiny island in the lake; and showed us over the "Silver Pavilion"—which, it seems, never was covered with silver at all, as its name "Ginkakuji" implies it was, for the ex-Shogun died before he was able to accomplish his wishes with regard to it.

[1] Murray's *Handbook*.

It has little interest beyond its picturesque appearance and an aged image of Kwannon in the upper story.

The little bonze then took us into the garden again, and finally brought us to two great conical heaps of sand. These are named the "Silver-Sand Platform," and the "Mound Facing the Moon." On the former Yoshimasa, this devoted disciple of beauty, "used to sit and hold æsthetic revels." On the smaller "he used to sit and moon-gaze."

In one of the apartments of the building near by there is a statue of Yoshimasa in priestly robes, marvellously lifelike. If it be a true portrait of the ex-Shogun it must depict him in his fighting days, for it resembles rather a fierce warrior in disguise than a fastidious, moon-gazing priest. It would be interesting to know what kind of æsthetic revelry the monarch indulged in. If, however, the elaborate system of etiquette, called "Cha-no-yu," which he perfected in his retirement here, be like his sand-heap revels, then it is easy to see how he could have indulged in them, to his heart's content, without disturbing the surface of his "platform," for anything more dignified and stately than this ceremonial it would be impossible to imagine. To Yoshimasa and his code of etiquette, which is followed to this day by the Japanese upper classes, must be largely credited that superb ease of manner and absence of self-consciousness that enables the Japanese lady to be the very embodiment of composure in all her actions. The inflexible code of Cha-no-yu, prescribing minutely her every movement in the intricate tea-ceremony, supplies rules that govern her deportment in every possible situation in which she is ever likely to be placed. To anyone versed in the art, lack of self-possession under any circumstances would be impossible; and none but the most ultra-refined of races could ever have evolved it. Though I have many times seen its formalities performed, to attempt to describe them with any degree of justice is beyond me. Some even who have taken lessons in the art, have tried and failed. They have merely described its forms, but left them devoid of all the poetry, and beauty, and culture which they mirror. One must

HIGASHI HONGWANJI TEMPLE, KYOTO

see a *Japanese lady* perform the tea-ceremonial to realise its æsthetic beauty—a foreigner can only burlesque it either in performance or description.

Japanese Buddhism is divided into six principal sects. In order of their numerical strength they are: Zen; Shin, or Monto, or Hongwanji; Shingon; Jōdō; Nichiren; Tendai. The Shin sect, whilst not the most numerous, raise the most imposing edifices from the standpoint of linear proportion. Their temples are always well in the heart of the city. Higashi Hongwanji, or Eastern Hongwanji, in the southern part of Kyoto, is not only the largest, but one of the newest and grandest temples in Japan.

One finds old temples, and grand temples, and magnificent temples in many Japanese cities; but it is not everywhere, nor indeed anywhere else than in Kyoto, that one can see what a Buddhist temple of truly majestic proportions looks like when almost new. Such, however, is Higashi Hongwanji, for it was completed as recently as 1895, after eight years of building— the original edifice having been destroyed by fire during the revolutionary struggles in 1864.

At each of the two gates in the massive fifteen-foot wall which surrounds the courtyards, there is a pair of superb bronze lanterns, deeply carved; and in the enclosure an immense lotus-flower of bronze serves as a fountain, from which pure water flows for the use of worshippers before entering to their devotions. The lotus is the sacred emblem of Buddhism, and fountains in the shape of its blossom are to be found in many Buddhist temples.

For simple beauty and grandeur Higashi Hongwanji's buildings are perhaps more impressive than any others in Kyoto. The Daishi-dō, or Founder's Hall, rears its enormous roof in sweeping curves one hundred and twenty-six feet above the ground; and ninety-six enormous boles cut from keyaki trees—the wood of which is so hard as to set time at defiance—support it.

That a great temple like this could rise, more magnificent than ever, out of the ashes of its predecessor, shows

P

how solid are the foundations on which Japanese Buddhism rests.

When the call for contributions went forth, those who had money to give, gave it; and those who had none, but yet were strong of muscle or skilful with their hands, gave their labour to the rearing of the great edifice. And the women, in thousands —not to be behindhand with the men in bestowing what they could—sheared off their raven locks to be woven into twenty-nine immense hawsers with which the ponderous pillars and beams were hoisted into place. These cables of human hair (the largest of which is sixteen inches in circumference, and nearly a hundred yards in length) are preserved as relics in the temple—an eloquent message to future generations of the sacrifice that the women of Meiji made for the creed in which they lived and died.

Higashi Hongwanji contains no old art treasures, as those it formerly possessed were all destroyed when the previous buildings were burnt. Its interest lies in its magnificent and well-balanced proportions, and the proof it affords that the Buddhist architect of to-day is as skilful as any of his predecessors. Not the least interesting of its sights is the pavilion in the courtyard, which shelters a huge bronze bell.

The Shin Buddhists have another temple, smaller, but more interesting to the artist and lover of old-time things— Nishi Hongwanji, or Western Hongwanji. Its apartments are a veritable treasure-house of old Japanese art. Never have I trod shoeless over cold winter floors and chilly mats more willingly and reverently than through this pageantry of treasure. The main buildings, splendid as they are with coffered ceilings, arabesqued cornices, golden walls, carved cedar doors and ramma, and gilt and painted shrines, are yet eclipsed in interest by the sumptuous feast of art in the state apartments of the Abbot's palace.

Here are masterpieces of the Kano, and other schools, on sliding screens, and doors, and walls. There are wild geese and monkeys by Ryōku; palm-trees and horses by Hidenōbu; a heron and a willow-tree, and a sleeping cat and peonies by

A BUDDHIST PRIEST AND PRAYING-WHEEL

Ryōtaku; Chinese screens by Kano Kōi; waves by Kōkei; tigers by Eitoku; deer and maple-trees by Yoshimura Ranshu; bamboos, with sparrows on a gold ground, by Maruyama Ozui; chrysanthemums by Kaihoku Yusetsu; wistarias by Naozané; and a whole gallery of works, by other artists, which would take some days to examine thoroughly.

Hidari Jingoro, most famous of all Japanese wood-carvers, is well represented, as he is in most temples of any note. Indeed, the short span of this left-handed artist's days (1594–1634) must have been worthy of a more strenuous era, estimated by the numerous works he left. One of his carvings on the Higurashi-no-Mon, or "Sunrise-till-Dark Gate," so called because a whole day and night might be spent in examining it, represents "Kyo-yo, a hero of early Chinese legend, who, having rejected the Emperor Yao's proposal to resign the throne to him, is washing his ear at a waterfall to get rid of the pollution caused by the ventilation of so preposterous an idea; the owner of the cow opposite is supposed to have quarrelled with him for thus defiling the stream at which he was watering his beast." [1]

From room to room, each as beautiful or more so than the one we had left, the old bonze led us, over twittering "nightingale floors" and through many painted doors, stopping to comment at every few steps on some famous work of art or point of interest.

At length we were conducted to the garden. This was one of the favourite pleasure-grounds of Hidéyoshi, most poetical of Japanese warriors. When he was not busy with schemes for the conquest of Korea or the invasion of China, here he used to come and restore his jaded body with rest, and feast his æsthetic soul with the beauty of O Tsuki San, the Lady Moon.

The pretty winding lake was crossed with stone and rustic bridges. Ducks sported in the water, and old stone lanterns peeped from herbaceous thickets or maple bowers, and were reflected on the surface. Palms, and banana-trees with elephantine leaves, gave the garden a tropical look, and but for the temple vistas through the foliage, one might imagine one-

[1] Murray's *Handbook*.

self in Ceylon. There was a Buddha in a shady nook, and great red carp gleamed in the water at its foot. They followed our movements round the pond until the old priest—standing on the bridge, hewn from a single stone, that spanned an arm of the pool—threw them handfuls of boiled wheat, which they gobbled up noisily.

In the temple courtyard there is a fine icho-tree, whose leaves, should a conflagration threaten danger, would immediately become fountains of gushing water, and thus preserve the sacred edifice from harm.

Although there is no praying-wheel in any of the Kyoto temples, I have seen several in other parts of Japan, the finest being a pair at the great temple of Zenkoji at Nagano, and it is perhaps opportune to refer to it here.

Every one has heard of the instrument—I might say the time-saving instrument—of devotion so popular with the Thibetan Buddhists. And every one knows that it is a little box of prayers which is whirled round by a handle held in the hand, the whirler laying up for himself as great a store of merit each time he whirls as if he recited the whole of the prayers with which the box is filled.

It is the Buddhist belief that death does not alter the continuity of life but merely alters its form. Death and rebirth follow each other in constant succession. According as a man has sowed in this life so shall he reap in the next, and so on until the final break-up of the universe, or the attainment of Nirvana, which latter, being the reward of a perfect life, is the hope of all good Buddhists.

The conquest of all earthly desire is essential to the cessation of rebirths, and it is to this end that the help of the perfunctory prayer-wheel is enlisted.

Although the small whirling prayer-box of the Lama is well known, I do not think it is so widely known that there are other forms of this devotional contrivance; and I have found that many people who have travelled and even lived in Japan are unaware that it is used in that country. About this instrument, how can I possibly do better than quote the

AN AVENUE OF TORII AT INARI TEMPLE

words of my friend Professor B. H. Chamberlain.' In *Things Japanese* he says of the praying-wheel: "This instrument of devotion, so popular in Thibetan Buddhism, is comparatively rare in Japan, and is used in a slightly different manner, no prayers being written on it. Its *raison d'être*, so far as the Japanese are concerned, must be sought in the doctrine of Ingwa, according to which everything in this life is the outcome of actions performed in a previous state of existence. For example, a man goes blind; this results from some crime committed by him in his last avatar. He repents in this life, and his next life will be a happier one; or he does not repent, and he will then go from bad to worse in successive rebirths; in other words, the doctrine is that of evolution applied to ethics. This perpetual succession of cause and effect resembles the turning of a wheel. So the believer turns the praying-wheel, which thus becomes a symbol of human fate, with an entreaty to the compassionate god Jizo to let the misfortune roll by, the pious desire be accomplished, the evil disposition amended as swiftly as possible. Only the Tendai and Shingon sects of Buddhists use the praying-wheel—gosho guruma as they call it—whence its comparative rarity in Japan." The photograph shows the priest in the act of revolving the wheel.

As Chio-in, Kiyomizu, and the Hongwanji are the principal Buddhist temples in Kyoto, so Inari-no-Yashiro and Kitano-Tenjin are the most important Shinto shrines.

That Inari, about two miles from the heart of the city on the Fushimi road, should be particularly popular with the farming classes is not surprising, seeing that its patron deity is the Rice-goddess. There are probably more temples dedicated to Inari throughout Japan than to any other member of either the Shinto or Buddhist pantheons. They number many thousands, if one include the wayside shrines to be seen in every rural district. Inari's temples are distinguished by red torii, sometimes in great numbers, and by stone images of a pair of foxes. Popular superstition credits the fox with being the incarnate form in which the deity comes to earth. The fox is therefore held in great dread in Japan, as the peasantry believe it to have the power to enter the body of a human being and there comport itself much as the devils of the New Testament did before their exorcism caused the destruction of the Gadarene swine.

The first of Inari's many buildings stands at the end of a stone-flagged avenue of pine-trees, entered through a great vermilion torii. Under the heavily-thatched eaves hangs a large polished mirror of bronze. This device—which was borrowed from Buddhism and is repeated in the other buildings —seems to say to all who enter "Know Thyself," and therein it embodies the whole teachings of the Shinto creed. Shinto has no dogma nor moral code; it offers no sage admonitions for the avoidance of worldly pitfalls, nor holds out, to those who instinctively elude them, any hope of future reward. Its whole teachings are summed up in the exhortation to its adherents to follow their natural impulses and obey the Mikado's laws.

Shinto, or the "Way of the Gods," is based on the assumption that, in Japan, man is born with an instinct that teaches him to distinguish between right and wrong, and therefore there is no need for any code such as might be necessary for the guidance of less-favoured mortals. The mirror is its emblem, mutely exhorting its votaries to look into their hearts and see that they are as clean as a properly-regulated instinct should keep them.

There are no art works at Inari, nor are there in any other Shinto temple; simplicity is as much the key-note of the buildings as the creed, and the magnificent elaboration, gorgeous embellishment, and intricate ritual of the imported Indian religion finds little echo in the indigenous faith.[1]

The inevitable carved foxes are, of course, in evidence. There are several pairs of them, covered with wire to keep the birds from defiling them. There are some fine ishi-doro (stone

---

[1] The mortuary shrines to the Tokugawa Shoguns at Nikko owe their splendour to Buddhism, though many Shinto features were introduced when the latter was established as the State religion at the commencement of "The Enlightened Era."

lanterns), too, and a number of brass and bronze ones hang
in the various pavilions.

Broad stone courtyards and flights of steps lead to Inari's
many smaller shrines, and all day long the temple precincts
resound with the clapping of hands and jingling of bells, as
the worshippers bring their palms sharply together to invoke
attention, and rap the call-ropes against the hollow bronze
gongs to make assurance doubly sure that the deities are
heedful, before making their supplications.

The veranda of the main building is guarded by a pair
of carved and painted koma-inu and ama-inu. These very
ferocious-looking creatures, with nicely-groomed and curled
manes and tails, are an idea imported from Korea and
China. They are credited with the power to ward off the
attacks of evil spirits, and are to be found in many
Japanese temples.

At the Lama temple in Peking there is a very fine pair,
superbly carved in bronze; and an immense granite pair guard
the entrance to the Palace in Seoul, Korea.

In China they represent the Heavenly Dogs that devour
the sun at the time of eclipse; and the ball so often carved in
the mouth of one of the pair shows the orb of day undergoing
this experience. In Japan they do not appear to mean anything
in particular, having simply been taken over from their neighbours by the Japanese, together with the religion, as picturesque
and appropriate features. One of the pair always has its mouth
open and the other's lips are tightly closed. Opinions differ
as to which is the male and which the female, but a Japanese
friend offered the explanation that the female is always shown
with the mouth open, "as it is quite impossible for a woman
to keep her mouth shut."

Inari's courtyards are the haunt of fortune-tellers and
diviners, mendicant cripples, toy-sellers, and an old woman,
who for the sum of three sen (three farthings) will liberate
a small bird from a cage, thereby bringing to the donor of this
amount some merit for the kindly act. For the sum of threepence one might free the whole of her stock in trade, and when

I did so, giving the old beldame double payment, she was quite overwhelming with her benedictions.

The Japanese uranaisha, or fortune-teller, fills a very serious and material place in the estimation of the lower classes of the people. They resort to him in every conceivable form of trouble. For a trifling sum he dispenses advice to the love-lorn maiden or the unhappy wife; instructs mothers as to the probable outcome of the ailments afflicting their children; warns his patrons against, or gives his assent to, proposed journeys; counsels them in business undertakings; looks into the future for them, or lays bare the past; delineates character in their palms and faces; advises them in matrimonial affairs; indicates where lost articles can be found, and in a hundred ways comforts and assists them in distress.

With a small pile of books, and a joint of bamboo filled with his divining rods, he is to be found at more than one temple in most cities of any size. How much reliance may be placed on his advice and prognostications is a matter for the individual to decide. The following case, however, came within my own experience.

One November I left Japan for India, not knowing when I should return, but telling a faithful servant I should probably be back in the following June. I returned in May, arriving in Tokyo at 6 o'clock one day. The same evening I took the 7 o'clock train to Yokohama to engage my servant's services again. On arriving at his house he evinced little surprise at seeing me a month earlier than I had told him to expect me, and, on my asking the explanation, said that he had been several times lately to consult a uranaisha. Without telling the uranaisha where I was, or anything whatever about me, he simply questioned him if he could tell "where my master is." On two occasions the seer could tell him no more than that his master was many thousand ri away. On the third occasion he had received the information that his master was on the sea, returning to Japan. On the fourth occasion—that very evening at half-past five—he had gone again, and the diviner had told him that I was not ten ri away, and that he would see me again that night. At the moment he secured this information I was actually within ten ri, and I called, as the diviner said I would. This episode may be accounted for by coincidence, of course. I have simply stated the actual facts concerning it.

There are several uranaisha at Inari. The illustration shows one of them, in consultation with a woman of the peasant class, selecting his divining rods preparatory to instructing her in the matter concerning which she has come specially to Kyoto to see him, whilst her mother and rikisha runner stand by, anxiously awaiting the verdict of the oracle. The pair of ishidoro to which he has fastened his sign-banner are typical of the severity of the style of the stone lanterns at this temple.

The portrait reproduced is from a photograph of another of the Inari uranaisha, and it shows him recording the particulars of a client's .case.

The circuit of Inari's grounds is a good three miles' walk, and one may spend hours wandering amongst its many shrines and avenues of wooden torii, which in places are erected so close together as to form one long continuous arch—each torii almost touching its neighbour. There are many thousands of them in the temple grounds—indeed, tens of thousands, if one includes the miniatures that are stacked about the principal shrines—varying in height from six inches to fifteen feet. They are painted vermilion, with black at the base, and form a brilliant contrast to the deep green of the trees.

The torii, characteristic of every Shinto temple, is not as nationally distinctive as some protest. Its whole meaning is a matter of contention. Most authorities claim for it Japanese origin as a perch for sacred fowls (tori), which time has modified to a mere "symbolic ornament." Kipling claims it is Hindu; and at Alwar, in Rajputana, India, one Hindu temple that I visited has almost its exact counterpart. The beautiful pai-lo of China is the same idea in a more embellished form. Be its origin what it may, the torii is a very striking and effective structure, and its dignified lines are much beloved by native artists. The numerous torii at Inari are the gifts of devotees whose supplications have met with favourable response.

There are a score or more other temples in Kyoto in which one might ramble for days and ever be discovering some beautiful or curious feature, hitherto unnoticed. At Kitano Tenjin there are bronze bulls, which shine with a beautiful patina brought out by centuries of friction at the hands of those who rub them, as they rub Binzuru's image at Kiyomizu, to gain relief from their ailments; and there is a fine old oratory round which to run a hundred laps is a penance that purifies the heart as effectually as it strengthens the body. Sometimes a dozen zealots may be seen vying with each other in the task.

Myōshinji, whose massive buildings lie deep in groves of fine old pine-trees, has many works of art, and a revolving bookcase, to turn which lays up as great a store of merit as if one read the whole of the scriptures it contains. Daitokuji boasts of a larger number of valuable kakemono than any other temple in Japan, and has an entire set of sliding doors, dividing room from room, painted by the famous Kano Ten-yu. Uzamasa is famous for its statuary. Kōdaiji was beloved by Hidéyoshi, who used to sit on a certain spot in its galleries and revel in the beauty of the moon, as he also did at Nishi Hongwanji. Eikwandō is embosomed in groves of maple-trees, and Shimo-Gamo has groves that are more beautiful and grander still. Here on the 15th May, at the annual festival, horse-races, in which the priests take part, are held on the broad reaches of turf among its splendid cryptomeria-trees; and a grand procession of warriors, with armour and accoutrements of feudal days, leaves the Imperial Palace to visit the old temple, just as it did in the days of old when the Mikado came in person.

So holy is this procession that no one in the crowd may have his head above another's; and not all the War Office and other official permits I possessed could gain for me the privilege of an elevated position from which to photograph it.

The stately old buildings of the Kurodani monastery, whose ponderous keyaki-wood doors are strapped and bossed with bronze, contain a blaze of golden glory in embroidered

H.G.P.

PORTRAIT OF A URANAISHA

silken banners, and its state apartments are as rich in art as its situation is in natural beauty.

At such places as Kurodani, Chio-in, and Eikwandō, one goes not only to see the temples themselves, but also to enjoy the perfect harmony with which the hand of time has clothed their surroundings. None but the most artistic of peoples could have designed or conceived such grand, reposeful settings; and the passing of the centuries has but added the soft charm that only time can give. There is an atmosphere of simple dignity about these temples that touches the very soul. One approaches them with reverence. One cannot enter them without being purified in spirit; for thoughts are elevated to loftier planes, and no believer in the faith these grand old structures adorn, nor any other believer either, could ever seek their precincts without deriving some benefit from the act. All their beauty, and the careful and imperceptible merging of the art of man with the handiwork of nature, is planned to calm the spirit and bring rest and joy to the troubled heart. Anger is dispelled, grief softened, and anguish tempered to him who roams their tranquil grounds with reverent mind, and a feeling of contentment and rest enters into his soul.

This is truly the zenith of the art of raising a sanctuary— to invest it with the atmosphere of peace.

An old English gentleman, whom I met at Kurodani, as much enchanted with this lovely land as I, said to me: "Though you love them too, you cannot feel such joy as these beautiful places bring to me, for you are too young a man, and are storing up a fund of memories for the days when strength has departed. I am old, and the peace and restfulness of these temples is to me the foreshadowing of the peace I soon must find for ever. I am glad I came to this gentle land, and would ask no kindlier fate than to end my days amidst such beautiful surroundings."

CHAPTER XIV

THE ARTIST-CRAFTSMEN OF KYOTO

In the old-time houses that line Kyoto's old-time streets ancient arts are perpetuated and kept ever young. Arts, too, that are not yet middle-aged, and others that are as yet but in their cradles, find in Kyoto the inspiration to give them their fairest and noblest expression. Bronzes, embroideries, silks, pottery and porcelain, damascene, cloisonné, and a number of other products for which Japan is noted, come mainly from Kyoto; and visiting the places where these are made is as interesting as "doing" the regulation sights.

Many and many a happy hour have I spent with Kyoto artist-craftsmen. About Kurōda alone I could write many pages, but must content myself with relating a few simple incidents.

Kurōda is a bronze-inlayer whose only compeer is Jōmi. He is a very tall, stern-looking, clean-shaven man, and speaks English fluently with a deep bass voice. Those who fail to visit Kyoto learn nothing of the artistic marvels created under his roof, for his masterpieces are never seen in any shop. Like a few others of his contemporaries, he does not sell his best work to the trade, for his output is small, and he finds a market for it all with visiting connoisseurs.

At either Kurōda's or Jōmi's one may see triumphs of the bronze-worker's art superior to anything ever produced by Nagatsuné, Jinpo, Toshiyoshi, or any of the old-time masters, for though many native crafts are being degraded by appealing to vulgar foreign taste, the product of the bronze-workers—one of the most beautiful of all Japanese arts—excels that of the old-time days.

I owe much to Kurōda for what he taught me. Though

I had spent a lot of time in the shops of other metal-workers, I had been groping in the dark until I met him. One day he said to me: "Very few foreigners understand anything about bronze, though most of them think they do. To show my finest work to them is usually a thankless task, as many cannot see why one piece should be worth four or five times as much as another that looks almost exactly like it. Even an educated Japanese does not know anything about the fine arts of Japan unless he be a collector."

With that he went to a near-by shelf, and, after careful deliberation, selected a box from a number of similar-looking ones of various sizes, and, opening it, produced a bag of brocaded silk, from which he drew out a bronze plaque.

"Now what do you think of that?" he asked, handing it to me.

I carefully examined it. The bronze was of a rich golden-brown colour, with an exquisite patina, and was inlaid in relief with silver and gold, and with shakudo and other alloys of bronze.

The design represented the famous Bay of Enōura, from Shizu-ura by the Izu peninsula. Silver-tipped waves were lapping the shore, and out on the ocean two golden junks were running before the wind, with silver sails bellying to the breeze. By the beach there was a grove of old pines, in various alloys, and in the distance Fuji-san's snowy crest, of silver, floated in the sky above clouds of shibuichi (a grey alloy of silver and bronze). The price was £8.

I had certainly never seen anything more beautiful, either in design or workmanship, in any shop I had previously visited, and said so.

"Do you know what I think of it?" Kurōda replied, and continued without waiting for an answer: "What you are looking at is rubbish. No Japanese collector would bestow a second glance on it. Now I will show you what a Japanese, *who knows*, would call good work."

With that he opened another box, and brought forth another plaque of like size, about seven inches in diameter,

and handed it to me. The design was the same, yet not the
same. The composition of the picture was different, though
the view was still Enōura Bay, with Fuji and the junks and
pine-trees. But it was not the difference in the composition
that struck me so much as the surpassing beauty of the workmanship. To examine these pieces, side by side, was in itself
an education. One piece was beautiful, the other was incom-
parably beautiful. There was as much difference between
them as there is between a cut-glass bowl made by hand and
another pressed in a mould. This difference was not apparent
at the first glance, and only by careful scrutiny could I see the
immense amount of skill lavished upon the one, which the
other lacked. The price of the second plaque was £30. Though
the thicker gold and silver used, and the better quality of the
bronze, increased the value, yet the extra cost was mainly due
to the workmanship expended on it.

Kurōda told me that the best pieces of his work were bought
by English and French visitors. Small vases and plaques are
the favourite pieces, but if one desires something combining
beauty with practical utility one may buy a cigarette- or card-
case of shibuichi, inlaid in relief with some such simple design
as a peasant carrying a load of firewood, or a pair of fighting-
cocks; but one must pay at least £15 to £20 for it if one wants
the finest work. This case, however, will be "a joy for ever"
to its owner, as he will always have the satisfaction of knowing
that it is a sample of the best art of its kind.

At Jōmi's one can see inlaid work no less perfect than
Kurōda's; and Jōmi is also the king of workers in beaten copper.

Jōmi gave me one day as instructive a lesson in beaten-
copper work as Kurōda gave me in bronze. He showed me two
quite plain but very tastefully designed vases, globular shaped,
with long thin necks. The bodies were about four inches in
diameter, and the necks perhaps six inches long and half an
inch thick. They were to all intents and purposes a pair, exactly
alike, yet one was five times the price of the other. The reason
was that, though both were beaten out of a flat sheet of copper,
one of them had the base brazed on, whilst the other was made

in one piece. One need not be an expert to realise that a copper vase, with a large round body, a base, and a long and very thin neck, beaten out of one single sheet of metal, must be about the acme of skill of the metal-beater's craft, and therefore worth much more than an apparently similar article in which the greatest difficulty was avoided by having a large open base through which to work.

One of Kyoto's most famous crafts is that of damascening. There are two makers whose products are equally good. Both bear the same name, Kōmai, though I was told they were not related.

I have a cigarette-case made by S. Kōmai. On the front of it there is an eagle sitting on a pine-tree, its feathers bristling with anger at the intrusion of two small birds that have approached. They did not know that their enemy was hidden in the tree, but, having just detected him, their mouths are open, crying with fear. The eagle and the tree are beautifully worked in gold of various shades, the branches are heavily laden with silver snow, and a few silver flakes are falling. Every feather and pine-needle is picked out and hammered into the steel, and the bark of the tree is wonderfully natural in its grain. At the back of the case there is a fiery dragon, writhing with rage, inlaid with gold of half a dozen different colours, every scale being inlaid separately, clean cut and free of its neighbours. Inside the case there is a golden outline of Fuji with the snow-cap overlaid with silver.

I do not think I ever fully appreciated this example of Japanese art until after I had visited the famous damascene works in Spain—the great sword factory at Toledo. One day when I was going through the inlaying rooms, I took out my case, and laid it on the table of the head workman. The man picked it up with an ejaculation of surprise, glanced at it, and then without a word went off with it to another room.

In five minutes he came back with half a dozen other men —the heads of various departments. For half an hour these experts subjected the case to the closest scrutiny with magnifying glasses, and with sighs admitted they had never seen

anything like it—that no one in Spain could execute anything
approaching it, either for beauty of design or perfection of
finish. Since that day this masterpiece of the Japanese metal
worker's art has been more precious in my sight, for my own
estimate of its merits has been confirmed by the foremost
experts of Europe.

Almost the only Japanese art not represented in Kyoto at
its best is ivory-carving. For ivories one must go to Tokyo
—to Toyama's, Maruki's, or Kanéda's. The two former deal
in the highly polished carvings, known all over the world so
well, and to be found in the cabinets of every European collector.
But Kanéda has brought the art of ivory-carving to a higher
degree of beauty. One finds no polished pieces in his house.
He abhors the high finish and colouring by which his contemporaries gain much of their effect, and finishes all his work
with a matt surface, pure white. Of the beauty of this it is
sufficient to say that he has taken the highest awards wherever
he has exhibited. Buffalo, Paris, St. Louis, all gave him the
gold medal, and the international expositions held at Osaka
and Tokyo followed suit.

Kanéda is not, however, the only artist now making
matt-finished ivories. Many other sculptors have imitated
his work—perhaps the best of all commendations of its
merit—but he is *facile princeps* of all the ivory-workers
of Japan.

He is equally skilful in bronze, and his chief delight is in
carving elephants. Like many others of the foremost Japanese
artists, he is now an old man, and does little himself beyond
supervising the artists who work under his instruction. The
work produced by him and his pupils in carving elephants in
ivory is unequalled; but Nogawa of Kyoto runs him very close
in bronze. Like Kanéda's, Nogawa's elephants seem positively
to live. One of Kanéda's artists—Kōmei Ishikawa, the most
skilful ivory-worker in Japan—will take a three-foot tusk and
carve it into a single file of elephants, so lifelike that they
almost seem to move along the thin strip left as a base; and
Nogawa's head artist will take a rough bronze casting of a

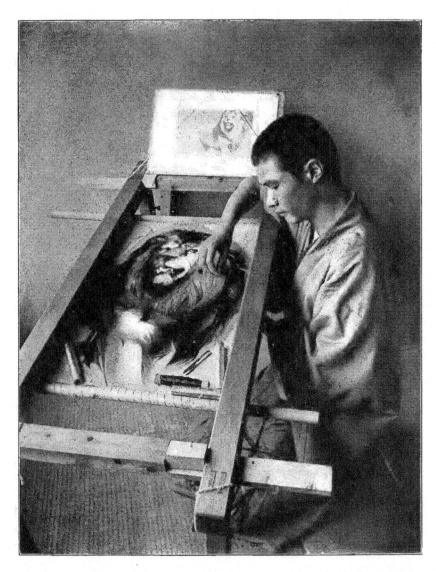

THE EMBROIDERER

pachyderm and fashion it with a tiny hammer and chisels till it, also, seems to pulsate with the breath of life.

At Delhi, in India, I have seen elephants, wonderfully carved in ivory, carrying a field-gun with its carriage and all the trappings. Every link of every chain was free, and each separate trapping could be removed and set up separately. But with it all, and notwithstanding that the Hindu has elephants every day before his eyes, there was not the *life* that the innate art of the Japanese enables him to instil into his image of an animal he never sees.

The Chinese, too, do miracles with ivory. In Canton I have seen a native take a cube cut from a tusk, and so manipulate it with various tiny tools that when it left his hands the solid mass had become a series of twenty hollow ivory balls, diminishing in size from a diameter of four inches to half an inch, each beautifully carved and revolving freely within the next larger one. The balls had not been cut open; each smaller ball was carved inside its larger neighbour through the ornamental perforations with which each ball was decorated. Surely this is the most surpassing skill; but it is the skill of the dexterous craftsman, not that of the artist. Kōmei Ishikawa could probably not execute such a piece of work for any sum of money, but he can do what no Chinese sculptor can even approximately accomplish—make a piece of ivory throb with life and animation—a more artistic effort than the Chinaman's concentric balls.

The wondrous ability of the Japanese in portraying animals is not confined to carvings. One may see at Nishimura's or Iida's, the great silk-merchants of Kyoto, such marvellous embroideries of lions and tigers that only the closest inspection proves them to be the work of the needle and not of the brush. The effect is only gained at the expense of a million or so of separate stitches. One piece at Nishimura's held particular fascination for me. It represented a tiger bounding out of a bamboo thicket. The creature appeared to be actually springing from the picture. Its jaws were open, and the fierce gleam in its eyes was startlingly realistic.

o

This wonderful example of the work of the needle was made by one Yōzo Nagara, who is regarded as the foremost exponent of the art of needlework in Japan. In order to increase the realism of the effect such pieces are not finished flat, but, by stitching over and over again, and gradually bringing the picture out in high relief by padding it in places with much stitching underneath, such solidity is given to the subject that it often seems to be the work of the sculptor and painter combined. Only close scrutiny betrays the embroiderer's hand.

I had the opportunity of seeing Nagara at work at his home, embroidering the head of a lion. He informed me that the foundation stitches were, in places, covered fully one hundred times before the desired effect of depth and richness was imparted to the mane.

The most expert Kyoto embroiderers are all men. Women are employed only for the coarser work.

Chinese embroiderers show unequalled taste in their choice of colours, but they have not the skill to hold the mirror up to nature as have the Japanese. In many of the arts that Japan has learnt from China—and China is to Japan what ancient Greece was to all the rest of Europe—inherent love of anything beautiful in nature has enabled the Japanese to counterfeit that beauty, by a hundred different means, to a degree of perfection the Chinese have seldom reached. The pupil has outclassed the master.

For centuries rigid seclusion from the rest of the world kept the art of the Japanese free from the contamination of foreign ideas. They founded their schools on Chinese lines, but built up and improved upon these until they had created an individual art of their own, which, whilst the Chinese origin is often apparent, is yet distinct in character and unique. In Europe a work of art executed in one country frequently might have been made just as well in several others. Not so, however, the work of the modern Japanese artist, who has broken the fetters of convention which kept the art of his country hide-bound for so long. His work shows character that cannot be counterfeited by a foreigner. Even Whistler's attempts are but mere parodies of Hiroshigé's bold and masterly strokes.

The Japanese embroiderer, who is true to his own traditions, can show needlework more beautiful in design and execution than any the world has seen, and the art is happily one that has not retrograded. But it is greatly to be regretted that so much artistic talent is wasted on mere slavish imitation.

The commercial maelstrom which has gathered Japan into its whirling vortex has produced a set of knights of the needle who cannot originate, but whose skill enables them to copy with absolute truth and fidelity anything that is set before them, be it in monochrome or colour. I saw at Nishimura's facsimiles of Landseer's works in monochrome so faithful to the copy that it was beyond my power to detect, except by close inspection, which was the original engraving and which its silken presentment. I saw, too, Landseer's "Dignity and Impudence" in colours so true to the painting beside it, that, from a distance of but a few feet, one would declare them both works by the same brush. It is depressing that such commendable talent should be applied to mere imitation.

The potters and pottery-painters of Kyoto are no less interesting than the embroiderers and metal-workers.

Awata is the centre from which the highly decorated ware, called "Satsuma" in American and European shops, is shipped in immense quantities all over the world. It is a cream-coloured faience, covered with a minutely-crackled glaze, an imitation of the famous old pottery formerly produced at Kagoshima in the province of Satsuma.

This Awata ware is decorated in many different styles, and for exportation in quantity nothing more inartistic is produced in all Japan. At a dozen large establishments the whole floors of rooms are littered with vases and urns. Here men and women and boys and girls, working side by side, quickly brush in the ground-work and trace designs, each finishing many pieces daily, and having no scruples in using the aerograph in the process — so debased have modern methods

become in the race for wealth by catering for the most
vulgar foreign taste.

At Yasuda's or Kinkosan's one may see the whole process
of pottery-making from the mixing of the clay to the packing
of the finished product.   The courteous proprietor of each of
these establishments deputes an assistant to take visitors round
and answer any questions.   In turn one sees the grinding-
wheels; the mixing-vats, where the clay is slaked and cleansed,
and made ready for the potters; the throwing-wheels, kilns,
and painting-rooms.

One old potter at Kinkosan's always interested me greatly.
In spring, summer, autumn, and winter I have seen him at
his wheel, his raiment growing scantier as the weather became
warmer, until August found him with nothing but a loin-cloth
and a few medical plasters to cover his rheumatic bones.
Many an hour I have spent watching him slicing off lumps of
clay and slapping them on to his throwing-wheel, which, with
a few deft turns of his hand, he set spinning rapidly on its
axis.   Then, as if he were some necromancer casting a magic
spell upon it, "The shapeless lifeless clay rose up to meet the
master's hand," and I almost expected the old fellow to mutter
some incantation as, with fingers and spatula, he quickly made
it swell out and hollowed it, and narrowed it again for the neck,
and swelled it again for the lip, until, almost before my fascinated gaze could take it in, hey! presto! the thing was done.
Then, taking a piece of wire, he cut it loose from the wheel and
placed it on the floor beside him—a graceful vase, matching
its fellows in all proportions to the fraction of an inch.

Near by the potters' sheds are the drying-rooms, where
the pieces are left for several days to dry out without artificial
aid.   Then there are the dipping-rooms, where the glaze is
applied after the first, and before the second firing.   The kilns
are always interesting.   Some of them are open, either receiving or being relieved of their fragile store, whilst others are
being carefully watched by practised old Palissys who continually poke fresh sticks of fuel through tiny loopholes
into the sealed-up fires.

A POTTER AT HIS WHEEL

At Yasuda's and Kinkosan's, besides the daubers—who apply to this beautiful pottery the disfigurement which the markets of Europe and America demand, but which no Japanese can bear the sight of—there are artists who adorn a limited number of pieces with paintings of exquisite beauty. At Kinkosan's these artists work in little houses in the gardens, where weeks, and sometimes months, are spent in the minute embellishment of a single vase. Lovely landscapes, and scenes from legend and history, appear in ovals and vignettes on a background of deep and lustrous blue, and gold is only used to give enrichment.

The work of the best Kyoto pottery artists, when examined under a magnifying glass, shows every detail perfect—every twig of every tree, and every feather of every chanticleer painted true to nature.

No one can see Kinkosan's show-rooms without wondering at the exceeding richness and beauty of the decorated blue ware which has justly earned for him the foremost place among the potters of Kyoto. Whilst he caters for uncultivated foreign taste, it is also his aim to keep up the standard of Japanese miniature painting. It came as a rude shock to me, therefore, when one day I saw in a Japanese shop in London some of Kinkosan's latest productions, which for bad taste and faulty painting were among the worst efforts I have ever seen turned out by any Japanese. The beautiful blue background was there, but the gold enrichment had become a gaudy plastering, and instead of charming Japanese scenes in the vignettes there were European landscapes, with swans or geese (one could not tell which they were intended for), and trees of which it was impossible to name the species. It is sad that Japan should sink to such debasing of her art, instead of educating her patrons to the standard of her own.

At the Kinkosan works an incident occurred one day which was the most remarkable instance of the Japanese proneness for imitation that has come within my experience. As it intimately concerned myself, I may appropriately relate it here.

Shortly after I had published in Tokyo, under the title

Fuji-San, a book containing a series of my photographic studies of the great sacred mountain—each one of which was taken from an entirely new viewpoint, which I had myself sought out and discovered during many weeks devoted to the work—I was paying a final visit to the Kinkosan works, before leaving Japan for India. Mr. Kinkosan himself conducted me to a room where he told me he had a great surprise for me. He had, indeed! There, with a copy of my book open before him, was his finest "Satsuma" artist, busily engaged on an miniature painting of one of my photographs of the mountain, which he was reproducing in gold and colours on a European-style tea-plate! Seven others were already finished, and I was told that the complete set would consist of a dozen. Though all my photographs are copyrighted in Japan, and this was an obvious infringement of them, I felt that the only attitude to adopt in the circumstances was one of "Shikata ga nai" (It can't be helped), and to comfort myself with the solace that imitation is the sincerest form of flattery.

When there is so much that is commendable, and even incomparable, in Japanese art, when conforming to its own traditions, it is depressing that modern artists should not be above slavish imitation of the work of a foreigner—with the camera.

That this commercial instinct of the Japanese, as exemplified at Kinkosan's, has not yet completely killed the old spirit of the days when a man worked for little beyond the sheer love of art, the following incident will show.

A few years ago one of these old Kyoto pottery-painters, who works alone in his own home, one day visited a foreign merchant in Kobe. Entering the merchant's office, and receiving permission to show his wares, he brought forth from his bundle some ten or a dozen small boxes, from each of which he extracted a dainty piece of minutely-painted pottery. These he tenderly and modestly arranged upon the floor, and, kneeling beside them, submitted each in turn for examination. When all had been appraised and a price quoted for each separate piece, the prospective buyer, indicating them with his foot,

A POTTERY PAINTER

remarked, "How much reduction will you make if I buy the whole lot?" The old man sprang up with anger blazing in his eyes, saying, "Not all the money you have would buy them now," and, quickly packing them up, he bowed and left the house.

This incident was related to me by a friend of the baffled buyer. There is no greater affront one can offer in a Japanese house than to use one's foot to denote an object; and when this old painter, born and bred in an atmosphere of strict etiquette—as even pottery-painters are in Japan—saw the work, over which he had bestowed so many weeks of jealous care, thus, as he thought, abused, he preferred to lose the sale rather than that the little pieces he loved should pass into the hands of any one who regarded them so lightly.

The art of making cloisonné enamel, whilst not modern, has yet been brought by a few of its present-day exponents in Kyoto to a state of perfection never hitherto attained in Japan or any other land. In a short paragraph in *Things Japanese* Professor B. H. Chamberlain says: "The art first became known in Japan some three hundred years ago, but it has only been brought to perfection within the last quarter of a century. Mr. Namikawa, the great cloisonné maker of Kyoto, will show visitors specimens that look almost antediluvian in roughness and simplicity, but date back no farther than 1873."

It was not, however, to Namikawa's that I first went. In other towns I had seen the process, and I had also visited several other makers in Kyoto before the above paragraph came before my eyes. When I read it I decided immediately to visit the famous artist, and when my call was over I was glad I had seen the other places first, as I was thus better able to appreciate the excellence of the workmanship which has placed the Namikawa product in a class which few of his contemporaries ever reach.

As I was whirled rapidly along in a rikisha, passing through street after street of two-storied houses with tiled roofs, each almost a counterpart of its neighbours, there was little outward show to indicate the treasures of art which might be concealed behind those wooden walls and paper windows. Indeed, the only visible clues to what investigation would reveal were often but simple boards on which were painted such names as "Kōmai," "Kuroda," "Jōmi," etc. To the initiated, however, these names mean much, for they are, as already shown, names to conjure with in the world of art—the patronymics of some of the greatest artist-craftsmen the century has produced.

My sturdy kurumaya, having received his instructions, hesitated before none of these, but trotted rapidly on until he finally turned into a quiet side-lane in the Awata district, and with a jerk pulled up and dropped the shafts before a private house. I thought there must be some mistake, but with a good-natured smile that covered his whole face, as he wiped the great beads of perspiration from his forehead and from amongst his short bristly hair, he pointed to a tiny placard, but a few inches long, by the entrance gate, bearing the simple inscription: "Y. Namikawa—Cloisonné."

The door was immediately opened, and I was greeted with a "Good morning" by a young man who conducted me past a pretty glimpse of garden into a room typically Japanese, except that it was furnished with a large cabinet and a graceful Chinese blackwood table.

Here I met Mr. Namikawa, a man of quiet speech and courteous manner, whose refined classical features betrayed the artist. He spoke no English, but relied entirely on the services of his interpreter, who invited me to partake of the tea which had been prepared immediately upon my entering the house.

There are still to be found in Kyoto, and elsewhere in Japan, a few of the old-time artist-craftsmen who cannot reconcile themselves to modern business methods, and with them the purchase of a small *objet d'art* may take an entire afternoon. The motive of the visit, although perfectly apparent from the outset, must be broached—or at least would be so by a Japanese—in the most delicate manner possible; and only after much discussion, and careful expression and veiling of

opinion, could a price be finally agreed upon at which the coveted possession would change hands.

There, however, is none of this beating about the bush with Namikawa. He knows what you have come for, and he also knows that the average foreign customer may likely enough have planned to visit half a dozen other—I was about to write "shops," but just checked myself in time—artists' houses the same afternoon.

Namikawa is at the same time an artist and a man of business; therefore, whilst I sipped the tea, he set about the selection of sundry little boxes from a cabinet near by. When he had chosen about a dozen, he placed them upon the table before me and forthwith proceeded to open one. He produced therefrom a little bundle done up in yellow cheese-cloth. Removing this, there was yet more cheese-cloth, and after that a piece of silk. Unwrapping the silk, he disclosed to view a piece of cloisonné of such design and colouring that the finest I had hitherto seen seemed but crude in comparison. In turn he opened the other boxes, and from each brought forth a masterpiece.

There were tiny vases of which the groundwork was of Crown Derby yellow; others in their colouring suggested Royal Worcester, only the designs were essentially Japanese. There were little jars and caskets of which the prevailing tints were delicate cornflower and peacock blues. There were groundworks of red and olive green, and of ultramarine and deep purple. One and all were decorated with designs more beautiful than any I had previously seen, and each was mounted on its own tiny stand of carved blackwood, as dainty in its way as the piece itself.

In Japan it is not the custom to display the finest work at first. The Japanese know that to show a fine work of art to the uninitiated is often a thankless task—as indeed Kurōda had told me; therefore only where genuine interest is shown are the most cherished pieces brought forth. Besides, too, there is nothing the Japanese likes better than to have something still "up his sleeve," and in this he shows a weakness that is, after all, but human. The visitor's knowledge and the quality of his interest are quickly gauged by these Kyoto artists. There is no deceiving them. Pretence of knowledge is of no avail. The real connoisseur reveals himself in every glance, just as the pretender betrays himself by every word. He who is anxious to learn is gladly welcomed, however, even though he be not a buyer.

Though Namikawa produced other and larger pieces, it was not until one of my further visits, many months later, that I saw the very climax of his skill—a pair of vases decorated with an old-time feudal procession, an order from the Emperor which had taken his foremost artist over a year to complete.

Namikawa's output is so small that the demand for it from visiting connoisseurs and collectors is sometimes more than equal to the supply. There is no catering for the trade. That is left to those who follow in his footsteps—who seek to imitate his methods and effects. As the pieces stood on the table they ranged in price from five to fifty pounds, a large piece of the latter value being about fifteen inches high, and decorated, on a deep blue ground, with a design of white and purple drooping wistarias.

The larger pieces were in no way inferior to the smaller ones, though the making of a perfect piece of large size is well-nigh an impossibility, as some tiny speck or minute flaw is almost certain to appear; yet careful examination showed that even in the largest there was such perfection as I had not seen before.

It seemed almost sacrilege to remove any of the pieces from the care of their creator and from the environment which became them so well; but I felt that henceforth life would be worth living only in the companionship of a modest but exquisite little vase, of which forthwith I became the proud possessor.

Whilst I was inspecting each vase, and casket, and urn in turn, Namikawa slid open one of the wood-and-paper shoji to admit more air, for the day was warm. Involuntarily glancing up I beheld a most charming scene—the essence of all that

is æsthetic, restful, and refined in a Japanese garden. There was a little lake with rustic bridges, and miniature islands clad with dwarf pine-trees of that rugged, crawling kind that one sees only in Japan; and out over the water, a few inches from the surface, they stretched their gnarled and tortured limbs towards others of their kind which strove from the opposite shore to meet them.

The verandah projected over the lake, and as my host stepped on to it, from every part of the pond great carp, black, spotted, and gold, lashed the water to foam as they rushed literally to their master's feet. He cast a handful of biscuits to them, and a frantic struggle ensued as the fish crowded to the surface noisily gobbling up the tit-bits.

Handing some of the biscuits to me, he invited me to feed them from my hand. Lying down on the porch I could just reach the water, and I found them so tame that they fearlessly took pieces from my fingers, and even permitted me to stroke them on the back.

Under the shelter of a dwarf pine, on a tiny island in front, a little tortoise was gazing steadily at us. I threw a piece of biscuit to it, but it did not move. I tossed another piece but it never stirred.

Namikawa, laughing, remarked, "It cannot eat. It is bronze."

Each shrub, each bridge, each stone lantern, and even each stone itself, was so placed in the garden as to help the composition of the picture.

Here was surely the highest exposition of the landscape gardener's skill, for although the entire enclosure could not have exceeded thirty yards in length, and half as much in width, yet so clever was the arrangement of the water and the trees as to suggest a large area unseen, and even the trees themselves were so arranged and controlled in growth as to make the apparent size of the garden much greater than the real.

Namikawa then invited me to inspect his workshop. Conducting me out into the garden and round the miniature

lake, he led me to another building, which was open to the
light on two sides, and furnished with running white curtains
to soften and diffuse, if necessary, the strong glare of the sun.
This was the workshop.

I had not expected to see a large one, for in Japan such are
seldom found, and many of the greatest masterpieces have
been created in a humble home, where a lone individual toiled
week after week, month after month, and in many cases year
after year, on a single piece, until at length it stood complete
—a master's work of art.

I had heard of many such cases, and I was not surprised,
therefore, to find Namikawa's entire staff in one room.

Some weeks before, I had seen, in Yokohama, a cloisonné
factory where the artisans worked on dirty wooden floors,
designing and enamelling beautiful floral vases.   In other
rooms figures, naked save for a loin-cloth, scrubbed, and
ground, and polished huge urns, in some cases as big as the
scrubbing figures themselves; and by the side of kilns, which
gleamed dull red, old and practised men stood and watched,
the sweat dripping from their half-nude bodies.

And in Kyoto I had visited the Takatani factory, where
an enormous demand from Europe and America for cheap
ware is catered for—the work being done by young girls and
children, who laid the enamel paste on with spoons, each
completing many pieces in a day.

Those were "factories" almost in the European sense,
where the love of the lone individual of the old days, who
wanted little and lived simply, content with the beauty created
by his own hands—his craft his life and joy as well as occupation—had degenerated into the equivalent of the modern
industrialism of the West, in the race for wealth which is
sounding the death-knell of much that is best in Japanese art.

But here were no such scenes.

Instead, I saw a spotless studio, twenty feet in length, the
floor covered with padded mats, on which, bending over tiny
tables, were ten artists, so intent on their occupation that our
intrusion caused but a momentary glance. Close by them were

NAMIKAWA'S WORKROOM AND STAFF

two figures, rubbing and polishing. This was Namikawa's entire staff.

In this room could be seen the whole process by which the enamelled ware, called "cloisonné," was produced—except the firing. Each artist was at work on some delicate little vase or dainty casket, which was surely, yet almost imperceptibly, assuming beautiful outlines and colouring on its shape. At one table a bronze vase was receiving its decorative design, not from a copy, but fresh from the brain of the artist, who sketched it with a brush and Chinese ink. At another table an artist was cutting small particles of gold wire, flattened into ribbon a sixteenth of an inch in width. After carefully bending and twisting the particles to the shape of the minute portion of the design they were to cover, he then fastened them in place with a touch of liquid cement. At yet another table the wiring of a design had just been finished—the silver vase which formed the base being beautifully filigreed in relief with gold ribbon. Namikawa's fame rests as much on the lustre and purity of his monochrome backgrounds as on the decoration of his ware; this gold enrichment, therefore, covered but a portion of the surface. It was simply a spray or two of cherry-blossoms, among which some tiny birds were playing. That was all; yet even in this state, as it stood ready for the insertion of the enamels, it was a thing of beauty, for every feather in the diminutive wings and breasts was worked, and every petal, calyx, stamen, and pistil of every blossom was carefully outlined in gold, forming, for the reception of the coloured paste, a network of minute cells, or cloisons, from which the art derives its name.

At other tables the enamel was being applied. The paste, with which the tiny cells are filled, is composed of mineral powders of various colours, which produce the desired tints when mixed with a flux that fuses them in the furnace into vitrified enamel.

In the finest cloisonné the cells are only partially filled at first. The piece is then fired. Then more paste is applied, and it is fired again. Perhaps it may be seven times treated thus

before the final application of the paste, and this last coating
is the most important. On it very largely depends not only
the effect of the other coats, but also the appearance of the
surface. It determines whether the surface shall be of flawless
lustre, or pitted with minute holes.

After this last filling and firing the vase presents a very
rough appearance, for the final fusion has run the enamels
together, as the cells were filled higher than the brim. There
is little in its appearance at the present stage to indicate the
beauty and brilliancy lying below. It is like a rare stone before
it emerges from the hands of the lapidary.

The vase must now be ground with pumice-stone and
water for many days, sometimes for weeks, to reduce the
uneven face to the same thickness all over. This is all done by
hand, and calls for great skill and watchfulness, for were it
ground thinner in one place than another the light would not
be evenly reflected by the brilliant surface, and all the preceding work would be ruined. No lathes are used for the work;
gentle rubbing by hand is the only process employed. This
grinding is accomplished so slowly that an hour's work scarcely
leaves any perceptible impression. As the surface day by day
becomes finer, pumice of softer and smoother quality is chosen,
and the final pieces used are soft as silk. After the pumice,
there follows more rubbing with smooth-faced stone and
horn, and finally with oxide of iron and rouge, which polishes
the surface to the lustre of a lens.

Namikawa then makes his final inspection of the vase,
though every day of its growth it has been under his watchful
eye, and if pronounced perfect and worthy of bearing his name,
it passes on to the silversmith for the addition of its metal
rim round the base and lip, and to have the engraved name-
plate attached to the base. On its return it is wrapped in
silk and yellow cheese-cloth, and consigned to the cabinet
in his house—not to remain there long, however, for it soon
passes into the hands of some travelling connoisseur.

One end of the room was shelved for the reception of the
bronze and silver vases that are used as foundation for the

enamel-work, and for some hundreds of bottles filled with mineral powders of every shade and colour. These were the materials for the enamel. The intimate knowledge of these powders can only be obtained by years of experiment and study, for the colours change completely when in a state of fusion. Not only must the artist know the shade of colour he desires, but how ultimately to obtain that shade by using a powder of a totally different hue.

After inspecting the workshop I was shown the firing-room, and here, too, everything was clean and neat. Namikawa himself attends to the firing—perhaps the most important part of the whole process, for on it depends the success or failure of all the work preceding it. Any error in the degree of heat might ruin all. On the fusing depend not only the proper setting and colour of the enamel, but also the richness of lustre and freedom from air-holes in its surface.

I learnt that some colours present much greater difficulties than others to fuse successfully, and that large monochrome surfaces require more skill than small cloisons. I was shown one piece, of which the design was a maple-tree in autumn tints on a yellow ground; the grading of the colour and the veining on the leaves were exquisite, and had taken many days of care to prepare for the final firing and polishing. Apparently it would be well worthy of a place in the cabinet; but as the pumice ground the surface down, and the details became clearer day by day, unsightly marks began to appear, and it had emerged from the kiln, not beautified, but marred and ruined. Thus it is that the finest specimens of cloisonné are so dear. The purchaser of the ultimate perfect piece must needs pay also for those ruined in the endeavour to produce it.

Namikawa's artists do not work by set hours, but only when the inspiration and desire for work is upon them. I have seldom, however, during my dozen or so visits, found a vacant place at the tables in the workroom. He has a name-sake in Tokyo—a cloisonné-maker no less famous than himself, but no relation. The Tokyo Namikawa makes the decorations bestowed by Imperial favour, of which the Order of the Rising

Sun is the most perfect specimen of enamel-work in the world, and—I have it on the authority of a well-known Piccadilly jeweller—quite impossible to duplicate in England.

But the Tokyo Namikawa withdraws the wiring from his pieces, thus producing an impressionist effect, for the enamels run together slightly in the fusing. Beautiful as the results obtained are, they have more the appearance of ceramic work, and should be regarded as an entirely separate art—as indeed the inventor justly claims for them.

CHAPTER XV

UJI AND THE FIREFLIES

TEA, as everybody knows, is the national beverage of Japan, though of late years beer is running it pretty close for first place in popular favour. Price is against the latter, however, and as long as tea can be produced of any grade and quality to suit any purse and palate there is little danger of its supremacy being seriously assailed, even though breweries are fast becoming as conspicuous features in certain cities as are tea plantations in certain rural districts. The popular palate, however, must be ruled by the popular purse; and the Japanese purse is larger in dimensions than in resources.

Japanese beer costs sixpence a bottle, whereas, even at the railway stations, tea may be bought for three sen (three farthings) a pot—including the pot and a cup as well. This, it must be admitted, is not an exorbitant sum. Where the potter's profit for "thumping his wet clay" comes in at this price it is difficult to see. As for the infusion which such a pot contains—ah well! I would not be guilty of betraying our friends the Japanese. Sufficient let it be to say that tea may be purchased in Japan for fifteen shillings per pound; a like quantity may also be bought for the sum of fifteen farthings; and it is not the most expensive variety that is vended on the trains.

The country round about Uji is the most famous tea-growing district in Japan; every hill-side near the little town is covered with the most valuable of all Far Eastern shrubs. At the end of April, and during the early part of May, when the "first picking" of the leaves takes place, the country-side presents a most extraordinary appearance, entire hill-sides being completely covered in with grass matting to preserve

R   243

the delicate young shoots from injury by the heat of the sun. The tenderest leaves of the new shoots produce the choicest tea. Only the wealthy classes, however, can afford it, as it commands a high price: as much as thirty shillings per pound is no uncommon figure realised for the very limited quantity of this quality. After this delicate growth is gathered, the bushes are picked over many times for gradually cheapening grades, until the final picking yields little else but coarse, hard leaves and tough stems. The shrubs are then permitted to rest for a month, when the "second picking" takes place. Sometimes there is a "third picking," but neither of these crops produces the superfine quality given by the first picking of the first crop.

The tea-bushes are grown in rows; if on a slope the hill-side is terraced. The shrubs are not allowed to attain a greater height than three or four feet, though some of them, it is said, are double centenarians. Vigorous pruning, as well as the stripping of the leaves, keeps the bushes dwarfed.

In the illustration the terraced hill-sides are covered with tea-bushes, whilst the valley below, divided up into small fields from which the barley crop has just been harvested, is flooded with water for the reception of the rice shoots.

The barley is cut in May; the fields are then dug up to a depth of eighteen inches, and flooded with water from an intricate irrigation system which turns them into soft mud. The mud is then strewn with manure and lime, and worked over and over again until it is of the consistency of slime, when it is carefully levelled, and flooded with running water to a depth of two or three inches. The best rice is grown where the water well covers the mud, and this necessitates much skill in arranging the irrigation channels so that a limited quantity of water may do duty for a large area. To facilitate this the fields are networked with earth dams, splitting them up into small divisions, from which the water, regulated so as to cover the surface thoroughly, trickles to the next lower division, and so on, until a whole hill-side may be covered with slowly moving sheets of water.

The manuring of the ground—and manuring is a necessity, for no sooner is one crop out than another goes in, and this has been going on for centuries—is what enables Japanese cities to dispense entirely with a sewerage system. The sewage of the city is nightly, and even daily, carted from the towns to the surrounding rural districts. The carts are drawn by human labour, and leave an aroma in their wake—to which the native olfactory nerves seem to be proof, but which to the sensitive European robs travelling in the country districts of Japan of much of its pleasure.

The rice is sown broadcast in small beds in April. In June the young shoots are transplanted to the mud fields in rows, about a foot apart each way, some four or five shoots being pricked into each hole. This is very rapidly done, and at this season the rice-fields are busy with men and women working nearly knee-deep in the mud. In some districts strings are used as guides to keep the rows even; in others these are dispensed with, and it is quite remarkable how uniformly the rows are planted by labourers working without this guide. Whichever way you look across a well-planted Japanese rice-field the lines are straight—in true quincunx formation.

When the summer comes with its grateful heat the sprouts spread out and the whole field becomes vivid green; as the shoots grow higher the separating divisions of the fields are lost to view, and a rice-grown valley seen from a short distance appears as smooth and even as if covered with velvet turf. The measure of heat given out by the summer sun regulates the harvest season. In an average year the crop is reaped in October; but after a cool and rainy summer it may be November before it is cut. One year—when the whole summer had been almost one continuous downpour of chilly rain—I saw hundreds of acres of rice uncut at the end of November. There had not been sufficient sun to bring the grain to the "dough," let alone ripen it, and the crop in many districts was not worth the cutting, and was of more value to be turned under again as fertiliser for the ensuing barley-crop.

Such years bring terrible distress, for the rice-crop is the staple wealth of the country. Japanese rice is the finest the earth produces, as well it should be, seeing the extraordinary attention that it gets. I have even seen peasants carefully going over the crop with a lantern in the dead of night, and with a horsehair switch brushing away the insects. But rice is seldom eaten by the poorer classes. Barley and millet are their staff of life. The rice they produce is far too valuable for their own consumption, and most of it is exported, chiefly to China, where it is esteemed as a luxury.

In late autumn the roads through every rice district in Japan are hedged with sheaves of rice, and before every farm-house the women-folk are busy with the flails. No modern threshing machinery is known here, and even if it were it would be of little avail, for each individual's crop is small and his labour of little worth. The time is far distant yet when it will be cheaper for the Japanese farmer to invest his savings in costly machines rather than to thresh his crops by the hands of the family he rears. Flails of the most primitive type are used, and heading is done by pulling the stalks, in handfuls, through large iron combs, which tear off the ears, leaving the straw to be applied to a hundred domestic purposes, or sold for use in various arts. Barley is not sown in Japan as we sow it, broadcast or in drills, but in carefully-tended, deeply-worked, hilled-up rows—as we grow potatoes. A Japanese barley-crop is a very symmetrical and beautiful sight, and furnishes abundant proof of the amount of time the peasantry give to work which produces but a small return.

Uji, however, is famous for a prettier sight than any of its farming scenes.

In the June evenings special trains run from Kyoto and Osaka crowded with visitors to see the fireflies on the Uji river which gather in prodigious numbers and engage in combat. A popular legend affirms that the insects are the ghosts of the Taira and Minamoto soldiers who perished at Dan-no-oura; and that the encounter is fought over again by the warriors in their insect shapes on every anniversary

of the historic conflict. It is called Hotaru Kassen, or the
" Firefly Battle."

The battle takes place, however, many times during the
month of June, and one evening I went to see it with some
Japanese friends. We engaged a boat, and as we proceeded to
a likely spot for the conflict there were thousands of fireflies
blinking among the trees and over the river. These, my friends
assured me, were gathering for the fray, which would surely
begin as the darkness grew deeper.

Many boats besides ours were out on the river, and the
twang of samisens rang over the water, giving just the Japanese
flavour to the evening to make it perfect, until a youth in a
boat near by, doubtless inspired by the romance in the air,
the sweet scent of the pines, and the glimmer of the fireflies,
burst forth into song—or what was doubtless intended for a
song. It was one of those wailing Japanese ballads, half soprano,
half falsetto, and had it been intended for a music-hall imitation of a tom-cat on the tiles, would have been a clever
performance; but as a song the effort seemed to me deserving
of less emphatic commendation. I was assured, however, by
my friends that the singer's voice was an unusually good one.
How different are the standpoints of East and West in such
matters! One has to suffer such hardships occasionally in
Japan; happily, there are many compensations for what must
be endured from the native vocal propensities.

We had chosen a most favourable evening for our visit.
There was no moon, and even the sky was cloudy, so that it
was very dark; there was not a breath of wind, and the glen
was hot and sultry.

As the night fell the fireflies rapidly increased in numbers,
reminding me vividly of a remarkable entomological phenomenon which I had seen a few years before in Java. Trains
do not run after dark in the Dutch colony. One must therefore
break the journey from Batavia to Sourabaya at a place called
Maos, where all trains lie up for the night. As we descended
from the hills to the swamps in the midst of which the town
is situated, day quickly gave way to night, and with the advent

of darkness fireflies commenced to appear. At first they came
in twos and threes, then in scores, then by hundreds and
thousands, and finally by untold millions. The sight was of
bewildering beauty. The whole night seemed to be filled with
showers of sparks—as I have seen them fly upwards when the
roof of a burning building fell into the flames—and the rice-
fields were illuminated by the glare for a mile on either side
of the train. At times a vast swarm of the tiny creatures would,
with one accord, flash their lights in unison. One moment all
would be black as pitch, the next a veritable blaze of fire would
burst out. This would be continued for some seconds. Then,
as if at the word of command, all would go as they pleased,
only to line up into unison again a little later. What instinct
is it that guides them? I have remarked precisely the same
unity among myriads of frogs croaking in a marsh. At a
moment's notice all the thousands of throats would cease their
song as if at some preconcerted signal; then every voice of
the chorus would burst out again almost at the same instant.

This spirit of unity was amongst the Uji fireflies, too.
Vast battalions of them had gathered by eleven o'clock and
the battle was at its height. The intermittent flashes were
controlled with the same spontaneous accord as I had seen
in Java. The insects congregated by thousands, and blazed
forth in concert. Then they gathered in vast opposing forces
and hurled themselves against each other.

It was a wondrous spectacle as the fiery insect waves
surged together, and after each clash the river sparkled with
the intermittent glow-lights of the fallen wounded. The dead
and dying were gobbled up by the fish, which must have had
a sumptuous meal that night, and reinforcements rushed in
from all sides to fill the gaps in the ranks.

For an hour the battle waged, until, with common accord,
the decimated armies dispersed, scattering to all the points
of the compass. This was the signal for the assembled spectators
to scatter to the railway-station or to their lodgings.

THE KOBUKUJI PAGODA

CHAPTER XVI

NARA—THE HEART OF OLD JAPAN

A JAPANESE proverb says, "Never use the word 'magnificent' till you have seen Nikko." They should have added, "Nor the word 'peaceful' till you have been to Nara."

Nara is the very heart of old Japan. The capital, which in ancient times was removed to a new site on the death of each Mikado—but was always situated somewhere in the provinces of Yamato, Yamashiro, or Settsu—came to its first permanent stop at Nara in A.D. 709, and Nara continued to be the seat of government until the Court was moved to Kyoto in 784. At that time, we are told, the city was ten times larger than at present. But though it is nearly twelve hundred years since Nara's glory departed, the passing centuries have been reverent and gentle. They have cherished the city's environs and the monuments embosomed in them, instead of harming them, and they have clothed them with the sweet serenity of honourable old age. For miles around Nara is haunted with the ghosts of the old prosperous days—ghosts as thickly cloaked with history as they are now overgrown with moss and lichens.

As one leaves the railway station (the very name of such a thing sounds almost sacrilege here) the eye is arrested by a stately pagoda standing on an eminence in the grounds of Kōbukuji temple. It completely dominates the landscape with its tiers of dark-grey roofs standing out in contrast to the cedar-clad mountains beyond it.

To the Japanese—who are very fond of embodying abstruse and abstract ideas into concrete forms—a five-storied pagoda is emblematical of the emptiness of life. Five is a mystic number. The pagoda has five stories. The universe has five elements. The body has five senses (which are, however, to

the Japanese mind, enclosed in a sixth sense—the body itself).
Everything in the world is composed out of one or more of
the five elements—fire, earth, water, air, and ether. The
human body especially is a combination of these elements,
to which, when life is extinct, the body returns. Thus does
the pagoda typify the instability of all earthly forms. The
body, being but worthless, temporary trash, should be re-
solutely combated and mortified, and care given only to the
soul. All this and more is borne to the Japanese mind by a
five-storied pagoda.

The Kōbukuji pagoda overlooks a pond called Sarasawa-
no-iké, about which there is, of course, a legend. There was
once a lovely maiden, who, though beloved by all the gentlemen of the Court, rejected all their offers, as she had eyes for
the Mikado alone. For a time she found favour in his sight,
but "the heart of man is fickle as the April weather," the
Japanese say, and the Mikado's heart was after all but a mortal
one, though it pulsed with the blood of gods. He neglected his
beautiful mistress, until she, unable to endure his indifference
longer, stole out of the palace one night and drowned herself
in the garden lake. Her spirit still haunts its shores on dark
nights, and you can hear her sighs as the breezes play softly
in the trembling osiers round her grave.

There are many famous temples at Nara, but it is Kasuga-
no-miya, one of the most beautiful old Shinto shrines in Japan,
which draws many thousands of pilgrims here annually.
Kasuga lies deep in the heart of a fine old park. To reach it
one must go through the great vermilion torii, which forms
the park gate, and proceed for well-nigh a mile along a gravelled
avenue of lofty cryptomeria-trees. As soon as rikisha wheels
are heard, deer come bounding out of the bracken and turfy
shades from every side, to beg with great, soft, appealing eyes
for a few of the barley-cakes which comely little country
musumés sell at stalls along the wayside. Long immunity from
molestation has made the gentle creatures very friendly, and
they will nibble from one's hand, or even thrust their noses
deep into one's pockets, searching for some tasty morsel.

Deer are, of course, quite in harmony with English ideas of such places; but an exceedingly charming and purely Japanese feature of this avenue is the great number of old stone lanterns among the trees. They are votive offerings to the temple from wealthy followers of the faith—many of them the gifts of Daimyos—and their numbers are not to be summed in dozens, nor yet in scores nor hundreds; in thousands alone can their aggregate be found. In places they stand so close together as almost to touch each other, and in ranks of many rows. These ishi-doro, thickly splotched with moss and lichens, are the most decorative ornaments imaginable, with the sunlight filtering through the branches overhead and forming soft symphonies of light and shade about them. But their virtue as dispellers of gloom is far outweighed, as is intended, by their fine artistic effect. They are not designed for service, except on very special occasions, and are only lighted for the yearly festival, or when some wealthy visitor makes a substantial donation for the purpose; even then it can scarcely be possible to light them all.

Never having been at Nara on the occasion of its annual matsuri, the 17th December, and as no Midas has appeared during any of my visits, I have not seen the lanterns lighted, much to my regret. I found, however, that several dozens of them were lit each night beside the main gates of the temple when the weather was fair. Small saucers of oil, with floating wicks, were placed in them, and when the wicks were lighted and the little wooden frames—covered with rice-paper to shield the flame—were in place, each lantern shed a soft mysterious glimmer all around it.

The atmosphere of peace and restfulness that encompasses Nara comes to a focus at the temple of Kasuga. It is the peace of many centuries. In A.D. 767 the temple was founded and dedicated to Kamatari, the ancestor of the Fujiwara family, which rose to be the most illustrious in Japan. The picturesqueness of the temple buildings, and the beauty of their surroundings, make a deeper and stronger appeal than their mere association with this great name. The lofty

cryptomerias rear their heads highest here, and among the
brown shades of their mossy, gravelled aisles great splashes
of white and vivid colour are painted into the picture with
grand effect.   These are the gateways and pavilions of the
temple, finished in snowy white and vermilion.

Massive roofs of thatch, a yard thick, crown all the
buildings, and every colonnade, gallery, and courtyard is kept
as fresh and clean as ever it was a thousand years ago.

It is said that all the temple buildings are demolished, and
rebuilt exactly as before, every twenty years—like the temples
of the Shinto Mecca, Isé—a practice which has been adhered
to ever since their foundation.   They are, therefore, incom-
parably more beautiful now than they ever could have been
in the zenith of Nara's history; for Time has worked marvels
in their surroundings, and, with the assistance of his handmaid
Nature, has enveloped them with an atmosphere of repose
and beauty indescribable.   One cannot help but feel that this
is hallowed ground; the very air is heavy with the odour
of sanctity.

Giant wistaria vines have crept to the very utmost branches
of the trees, and in May the tall cedars themselves seem to burst
forth into clusters of drooping purple blooms.   Through many
an opening in the floral arches overhead the sun throws long
shafts of light, which touch the pendent blossoms, and then,
glancing downwards, melt moss and gravel into golden pools,
or, searching out some spot on the brilliant lacquer, make it
glow with ruddy fire as the great orb himself glows at daybreak.

The deer roam undisturbed about the mossy, lanterned
avenues, and form charming pictures as they stand framed in
the burning lines of some vermilion gateway.   Fearing no
rebuffs, they even wander into the temple courtyards to be
petted by the little daughters of the priests, whose duty it is
to go through the stately measures of the ancient religious
dance, kagura.   The priests are born, live out their lives, die,
and are buried in the heavily-scented shade of the towering
cryptomeria-trees, and their children succeed them to live
and die here also.

Kasuga's galleries and colonnades are hung with innumerable lanterns of carved and fretted brass and bronze. There are almost as many round its courtyards as there are ishi-doro in the gravelled avenues, and every gentle zephyr sets them swinging. When these are all lighted the temple must be an even more beautiful and wonderful sight than in the daytime.

Pilgrims are ever haunting the sacred precincts. With slow step, and eyes bright with happiness, they softly tread the avenues, kneel before every shrine, and rest at every stall to feed the deer that nose around them. With staff, broad-brimmed hat, and tinkling bell, they come to Nara from the uttermost parts of Japan, just as they flock to Fuji and every place of holy fame throughout the land.

They come alone, and they come in bands; but to one and all the visit is the attainment of a life-long desire. Most are members of some pilgrims' club, who, when the lot falls to them to undertake the pilgrimage, believe in their hearts that they have received a special call from the gods to visit them. It is easy, therefore, to explain the beatitude written on their faces and the light of happiness in their eyes.

Such a pilgrim is the old man in the picture. "Years bow his back, a staff supports his tread," yet he had come on foot nearly two hundred miles to this holy place. Poor and simple though he was, he was kind and gentle of speech, and, like his fellows all the country over, courteous and respectful. His staff and broad hat of kaia grass proclaim his mission. His kit he carries on his back, and his kindly, smiling face is a faithful index to his contented, gentle soul. At each shrine he visits he receives from the priests some little token, and the temple stamp is impressed upon some portion of his raiment. His needs are few and of the simplest, and his daily expenses, all told, aggregate but a few pence. His progress is slow, and perhaps he may be many months upon the road before he reaches home again. But what of that? He is a type of the Old Japan, and in the days gone by the time spent on a pilgrimage, as on the production of a work of art, was never considered.

In a pavilion of the Tōdaiji temple hangs the Great Bell

of Nara,[1] and Tōdaiji is also the home of the Nara Daibutsu —a prodigious image of Buddha, the largest in Japan, though not to be compared with that at Kamakura as a work of art. This image dates from A.D. 749, and was completed, under the supervision of a priest named Gyōgi, in eight castings, which are brazed together. The head, however, was melted off during a conflagration, and the present one was made to replace it towards the end of the sixteenth century.

The great edifice containing the image was rebuilt about the year 1700, but two centuries have left their mark and it now looks somewhat shaky. In this respect it differs from any other temple at Nara. One of the great pillars which support the roof has a hole in its base, and those who are able to crawl through this hole are regarded with indulgence by the deity. The task is not an easy one, and if the divine favour be sought it is well to repair here in early youth. One thinks of the camel and the needle's eye when estimating a fat man's chances of accomplishing the feat.

Colossal figures of the Deva kings stand in niches at the principal gateway, and every pilgrim as he passes chews a sheet of rice-paper to pulp and tests his favour with the gods. He spits, or throws it at one of the figures, and if it sticks it augurs well for the fulfilment of the desire.

Ni-gwatsu-dō, the "Hall of the Second Moon," is another Buddhist temple, very picturesquely situated on the side of a hill, to which it clings by means of a scaffolding of piles. Its whole front is hung with metal lanterns, and huge ishi-doro stand in the grounds below. Fine old stone stairways, flanked with more lanterns, lead up to its balconies, where the pilgrims pause to admire the panorama over the park, and the beauty of the Yamato mountains.

There are other temples and beautiful sights far too numerous to detail here. Only a bulky volume could do duty to the manifold charms of Nara.

[1] Its dimensions are given on page 199.

CHAPTER XVII

THE RAPIDS OF THE KATSURA-GAWA

ONE lovely April morning, when all the land was sweet and smiling—for Nature had donned the very fairest of her dresses and decked herself with cherry-blossoms—two friends and I started for the Katsura-gawa. Though I had shot the rapids several times, I never tired of this beautiful river and the excitement of racing down its cataracts, for the brawling narrows and peaceful reaches, with their rocky gorges and forest-clad hills, had always some fresh beauty and some new secret to reveal.

From Hozu, the starting-point, to Arashiyama, at the foot of the rapids, is a distance of about thirteen miles, which is usually accomplished in an hour and a half if there is a fair river running. When the water rises above a certain mark at Hozu nothing will tempt the boatmen to essay the journey. On the other hand, if the river be too low much of the excitement of the trip is missing. If, however, one chooses a day when the water is just below the danger-point, even the most adventurous spirits will not complain of lack of excitement.

On the present trip the river was above normal, rather high than low. We had made all arrangements in advance, and when we reached Hozu we found the boat ready, and in charge of my favourite sendo, Naojiro, one of the finest boatmen in Japan—a splendid athletic fellow, lithe and active as a panther, whose honest, sunburnt face was always wreathed in smiles.

The boat was flat-bottomed, about thirty feet long, six feet wide, and a yard deep, with three thwarts to brace its straight sides. These Japanese river-boats are very flexible and frail-looking, but their staunchness is remarkable. They only draw two inches when empty, and about four when half a dozen people are on board; and when going over rough water the flat bottom yields and bends to the waves, until it seems the planks must surely open up and the craft be swamped. It is essential that the boats should be thus pliant; if built rigid they would speedily be buffeted to pieces by the constant bumping on the water.

Our crew consisted of four men, besides Naojiro, two of whom rowed with short sculls on the starboard side, and one on the port, whilst the fourth steered with a long yulo at the stern.

For the first mile the river is wide and the current slow. As we pushed out into mid-stream in bright sunshine, which was almost insufferably warm for the time of year, the limpid water was too tempting to be resisted, and a simultaneous and overpowering desire seized upon us. We looked at the crystal water and then at each other. There was no need for words. The wish was parent to the act. Bidding the boatmen go easy, we quickly stripped to the buff, and plunged headlong into the cool green depths. For half a mile we swam beside the boat, till swirling eddies began to appear upon the surface of the water, and the banks seemed to be rushing past as they closed in and steepened and the river narrowed for the first rapid. We much wanted to swim this first rapid, as it is an easy one, but the men declared they would be unable to stop the impetus of the boat after passing it, and we should be carried down the second race, which was too rough to attempt to swim. So, much reluctant, we had to get on board again—a feat which we found anything but easy to accomplish, and quite impossible without a helping hand, at the rate we were being borne along.

One of the men now took up his position in the bow, with a long bamboo pole to push the craft from any rock that might threaten; and the rowers rested on their oars as the boat slipped down the narrow, with only an occasional touch of the helmsman's yulo to guide it.

The gentle, smiling stream on whose placid bosom we had started now became a thing of moods. It danced and gurgled

with glee; then for a few brief moments it shrank back into itself, as if startled at its own audacity, and, hugging the overhanging rocks, became Nature's looking-glass, and mirrored snowy clouds, and beetling crags, and woodland foliage in its depths. It was but the transitory humour of a moment. The mood quickly changed again; the waters grew troubled and restless, and, lashing themselves into a passion, dashed in impotent rage against the rocks. Then they calmed once more and purred with pleasure, and the sun beat down with scorching power into the stilly glen, and the scenery grew weirdly beautiful—like that of old Chinese paintings.

But a distant murmur marked the approach of another change of mood. The murmur became a growl, and then an angry roar of fury, as the stream took the boat into its arms and drew it along with irresistible power. It was Fudo-no-taki, the "God-of-Wisdom Fall," that we were approaching, one of the finest of all the rapids—a long, narrow incline, about eight yards wide and a hundred yards in length, down which the river, gathering all its waters together, shoots with terrific force.

Naojiro now took the bow position, and, at his word, the rowers shipped their oars, and the helmsman, with a dip of his yulo, sent the boat straight for the curling vortex that rolled over the brink of the torrent.

In a twinkling we were dashing down the foaming chute at dizzy speed, the thin, pliant bottom of the boat rising and falling in undulations from stem to stern as it beat upon the waves. At the end of this watery slope there is a level reach, and as the descending flood meets it, is tossed in a great wave into the air. Over this the boat leapt, with the impulse it had gained, all quivering and trembling like a living thing, and well drenching us all with spray as the prow dug deep into the foam. With another bound it leapt into the smooth water beyond, and we drifted quietly along, amidst glorious scenery with pine and maple forests to the mountain-tops.

After a series of lesser rapids we came to Koya-no-taki, the "Hut Fall," with a great boulder in the middle of a horse-shoe curve, and a drop of five feet where the water sweeps over a submerged shelf of rock.

The now maddened river seethed and roared, and no other sound could be heard for the thunder of its waters, as straight towards the fall we flew. The captain never glanced behind him; he knew his men too well. Each was ready at his post, with pole poised in hand, and each knew the spot for which to aim. It seemed we must inevitably be dashed to pieces as the boulder raced towards us, but, just as the crash was imminent, Naojiro's pole flew out into a tiny hole in the slippery boulder's side. Simultaneously three other poles darted out as well. There was a jerk, a momentary vision of four figures putting forth their utmost strength and bending with all their strength against the rock, and the swirling waters rose level with the starboard gunwale, as for an instant our speed was checked, and the boiling current banked up against the boat. But it was only for a moment. The helmsman swung the stern round, and the great ungainly craft, grazing the boulder as it did so, took the curve and sprang over the waterfall like a fish.

It is wonderful how skilfully these Japanese boatmen dodge these death-traps. A fraction of a second's hesitation at such a place, and the boat would be broadside to the stream and dashed against some rock and overturned, and the strongest swimmer's skill could avail him little here.

At critical places all down the river, a keen observer may notice little niches in the rocks, just large enough to admit the top of a bamboo pole. These are not made by hand, but, incredible as it may seem, are worn by the poles themselves, by centuries of use in log rafting and taking merchandise down the river. They bear testimony to the necessity of gauging the distance to an inch in order to navigate a difficult place in safety.

Rapid after rapid followed in quick succession—Takase-no-taki, the "High Rapid," in the midst of lovely scenery; Shishi-no-kuchi-no-taki, the "Lion's-Mouth Fall"; and Nerito, named after the famous whirlpool at the entrance to the Inland Sea. Nerito is the most spectacular of all. It is a short rapid, but it has two difficult curves with rocky walls between which the roaring river sweeps at tremendous speed.

Our boat hesitated for an instant on the rounded lip of green water at the top of the fall, and then plunged for the precipitous wall on the left at such speed that this time it seemed no power could save us. But Naojiro's clever hand was ready, and his eye was focussed on a certain spot. Out shot his poised bamboo at the critical moment straight into a little crevice, and throwing his weight on to the pole, he sheered off the bow from the rock, and the boat went sweeping past the precipice, to be caught into the vortex again so easily that we loudly cheered him for such masterly handling of his craft. He turned round for a moment to show his good-natured, sunburnt face beaming with pleasure at our appreciation of his skill, as he thanked us "Domo arigato."

These boatmen do their work so unostentatiously and skilfully that it seems to be quite easy. What difficult feat when performed by an expert does not seem easy to the uninitiated? But Naojiro told me that he dared not let his attention wander for a second in such places, as if he slipped, or missed his mark, the boat would immediately be wrecked.

We passed many boats being towed up-stream, closely hugging the bank, with the trackers straining at the tow-ropes just as Hokusai painted them nearly a century ago. Again, some lonely fisherman standing on a jutting rock, with his straw coat thrown about him to protect him from the sun, and a broad hat of reeds on his head, was another Hokusai study. When one sees these quaint figures of rustic Japan in the flesh, one realises how true to life was the work of the old master.

The scenery became more beautiful still as we neared the journey's end. In the forests that clothed the mountain-sides cherry-trees in blossom were lovely colour-spots everywhere, and when the Kiyotaki came bounding and dancing to the parent river between rocky precipices—to which old bristling pine-trees clung tenaciously—we had to bid the boatmen stop for awhile that we might more leisurely absorb the beauty of it all. At the meeting of the waters a lofty bridge

s

leaps from cliff to cliff across the foaming tributary—a scene immortalised in art by Hiroshigé in one of his most famous paintings. After feasting our eyes long on this beautiful scene, we pushed off again and glided among tiny islets, and the river, expanding wide, became peaceful and almost still—as if the worn-out waters rested after the torments they had suffered.

We seemed to be floating on some mythical stream that flowed through Fields Elysian—where storms never raged, and winter's blighting hand never robbed the forests of their springtime beauty; and where the blessed might find rest and spend all Eternity drifting under the fragrant pine-trees, or basking in the sunshine by waters beautiful and musical as the fairest streams of Arcadia.

It was Arashiyama, beloved of poets and painters—one of the fairest spots in this land that Nature adorned when in the kindest of her moods. The mountain-side was pink and green with cherry-blossoms and pine and maple trees that strove to hide each other; and in the emerald river great trout sported among the blossoms reflected in its depths. Red old firs leant over the water, stooping to the mirror below them; and framed among the cherry-trees were dainty tea-houses with broad verandas, where lovers of the beautiful come and sit all day and feast their eyes on the sumptuous repast which Nature has provided.

In boats, yuloed lazily along by old sendos who had spent their lives upon the river, pleasure-parties, with faces uplifted, were gazing in wonder and rapture at the harmony of pink and green above them. Other pleasure-seekers were rambling along the avenued river-sides, and the twanging of samisens in the tea-houses told us that some of the nature-lovers were enjoying their æsthetic revels in the society of the merry geisha.

At Saga, a village on the eastern bank, we paid off our boatmen, and never did we pay money more willingly for any excursion in Japan. Here a row of restaurants faces the river, and a slender wooden bridge crosses it. Saga's one street is a bazaar of shops for the sale of walking-sticks and household

A GLEN ON THE KATSURA·GAWA

ornaments made of cherry-wood, and beautiful stones from the river. Stones of good shape, from celebrated places, are much sought after by the Japanese, who esteem such natural articles highly; for specimens resembling some well-known island, or famous rock, high prices can be obtained. I have seen a stone, well covered with a much-admired kind of moss, in a dealer's window in Tokyo, for which a hundred yen (ten pounds) was asked—and it was not more than a foot in length. At Saga, however, beautiful specimens from the river may be purchased for a few shillings.

Once I was invited by the courteous manager of the Miyako Hotel to accompany him in a trip *up* the river. This is even more interesting and exciting than the down-stream journey, for one has plenty of time to admire the scenery; moreover, the races and rapids—which the boat slips down so easily— present quite a different aspect when one is being towed slowly and laboriously up them.

We had my favourite crew, with Naojiro at the bow, and one extra man to tow, making six all told. No steersman was necessary, as the captain kept the boat clear of the rocks with his bamboo pole. The towing-lines varied in length from seventy to a hundred feet, so that each man had plenty of room to himself without interfering with the others.

It was May, and the azaleas, which covered many of the hill-sides, were a lovely contrast to the deep green of the woods. In the depths of the gorge the heat was scorching, and the trackers, stripped of everything save straw sandals and loin-cloths, resembled ivory carvings as their sleek bodies shone in the sun. With the agility of mountain-goats they leapt from rock to rock; but, though they put forth all their strength into the harness round their lusty chests, their clean-cut limbs never bulged with ugly knots of muscle.

At almost every touch of Naojiro's pole, at difficult places, it fitted into one of the little holes before referred to; and from time to time, when some rocky weir stood barrier before them, the trackers hauled in the ropes and crossed in the boat to the opposite shore. At one place they all came

aboard and took to the poles, with ourselves lending a hand to
help; but our united strength did not avail to keep the bow
to the stream, and the current, whirling the light craft round,
swept it broadside along towards a great boulder in the centre
of the river.

Here the amazing alertness of the men was manifested in
a thrilling manner. It was quite an unexpected incident, due
to the fact that the boat drew so much water, as, including my
camera-coolies, there were eleven people in it—an altogether
unprecedented number in taking a boat up the river. The
current swung us round so quickly, once the boat's head lost
the stream, that the peril was on us almost before we saw it.
But Naojiro saw, and gave a shout of warning, and in a twinkling all were on the side where danger threatened. Every pole
struck at once, and bent almost to the breaking point as the
men threw their weight and strength against the boulder,
round which the water rose high and boiled in baffled fury.
It was a breathless moment—but moment only, for the impact
was avoided, and we swept past the great stone, and well clear
of it, to safety; but admiration filled us at the skill these
sterling fellows had shown. Had we struck, nothing could
have prevented our undoing, for the current there was a good
twelve knots. We all got out, except the captain, and scrambled
over the rocks to the quiet water above this place, and the
boat, freed from our weight, was then easily pulled up without
more ado.

Then came Koya-no-taki, where the five-foot waterfall
bars the way. We thought it impossible to surmount this
formidable obstacle; but Naojiro only smiled and called to
his minions to haul in closer on the lines. Bracing his feet
against the starboard side and his pole against the rock, and
bending his supple body with all his strength of sinew to
the task, he gave a word of command to the trackers, who
pulled together with a will, lifting the prow up the watery
wall as if some unseen power below impelled it, and we
slid slowly to the higher level, scarcely shipping more than a
bucket of water in doing so.

At Nerito the straining trackers went on all-fours, gripping the rocks with hands and toes, and the torrent rose to the gunwale on either side. It seemed incredible that five men could pull so large and heavy a boat up such a swirling flood; but inch by inch they did it, and when, at length, we floated in the smooth green water at the top, and looked back on the roaring tumult, the feat seemed more wonderful still.

Once I attempted the up-stream journey with a less skilful crew and a smaller boat, for my favourites were engaged. At Koya-no-taki we met disaster. As he gave the word of command to pull, the captain missed his mark and sent the bow under the fall, nearly swamping us. At our shouts the trackers dropped the ropes, and the boat, full to the thwarts, was carried back with great force against a rock, which stove the top planks in for ten feet on one side. Fortunately, this rapid is a short one, and we drifted to shore in the reach below without further harm.

The men who pilot tourists down are all masters of their craft, and take pride in the fact that they have never lost a visitor's life. They dare not risk the revenue they get by this occupation, from both foreigners and Japanese, by entrusting the boats to unskilful hands. The men I had engaged on the day of this adventure were not master-hands, and told me so at the outset; but they were the only men available, as I had come without notice, and it is quite an unusual thing for any one to go *up* the rapids.

In these rugged volcanic islands every river is a torrent, and the men who make a living on them, and the fishermen around the coasts, are the class from which Japan recruits her tars. For agility, resource, and skill in their calling, I know no finer type of men in all the world. The boatmen of the Katsura-gawa are as picturesque as the scenes amidst which they labour are beautiful. Any visitor to Kyoto who omits to take this lovely trip misses some of the finest scenery, some of the most interesting people, and one of the most enjoyable and exhilarating experiences to be had in all Japan.

CHAPTER XVIII

HIKŌNÉ AND ITS CASTLE

THE province of Ōmi, one of the most celebrated in Japan, is equally renowned for the beauty of its scenery as for the web of historical memories and legend with which it is interwoven from end to end. Biwa-Ko, the largest of Japanese lakes, lies in its heart, filling about one-fifth of the whole province with its waters. Its length is thirty-six miles, thrice its greatest width, and the depth in places is said to be about fifty fathoms.

This is the lake which, according to tradition, fills the great depression that appeared in the earth during a violent seismic disturbance one night in the year 286 B.C., when Fuji-san burst upwards from the plains of Suruga. Tradition or fact, there is nothing geologically illogical about such an event in this volcanic-studded land, where the thin crust covering the eternal fires so frequently trembles; and it is only to be expected that a sheet of water which claims its origin in such an occurrence should have lived up to the remarkable circumstances of its birth by enshrining itself in beauty and legend. Some of the legends are to be found in most books on Japan; but about one of the most charming of Biwa's beauty spots I have never found more than a few lines in any book at all. Hikōné is its name—a little town standing on the east of Biwa's shores, a place about which my memory lingers fondly.

One early summer's day as I was whirled up to the porch of the Ha-kei-tei Hotel in a rikisha I was greeted by the assembled female staff with the customary chorus of welcome, only here the welcome seemed more than usually warm and sincere. As we entered the hotel grounds I could hear the shrill voice

REFLECTIONS

of the head maid-servant—who, as at most Japanese hotels, was more remarkable for her virtues and length of service than for her good looks—calling to the younger girls, as she detected the sound of rikisha wheels on the gravel. "O Kyaku-san! O Kyaku-san!" ("An honourable guest!") she cried, and as my kurumaya dropped the shafts at the great wide doorstep, the little neisans came running from every direction, with many bows, to take my luggage.

When I had removed my boots—for one never enters a Japanese native style hotel with boots on—one of the neisans led me to my room. As we passed along a dark corridor I had the misfortune to bump my head against a beam in its low ceiling. This mishap proved altogether too much for the composure of the little maid. She leaned against the wall, laughing till the tears filled her eyes, and the whole establishment, coming to see what was the matter, and finding me ruefully rubbing my pate, laughed as well. The little incident put us all on good terms at once, and every member of the domestic staff was soon my friend; and when one makes friends with the staff at a Japanese inn, they in turn do everything to make one's stay as pleasant as possible.

The hotel is entrancingly situated by a miniature lake in one of the most famous gardens in Japan; and the room to which I was shown was built out over the water with a veranda on three sides of it. This ornamental sheet of water is a facsimile of Lake Biwa, all the famous sights of which are duplicated in the miniature. There is a long rustic bridge representing "The Long Bridge of Seta"; a maple-clad hill stands for the mountain Ishiyama, and another one is Hirayama—the "evening snow" on the original of which is the second of the "Eight Sights of Ōmi" in native estimation. There is even a curiously-trained pine-tree as proxy for the veteran of Karasaki—the arboreal giant of Japan, and one of the most curious trees in the world. The "Karasaki-no-matsu," on the opposite shore of Lake Biwa, is not only the greatest pine-tree in Japan, but also the most sacred. This patriarch, though now not more than forty feet high, has branches which stretch their crooked length well over a hundred feet from the old trunk. They are supported on a forest of props, and are so low that one has to duck one's head to pass under them. All holes in the trunk are made water-tight with plaster, and a roof over the broken top keeps the rain from entering and hastening decay.

The pine in the Ha-kei-tei garden is not of any great age— a mere century or two—nor is it large, but it is very picturesque. During my stay two gardeners spent the greater part of three days going over all its branches and carefully plucking out about three-fourths of its needles. This was done with a double object—to give it that spiky appearance so greatly admired by the Japanese, and also to stunt its growth. Pine trees in Japanese gardens are subjected to this treatment every two months, and to root-pruning once a year.

The Ha-kei-tei garden was a never-ending source of delight to me. I was always finding some new and lovely peep through its maple-trees, or among its islands and the bays and gulfs and outlets of its lake. Every evening carp nibbled noisily at the lily leaves, and swallows fluttered over the surface of the lake. The swallows nested under the eaves of the hotel and even inside its porches. This is considered a lucky omen. No Japanese would think of disturbing a swallow which took up its abode in his house.

Another and larger hotel—the Raku-raku-tei—has a garden adjoining, but although it also has a "lake," no fish nibble at the lily leaves, for the lake is only an imaginary one, and has no water in it. This garden is in the severest Cha-no-yu style, and the lake is simply a bed of pebbles, with islands, bridges, overhanging pines, stepping-stones, and all—everything save water, which the imagination of this highly idealistic people easily supplies.

These gardens were formerly the pleasure-grounds of one of the most powerful feudal families, whose fine old castle stands on a hill overlooking them. The last feudal lord, or Daimyo, of the Hikōné clan was Ii-Kamon-no-Kami, the sage and diplomatic noble who acted as Regent for the young

Shogun Iémochi in the troublous times preceding the Reformation. For leaving this lovely country-seat and mixing himself up in politics he paid penalty with his life; he was assassinated in front of the General Staff Office in Tokyo on the 24th March, 1860. His castle (O-shiro) is one of the very few of such edifices now remaining in Japan. Shortly after the period of Meiji was inaugurated the Japanese, disgusted with everything of their own creation, were seized with a mania for razing all such structures to the ground. The destruction of Hikōné castle had already commenced, when it so happened that the Emperor Mutsohito, being at that time on a journey to Kyoto, passed this way, and seeing what the local officials had begun to do, he commanded them to desist. Thus the old castle was rescued from the fate which threatened it, and it stands to-day one of the finest and most picturesque feudal features of Japan.

It was the custom in the old days for a Daimyo, when he found his bones ripening with years, to abdicate in favour of his son. When such an event happened at Hikōné the ex-lord retired to one of the residences, now turned into hotels, in the castle grounds. It was in one of these charming houses that I now found myself, and as I stood by the shoji of my room on the evening of my arrival I wondered if any other place in the world could be more serenely restful. I stepped out on to the veranda, and immediately great carp, which had been loafing on the muddy bottom of the lake, glided up to the surface, just below me, sticking their heads almost out of the water in the expectation of being fed.

I wandered out into the garden among the maples and stone-lanterns, and found an almost hidden path, walled in on either side with blocks of rough-quarried stone. This led to a stairway in the outer wall of the castle, the steps of which ended in Biwa lake. It was one of the most beautiful and romantic spots I have ever seen. The reeds growing far out into the shallow water were full of frogs, and the very air was ringing with their croaking. Every now and then some solitary crow, flapping his way lazily overhead, would augment this evening chorus with a few hoarse caws; and the crickets, which were just tuning up for the night, added a shrill soprano accompaniment.

Rugged, purple mountains were reflected in the lake, the surface of which was broken only by the ever-widening ripples in the wake of a boat which was approaching, whilst the sendo sang a song as he slowly yuloed it. The boat came across the foreground of the picture, and pulled up at the mossy stairway where I stood. Imagination was beginning to conjure up all sorts of possibilities about it, and the tubs with which it was laden, when a coolie came down the stairway bearing two other similar tubs on a yoke across his shoulders. Alas! my dream was over, for the aroma which insulted the air told that his burden, and the cargo of the singing boatman's craft, was manure for the rice-crops. Such is Japan! Whilst there is "so much that appeals to the eye, there is also not a little that appeals to the nose," as Professor Chamberlain archly remarks; and these rude shocks to the senses are but too common.

I turned away and wandered over towards the hill on which the castle stands. Its slopes are thickly covered with pine and maple-woods, where the hawks breed unmolested and are always soaring in the skies. At the bottom of the hill there is a broad moat banked high with sloping walls of stone. The water is much overgrown with aquatic plants, and there are many curious bamboo fish-traps in it. As I stood beside the quaint old bridge—which stretches over the moat in a single span supported by many props—watching the afterglow playing pretty tricks of colour in the water, the daylight waned away, and I heard the tramp of men-at-arms and the sound of horses' hoofs coming down the roadway from the castle. First, through the gateway and across the bridge came swift outrunners to clear the way; then at the head of the band appeared mounted knights, clad *cap-à-pie* in lacquered armour —cuirass, morion, tasses, and all—and with swords stuck in their girdles and gleaming spears butted in their stirrups. Behind them marched the foot-soldiers, clad in armour too,

A FEUDAL CASTLE, FROM THE MOAT

with bows and arrows slung across their shoulders and a pair
of swords in every belt. On they came, making the old wooden
bridge shake and echo with their tramping, and swung along
the road with swaggering air and short quick steps towards
the town. In the middle of the train was a mettlesome cob,
ridden by a noble figure of a warrior clad in vermilion lacquer
and mail, with enormous wings spreading from his helmet
and white plumes dancing between them. I knew him for the
Daimyo at a glance. It was the feudal lord of Hikōné, going
off, perchance, to make a raid upon the Daimyo of some
neighbouring province. I watched them pass along the road
and disappear into the twilight, among the leaning pine-trees
and the cloud of dust raised by their feet. When the tramping
died away in the distance I turned hotel-wards along the bank
of the beautiful old moat, and into the dust which still hung
in the air—only it was not dust at all, but a film of night-mist
rising from the water, and the Daimyo and his samurai were
but a vision, born of the reverie into which I had fallen. A
few days before, I had seen, in Kyoto, a pageant of an old-time
feudal procession which once every year leaves the Imperial
Palace and proceeds to the ancient Shinto temple of Shimo
Gamo. Each participant was clad in armour to represent a
samurai or his feudal chief; and as I stood in the twilight on
this romantic spot, imagination, responding to the surroundings, had seized the opportunity to make them the setting
for a vision of the spectacle I had lately seen.

All night long, as I lay in comfortable futons on the floor
of the old Daimyo house, I had a vague consciousness of
samurai clattering down the hill, and of fish leaping in the
moat. There was nothing unreal about the sounds, however,
for whenever I woke up—as I did several times—I heard the
carp splashing in the lake, and the rats were scurrying noisily
over the thin, resounding boards of the ceiling overhead.

The next morning I went up to the castle, and apropos of
this visit I find these lines in my notebook:

" If I only make one visit to this castle it will always remain
in my mind in connection with a crowd of hundreds of school-

children who have come to picnic for the day in the castle
grounds. They are in the charge of their teachers, and are
running all over the old courtyard and woods, shouting
with delight.

"The natives have girded their loins to do justice to the
occasion, and justice is undoubtedly being done. The cake-
man, the fruit-man, the iced-drinks-man, the air-balloon-
man, the ice-cream-man and the toy-woman—all are here.
There is also an itinerant merchant who has a number of small
tubs of different coloured sweetstuffs, and when young Japan
presents his farthing, he gets a cockle-shell heaped up with
the sweetmeat in layers of blue, red, green, yellow, and white.
There is another old fellow, old as old can be, with face as
wrinkled as the rind of a musk-melon, whose trade it is to dip
from a bowl of batter a small portion, and spread it on the face
of a sheet of bronze laid over the glowing embers of a hibachi.
He flattens the sputtering mess out with a stick, until it is as
thin as a wafer, and in an instant it is cooked. Then he takes
in his hand a lump of sticky sugar and ground rice and rolls
it out between his palms till it is four inches long; this he lays
on the cookie and rolls all up together. About these stalls
children of assorted ages, from six to sixteen, flock like moths
around a candle, and the small coin of the realm is quickly
finding its way out of the purses in the children's girdles to
the pile of copper before each vendor."

But during this, my first, and subsequent visits to Hikōné
I made more than one visit to the castle, when it was quite
deserted, and explored every nook and corner of its halls and
garrets. In one of the rooms of the keep a fine display of old
armour is preserved. Several suits that belonged to the Daimyo
are magnificent examples of the Japanese armourers' art.
They are made of many small strips of iron, coated with
vermilion lacquer and fastened together with leather thongs
and silken cords. His helmets, kabuto, have immense horns
or wings—like those on the petasus of Mercury, only much
larger—and between them hangs an enormous white plume,
which, when in use, must have fallen well below his eyes.

There are swords and spears of such workmanship and mounting as to delight the soul of any one who loves such things, and many other valuable relics of the old-time days.

The keep, or what is usually called the "castle," was never at any time the residence of the Daimyo. It was simply a stronghold to which he and his family might retreat as a last resource if driven to bay. It is constructed of uncemented stone, each block being shaped to fit exactly amongst its neighbours. Within the castle compound, near the keep, there is a belfry with a fine old bronze bell, whose tone is of the sweetest and can be heard for many miles when the air is still. The compound is protected by a deep, dry moat, between high walls, and it is crossed by drawbridges, similar to those of our own feudal times.

Enclosed within the castle precincts there were formerly many houses where the Daimyo and his retainers dwelt, but these unfortunately had been pulled down before the Emperor stopped the work of destruction. The views from some of them must have been exceedingly beautiful, for the panorama overlooking the gardens below and Lake Biwa, with its numerous islands, and away over the rice-fields to the purple mountains, is one long to be remembered.

The largest of all the Japanese feudal strongholds was Ōsaka castle, the keep and buildings of which were burnt during the revolutionary struggles in 1868. Its walls, however, remain, and can certainly claim front rank among the mural wonders of the world.

To quote from the *Letters of Will Adams*, that brave Kentish navigator—the first Englishman to live in Japan—who in all his words and actions was such a gallant gentleman: "The stones are great, of an excellent quarry, and are cut so exactly to fit the place where they are laid, that no mortar is used, but onely earth cast betweene to fill up voyd creuises if any be."

Nobody could accuse the modest sailor of exaggeration, for some of the granite blocks in the castle walls are forty feet in length and ten feet high, and are said to be eight feet thick. The moat is in proportion to the leviathan stones in the walls; it varies from 250 to 360 feet in width.

Perhaps I may be permitted here to intrude an incident that occurred at Ōsaka. I had set up my camera by the moat to make a photograph, when I noticed some soldiers watching me from the walls. They disappeared and came back again with several others; then all retreated from view. Shortly afterwards I saw a commotion by the drawbridge; an officer and a number of men engaged in a discussion were carefully observing me. The officer then gave some instructions, and a squad of men marched over the bridge and along the moat-side in my direction. When they reached me, one of them, who spoke excellent English, thus addressed me:

"You must excuse me, but I must arrest you. It is forbidden to sketch the castle."

I therefore excused him and submitted to the inevitable, and was conducted, camera, cases, and all, into the castle. There I was given to understand by a sergeant that I had committed a serious offence in attempting to photograph the walls, and on my War Office permits being examined it was pointed out that although many other fortified areas were included in my permission to use a camera, Ōsaka was omitted. As Ōsaka is only a garrison town, and possesses no fortifications, I had not thought it necessary to stipulate for its mention in my permit to photograph in certain military areas. I explained this to my interrogator. He had, however, no power to release me until another officer came, and I was detained in the guard-room for several hours—the butt for the wit of the men, whose veneer of courtesy quickly rubbed off when they found they had the whip-hand of a foreigner for the time being.

Finally an officer, quite a young man, arrived and cross-examined me. After asking my name and nationality—both of which were clearly defined in my permit—he demanded to know if I were a Russian. On my assuring him that I was not, and that my country was stated in the document which I had

handed to him, he asked me, "Are you quite sure you are not a Russian?"

I told him there was no shadow of doubt in my mind on the point; which answer evoked the further question, "Who is your father?"

Becoming a little nettled at such vacuous interrogations, I replied that he was the son of my grandfather and was a good many thousand miles away at the moment, and that I did not consider it necessary to draw him into the matter at all.

After admonishing me, as he might have scolded a child, he graciously permitted me to go. In an hour I returned to the castle, and, handing my card to the sergeant of the guard, requested him to send it in to the Commandant. This he did, and I had the pleasure of being received and entertained with wine and cigars, and afterwards being shown all over the castle enclosure by the courteous old soldier, much to the chagrin of the lieutenant who had questioned me so ridiculously, and who, it seemed, was the Commandant's aide-de-camp. Japan is no exception to other countries in respect of the officiousness of underlings.

To return, however, to Hikōné, a very favourite amusement of the Japanese "upper crust," when visiting the province of Ōmi, is to go to a spot on the shores of Lake Biwa, near where the Seiri-gawa runs into the lake, and there watch the fishermen drag a net. There is a long stretch of shingly beach, where small tea-houses are to be found. In these houses those who seek this form of diversion sit and picnic, as they watch the fishermen get out a seine net of enormous length and take it out into the lake. It requires several boats to pull it, and an hour or more to cover an area sufficient to ensure a good catch. The net is then drawn in to the shore near the tea-houses, and the party select from the spoils such fish as they desire, which are cooked and eaten on the spot.

The pleasure-seekers, whether they come to see the fishing or the castle, never fail to visit the gardens, for above everything else the Japanese love a garden. Consequently there is seldom a day when the bright kimonos of geisha cannot be seen like pretty butterflies flitting amongst the trees. In the summer evenings their laughter, their songs and the twanging of their samisens sound merrily over the lake; and as they sit, with shoji open, watching the fire-flies flashing across the water, it needs little effort of imagination to turn the gay beauties into the dainty Japanese ladies who lived here in the old-time days.

CHAPTER XIX

THE GREAT VOLCANOES, ASO-SAN AND ASAMA-YAMA

THE Japanese archipelago is undoubtedly the most active centre of the world's seismic disturbances; and little wonder, for the islands bristle with volcanoes, and seethe with solfataras and hot-springs. Few are the weeks I have spent in the capital without experiencing at least one earthquake. I have even felt several in a night, and tremors for several nights in succession. The moment a "jishin" begins, one's thoughts fly to subterranean fires, and thence—what more natural than to volcanoes?

The two most active volcanoes in Japan are Aso-san and Asama-yama. Aso-san, in the heart of the island of Kyushiu, is not only the largest active volcano in Japan, but can boast that its ancient, outer crater is the largest on the earth. Aso is, however, far from the beaten track, and so is very seldom visited, as its ascent entails a four-days journey from the distant port of Nagasaki. But Asama can easily be ascended by any good walker in a three-days absence from Tokyo; and being so accessible, as well as the highest active volcano in Japan, a good many enthusiasts make the ascent every year.

The two volcanoes are as different in appearance as they are in temperament, and neither has any pretensions to the almost perfect outline of Fuji-san. The peerless Fuji has the comely form of youth, whereas Asama is rounded with age, and Aso's original crater is now filled with the accumulated ashes of centuries. Though only a fraction of Aso's once colossal crater is now active, even that fraction is larger than any other crater in Japan. Aso is, however, an even-tempered volcano, and it is not often that its steady cloud of smoke and steam varies in volume; whereas Asama is a fretful and irritable mountain, subject to exceedingly violent outbursts. Sometimes Asama is restless for days together, and explosions occur every few hours; then it calms itself and is peaceful for many weeks before the angry mood returns.

One hot August night I started for Kumamōtō, *en route* for Aso-san. Soon after leaving Nagasaki a thunderstorm broke, and raged with truly tropical severity. For over an hour the lightning was so incessant that the train was illuminated as though by daylight. In one minute I counted over seventy flashes; this was about the average of each minute for over an hour, and the noise of the train was completely drowned in the ceaseless overlapping crashes of the thunders. As we flew past hills and valleys and rice-fields in the night, every mile of that beautiful Kyushiu country was brilliantly illumined by the flickering lightning, whilst a deluge poured from the skies such as I have not seen equalled even in the tropical rains of Java. Then the flashes became less frequent, and the scenery was revealed in a series of brilliant pictures. At one moment a village was a typical scene of night, with only a light showing here and there. Then the lights disappeared, as though extinguished, and every house, and window, and bamboo fence stood out as clearly as if in sunlight. So the wonderful play of day and night continued for a further hour, dispelling all thoughts of sleep.

Early the next morning we arrived at the historic old town of Kumamōtō, and, after settling our things at a hotel, and having breakfast, we went out to see Suisenji park—one of the most celebrated pleasure-gardens in Japan. The weather was almost unbearably hot—over 90° F. in the shade—but the park was at its fairest. Gentle little neisans invited us to take tea as we entered the gates, but we ordered shaved ice and fruit syrup instead, and lay on the turf in the shade to sip it, whilst we revelled in the lovely summer scenes around us.

There was a large but very shallow lake, with water clear as the crystal of wisdom in the forehead of Buddha. It was studded with pretty islands, covered with dwarf trees, old

stone lanterns, and summer-houses; stone and rustic bridges stretched over the water, and temples, torii, crooked pines, and banana-trees were scattered about the garden everywhere. A miniature artificial Fuji-san graced the opposite shore of the lake, and beyond it the eternal smoke cloud of the great Aso rose into the heavens. The broiling August sun glinted on the brown and azure wings of a thousand dragon-flies darting about the surface of the lake, and great carp glided over the gravel and in and out about the water-plants, in water not a dozen inches deep; whilst the air shrilled with the unceasing screams of myriads of cicadas. Scores of tiny girls and boys were paddling in the water or scampering over the grass—innocent of a stitch of clothing—making the place echo with their happy shouts of laughter. The whole scene was an idyll of innocent happiness and beauty.

At one end of this Arcadian paradise the water deepens, and here a score of boys and adult men were bathing and frolicking about the banks—as naked as the children—whilst fair and dainty promenaders of all ages walked amongst them unembarrassed, not even noticing the nudity around them.

Early the next morning we started, by basha, on the twenty-mile journey to Toshita village, from which we were to make the ascent of the great volcano. The road is a very fine one, well drained and of excellent surface, and avenued with tall cryptomeria-trees the greater part of the way. The scenery too, in places, is magnificent. Nearing Toshita the road wound along the side of a deep gorge, every yard of the steep bank of which was wonderfully terraced with rice-fields. The air was filled with the soft murmur of tiny streams that fell everywhere from terrace to terrace, until they finally leapt over the cliffs into the foaming torrent a hundred yards below. The south bank of this stream—the Shira-kawa, or "White River"—is a precipice three hundred feet in height, above which thick forests clothe the mountains to their summits. In every mile at least a dozen streams danced down the slopes, adding to the humming of the waters that filled the air, and beautiful cascades sprang from the beetling cliffs on the opposite bank to fall in clouds of rainbowed mist into the rocky gorge.

The inn at Toshita is an unpretentious place, close by the river, and one goes to sleep lulled by the music of its waters.

We were up early the next morning to have a bathe in the public hot-spring, where we found a number of villagers already tubbing. Much curiosity was evinced as I entered the plunge, which is common to both sexes, and many observations were made on my personal appearance—especially by the ladies. My smattering of the language enabled me to gather that these comments chiefly concerned the colour of my skin, and with satisfaction I noted that they took a not unfavourable tone.

At eight we started on foot for the ten-mile walk to Aso's crater, with several coolies to carry my apparatus and luggage, for we intended to traverse the mountain and continue the journey across the island of Kyushiu to Beppu, on the Bungo Channel.

It was a glorious day, but fearfully hot. At the village of Tochinōki there are many baths, fed by hot-springs, where rounded youth and shrunken age of both sexes bathe together. Two years later, when I again visited this place in March, I saw wrinkled old fellows, whose skin was like a withered apple, lying sound asleep in the water, with their heads resting on the steps, and with flat stones placed on their bellies to keep their bodies submerged. They spend the entire winter in the warm water thus, seldom, if ever, donning their clothes. The water is said to be very efficacious for rheumatism, but it seems to have evil properties as well as virtue, for several of the bathers were piebald with pink and yellow patches.

Passing through the village we came to an open rolling moor, and the great volcano loomed straight ahead of us. I wish those who believe Japan to be "a land of birds without song," as one writer has so falsely described it, could see this moor in early spring-time. When I crossed it again on my subsequent visit in March the very skies seemed to ring with celestial music, and the air trembled with the melody of a

myriad unseen larks singing at the gates of heaven. I have never heard anything to compare with this birdland concert, in the British Isles or any other land. Every few seconds a tiny speck would appear far up in the blue, and the sweet piping notes and trills of one little voice of the chorus grew clearer and clearer as the tiny owner fluttered down, down, down—at times hovering almost still in the air—till the singer was lost to view in the grass. But still the little throat pulsed and throbbed out the lay of love, as the happy little creature wooed its mate upon the nest. Only in the mating season are larks inspired to pour forth such rapturous melody as this.

That day in March was one never to be forgotten. A perfect spring morning in the hills! The very air seemed to be charged with the romance and mystery of Old Japan, and pulsated with the trilling and warbling of a thousand larks.

But in August it was a different story. The heat was getting *terrific* as we went along at a good gait over the soft, springy turf, with the serrated edge of the great ash-hills, which encircle the inner crater, far above us and beckoning us on. This moor is inside, and now forms the floor of, the ancient crater; and the mountains all round us marked the lip of the original outer rim, which is fourteen miles from brim to brim.

The geysers of Yu-no-tani now appeared ahead, sending great billows of snowy steam high into the heavens—making a beautiful contrast to the azure of the sky, the yellow of the sunburnt grass, and the deep green of the forests which surround the springs. At a distance of two miles we could hear the geysers hissing, but as we drew nearer the sound grew rapidly louder, and changed from hissing to rumbling, and then to a deep booming that made the ear-drums tingle. Finally it grew into a deafening roar that shook the earth, as we stood beside great fissures from which steam shrieked at terrific pressure. There is power enough going to waste there to run all the factories in Osaka, if it could be harnessed. From the force with which the steam was emitted it seemed as though the rocks must momentarily be rent asunder, which is probably what would happen were it not that these vents are the earth's safety-valves.

Miles of black ash-hills, which reflected the 90°-in-the-shade heat into our faces with scorching power, now had to be traversed, and our clothing was soon as wringing wet as though we had been in a river. We should certainly have welcomed a dip in one at that stage of the journey. We passed many farms and rice-fields, for the ground is very rich, and wherever there is water abundant crops are grown. It is said there are over twenty thousand people living in the villages within the original outer crater walls.

When we reached the summit of the ash-hills which form the second lip, we rested and restored our wasted tissues with lunch, whilst enjoying the grand spectacle of the crater, only three miles away, pouring volumes of smoke and steam into the cloudless skies. Fortified by food and rest, we soon disposed of the remaining distance, passed the temples at the foot of the cone, and were plodding up to the crater's brink. It behoved us to be very careful how we stepped, for the ash deposited is of so soluble a nature that the recent storm had turned it into slippery mud, and we had more than one fall and long slide in the slime before reaching the brink. The crater lip is very dangerous as the bank dips towards the edge in places, and a fall might precipitate one into the abyss. The walls are not coloured like those of lava mountains, but are black precipices of accumulated ashes, with only occasional streaks of volcanic rock. Occasionally the clouds of vapour which floated up from the great pit parted, and we could see the crater bottom, with its thousand cracks and fissures, from which the steam hissed and roared—a most fascinating and magnificent spectacle. Once the wind veered for a few moments and we were quickly enveloped in the steam, which sent us running, sliding, and tumbling to get away from the suffocating fumes that gripped us in the throat and set up paroxysms of coughing; yet I saw butterflies flying across the abyss and emerging from the noxious vapours unharmed.

There were two separate craters active within the confines

of the walls, and two inactive cones, but the aspect of the crater changes every time the volcano has a fresh outburst. The highest point of Aso-san is Taka-daké, or "Falcon's Peak," 5630 feet above the sea. There are several others nearly as high, and from the north side they give a magnificently broken appearance to the mountain, which is quite unsuspected from the west. From the town of Boju the five serrated peaks of Aso-san, with the snowy steam-clouds rising heavenwards behind them, make no little pretence to grandeur.

We stayed on the mountain till long after the setting sun had turned the clouds of steam to fiery flames; then, as the moon rose over the jagged peaks, and shone with weird beauty through the ghostly vapours, we started on the journey down to Miyaji.

Every hour of the rest of the trip across Kyushiu was full of interest. The town of Takeda is most picturesquely situated in a hollow, surrounded by high hills which are pierced by over forty tunnels to render the town accessible. Only by passing through several in succession can the town be entered. There are pretty waterfalls near here, flowing over the tops of closely-packed, upright basaltic columns, and the scenery all round the little town is singularly beautiful.

But Beppu and Kanawa, at the end of the journey, were the most interesting places of all. They are situated on the shore of the Bungo Channel, the south-west entrance to the Inland Sea.

The whole of this neighbourhood is so volcanic that hot-springs abound almost everywhere. Beppu town is filled with public bath-houses; every private house has its hot-spring, and the sea-shore is bubbling with almost boiling water. The beach was swarming with men, women, and children who scooped out hollows in the sand, and lying down in them covered themselves so that only their heads could be seen. Thus they parboil themselves for hours, and even sleep there. I joined the crowd and tried this method, but found that the water which percolated into the hole I dug was so hot that I could not stand in it—much less lie down.

At Kanawa, a village a few miles away, the crust of the earth is so impregnated with volcanic heat that almost any-where steam can be tapped by punching a hole in the ground with a crow-bar. Almost every house has a row of holes outside which are used for cooking purposes. These have to be plugged up, when not in use, to keep the sulphurous steam from entering the buildings and asphyxiating the inmates.

The most extraordinary baths in all Japan are to be seen here. After soaking in the public plunge, the people crowd— a dozen or so at a time—into caves in which the heat is terrific. In half-an-hour they creep out, covered with mud which has fallen from the roof, and stand under jets of almost ice-cold water which come from other subterranean sources. This natural Turkish bath is said to be very efficacious for the cure of rheumatism.

There are many other baths at Kanawa, some of them arranged as long troughs about fifteen inches deep and wide enough for a bather to lie in at full length. In these the bathers recline side by side. There is one trough for men and another for women, but it is quite common to see old and young of both sexes soaking alongside each other and chatting sociably together.

There are less pleasant places at Kanawa also—one of them a sputtering, boiling bog of dark-green, sulphurous slime, and another of brilliant green, boiling sulphur-water —which I was told were favourite resorts of suicides. As I gazed into these awful sloughs I thought that the terrors of life must indeed be greater than fear of death to impel that last despairing plunge.

One gloomy afternoon in October, my friend Dennis Hurley and I left for Karuizawa, which is about six hours' journey by rail from Tokyo, to visit the volcano Asama-yama.

Asama is 8280 feet high, but as the village of Karuizawa, the starting-point for the ascent, is 3279 feet above sea-level, it leaves only some 5000 feet to be climbed after leaving the train; and after all it is a climb only in name, for this volcano

A PUBLIC BATH AT KANAWA

has spread itself in such a manner that it is merely a walk of several hours up a steady incline to the top.

The railway from Tokyo follows the Nakasendo—the old mountain highway of Japan, which in feudal days connected the capital of the Mikado at Kyoto with the Shogun's capital at Yedo—but there is no scenery of any remarkable interest until the town of Myōgi is reached. At this point the line enters a mountain region of truly mystifying beauty. For several miles the famous Myōgi-san on the left is a marvellous conglomeration of beetling crags, towering Gothic peaks and cliffs which lean far out from the vertical, seeming to menace everything below them with immediately impending destruction. The whole mountain was clothed in a glorious autumn garb of every shade of red and orange, blended with brown and green; and spiky pine-trees pertinaciously clung to the most impossible of its precipices, or bristled against the sky on the uttermost and most inaccessible of its pinnacles.

From Yokugawa onwards, the steep gradient—one in fifteen—renders traction by an ordinary locomotive impossible, so a steel rack is placed between the rails, into which cog-wheels in the bed of the engine engage. This is the Abt system, similar to that used on the Gornergrat and others of the mountain railways of Switzerland.

There are twenty-six tunnels in the next three miles, and sometimes only a few score feet separate one tunnel from the next. As we passed these openings, we caught fleeting glimpses of scenery, exquisitely beautiful, with burning autumn tints climbing high up the distorted shapes of the grim volcanic rocks; and, as the sunlight waned, the jagged pinnacles and spires stood out in uncanny silhouettes against a lurid sky.

We saw Asama, the object of our visit, for a few brief moments from the train, a faint smoke issuing from the summit; but night had fallen ere we reached our destination, cold and hungry, and, though the outline of the mountain could be seen in the darkened sky, we were too intent on finding a warm room, a good meal, and a hot bath, to feel much interest in it that night.

There were no rikishas at the station, and when we had tramped the mile to the inn we found the place shut up and apparently deserted, for there are few visitors at that time of the year. Only after repeated efforts could we succeed in making ourselves heard, but when at length the door, with a great clatter, was unbarred, we were welcomed with customary courtesy and a chorus of greetings from the host and two little smiling maids. They had hastily bundled out of the beds to which they had retired for warmth, and, with much bowing, apologised for keeping us waiting outside on such a frigid night.

The warmth of the welcome, whilst cheering to the spirit, did not, however, raise the temperature of the hotel; and we went shivering to our rooms, with maledictions on ourselves and on each other for having been so foolish as to disregard the advice we had been given in Tokyo—to telegraph ahead that we were coming. But braziers were quickly filled with glowing charcoal; hot tea was brought; warm baths were prepared; and as the mercury in the thermometer on the wall went up, so did our spirits, until at length, after a boiling hot tub, we sat down to a hastily prepared but excellent meal, fully resuscitated from our six hours' incarceration and fast in that chilly train.

There is nothing of any particular interest about Karuizawa itself, though the high location and cool air make it a favourite resort for residents of Tokyo during the hot summer months. It was the mountain, however, that we had come to see, and at this season of the year we were willing enough to give all the cool airs the place could boast for a few hours of grateful sunshine. And fortune was more than kind, for the morning after our arrival was clear and still—a lovely October day. Nothing could be wished for more, so at 7 A.M. we started out with a guide, and three coolies to carry our lunch and my heavy photographic apparatus and plates, which weighed about eighty pounds.

There had been a keen frost overnight, and in the crisp air the volcano stood out sharp in every detail, with a faint white vapour issuing from its rounded top. Scarcely had we started when one of the coolies shouted, and pointed to the mountain. On looking in that direction we saw a wonderful sight. A great ball of steam shot upwards from the crater and floated like a monster balloon up to the sky. This was immediately followed by clouds of dense, black fumes, mingled with great billows of vapour, which belched forth in bellying convolutions, and piled upon each other, higher and higher, until a pillar of smoke, ten thousand feet or more in height, floated over the mountain. A high air current then caught the top and flattened it out and tilted it, and finally the whole column drifted off lazily southwards staining the skies as grey as though a heavy rainstorm were passing. I have never seen a grander sight than that cyclopean pillar of writhing smoke and vapour pouring up into the vault of heaven on that sunny October morning.

We had not bargained for such marvellously good luck as this. To have a faultless day, and to find that the volcano was in an unusually fierce state of activity, was fortunate indeed, and well calculated to cheer the soul of any one bent on securing photographic results. Our host of the hotel came running after us, warning us to be very careful how we ascended the mountain, and exhorting us not to venture near the crater unless smoke was issuing freely. Reasons for this sage advice I will give later. We had, however, made up our minds to see the crater, and intended to look into it that day, be the risks what they might.

Leaving Karuizawa behind us, and passing through the quaint straggling village of Kotsukaké—the cottage roofs of which were covered with stones to weight them down in the strong winds which prevail here—the road led past rice-fields and sparkling streams with quaint water-wheeled mills; thence on to a beautifully-wooded, sloping moor, which soon changed to rolling hills of volcanic ash and scoriæ, overgrown with grotesque pines.

The hillsides were golden in the sun, and the silver-tipped kaia-grass, which flecked the gold, made a foreground of feathery beauty for every view. The frost had covered the trees and kaia with crystals, which scintillated like gems in the sunlight, and as we rapidly covered mile after mile through the lovely woodland, and ascended gradually higher and higher, the simple beauties of this undulating country seemed as charming as more showy landscapes, the praises of which have been sung by every writer on Japan.

The great mountain mass lay straight ahead, but since the explosion at 7 A.M. scarcely a trace of vapour had issued from the crater. At 10 A.M. we passed round the side of Ko-Asama, or "Baby Asama"—a small extinct volcano which lies at the base of its larger namesake—whose slopes were crimson with autumn tints. Shortly afterwards we reached the place where those who come on horseback must leave their steeds behind and proceed the rest of the way on foot, for, like most volcanoes in Japan, Asama-yama is sacred, and above this spot no horse may tread. From here to the summit it is simply a matter of walking over a bed of cinders and pumice, which gets steeper and looser as one nears the top. Ash is frequently ejected from the crater, and most of it falls on the upper part of the mountain, the accumulation of centuries accounting for the smooth, round appearance which the volcano presents when viewed from a distance.

The lower slopes are overgrown with a tangle of vines bearing small seedless grapes, from which the natives make a kind of jam. At 11.20 A.M., as we were toiling up this incline, another explosion occurred, and again vast clouds of smoke and steam belched out from the crater and rose thousands of feet into the air. A muffled roar, however, was the only sound which reached us at this distance. A gentle breeze had by this time sprung up, causing the smoke to drift off rapidly eastwards, and as it floated overhead a shower of ash fell around us.

We relieved our coolies of the contents of the lunch basket shortly after this, for the guide told us that the mountain was extremely dangerous when in such a mood, and ejected showers of stones with each explosion; it would therefore be unwise to tarry long enough at the summit to lunch there as we had proposed.

AT THE CRATER'S BRINK

At 1 P.M. we reached the top of the great ridge of the outer cone. The ground hereabouts was exceedingly soft from the quantity of fine ash that is intermittently deposited. It was studded with innumerable stones, some of which bore silent testimony to the soundness of the guide's warning, for they were quite warm, showing that they had been ejected in the recent explosion. There was a slight depression beyond this, and then another slope, which is the inner cone. The roar of the great cauldron could be heard as we arrived at this spot, but when we reached the summit a few minutes later, and stood on the crater's brink, a marvellous spectacle lay before us.

We saw an immense pit, six hundred feet or more across, and almost perfectly round, with perpendicular walls five hundred feet or so in height. These walls were burnt and scorched and stained with fire to every colour of the spectrum; and from a myriad cracks and crannies sulphurous jets of steam hissed out, each contributing to the filmy vapours that rose from the abyss. Through the thin steam the entire crater floor was visible. It was a huge solfatara, with numerous holes from which molten matter was spurting, and red-hot lava pools which now and then were licked by little tongues of flame.

The noise of the place was truly infernal. There is no other sound that can be likened to the sputtering, buzzing roar of a volcano. It is fearful to listen to—this vibrating, throbbing, pulsating boom of fiercely boiling lava. The crater seemed to be fermenting with suppressed rage; and one half expected that any moment it would burst open and loose the furies it could scarce restrain.

The whole summit of the volcano was covered with stones, some of which must have weighed a ton or more. Many of them had obviously been ejected quite recently, for the marks they had made in the soft ash were fresh, and some of the larger ones were still hot, having obviously been thrown out from the crater in the explosion that occurred during our ascent. The fresh ash, which falls after each such outburst,

speedily covers the stones, so that it is easy to see which have
been expelled most recently. Our coolies emphatically drew
our attention to the freshly-fallen ones, intimating that it
would be exceedingly hazardous to tarry at the summit very
long. But the intense interest of the place, and the wonderful
views to be had from the lofty vantage-point, made us disregard their warnings; there was so much to marvel at, and
all around us a glorious panorama of mountain scenery.

Eastwards, rugged mountains rose tier beyond tier, ending
with the craggy peaks of Myōgi-san, and farther north the
Nikko range. Northwards, were the Kotsuke range, the
mountainous district of Kusatsu, and Shirane-san; whilst
in the west that forbidding conglomeration of great barren
peaks, which the Rev. W. Weston has named "the Japanese
Alps," was a dream of light and shadow in the afternoon sun.
Southward, there rose the great Kōshu barrier, above which,
and far beyond it, the lovely snow-clad cone of Fuji towered
high, and surpassed in the beauty of almost faultless symmetry every peak within the range of vision.

Whilst absorbed in the contemplation of these beautiful
surroundings, and the wondrous red and purple colouring of
an ancient broken crater on the mountain's western side, the
time sped swiftly on, and it was not until three o'clock that
we prepared to leave.

Our coolies went on ahead, but Hurley and I stopped a
few moments for a last look at the crater, which we were
reluctant to leave. As we stood on the brink, gazing into
the abyss, there was a crash like a thunder-clap, and the
bed of the crater parted asunder and burst upwards, throwing
thousands of tons of rock against the walls. Masses of rock
were hurled against the cliffs and shivered to fragments with
reports like exploding shells, and showers of stones, whistling
past us, shot many hundreds of feet into the air.

I thought my last moment had surely come, for it seemed
we must inevitably be struck by the falling stones. My first
impulse was to seek safety in flight; but after running a few
paces it occurred to me that the stones were just as likely to

hit me running as standing still. Hurley, who had also started to run, stopped too, and we both waited for our fate. Just then the smoke, which rose from the crater immediately after the explosion, swept in a great cloud above us, so that we could not see the flying stones, or form any idea where they were likely to fall. I shall not soon forget those moments, as we gazed upwards, with arms involuntarily held tightly over our heads for protection, waiting for the descending missiles to drop out of the smoke-cloud and annihilate us.

And then the stones came clattering down—sticking, with sharp thuds, deep into the ash. It was fortunate for us that a mere sprinkling fell in our vicinity, in comparison with the hail of rock fragments that dropped not a hundred yards away.

No sooner, however, were we safely delivered from Scylla than the perils of Charybdis were upon us. The smoke that was belching from the crater's mouth now enveloped us, and in a moment we were choking with the sulphurous fumes. It was impossible to breathe, as, with hands tightly pressed over our mouths and nostrils, we blindly ran through the smoke for air. Fortune again was with us. In less than twenty paces we emerged suddenly from the asphyxiating smoke into brilliant sunlight, gasping and filling our lungs to their fullest extent with great draughts of sweet pure air. It was a happy thing for us that the strong breeze which was now blowing was coming from the south; thus, the smoke was blown from where we stood across the crater. Had it been blowing from the north we should have been unable to escape from the suffocating fumes.

Great black whorls of smoke belched from the crater, being emitted with such force and volume that they were pushed far back into the teeth of the wind; and several times we had to retreat quickly as they bellied out toward us. They rose to the heavens in writhing convolutions, and from the centre of the mass billows of snow-white steam puffed out, and bulged beyond the smoke. And as white and black rose higher and higher in turn, they mingled with each other, and soared up to the skies in a gradually diffusing pillar of grey,

which was tilted northwards by the wind and borne off rapidly
into the clouds above.

Here was a wonderful chance to secure a unique photograph, but on looking round for the coolies, I saw them madly
rushing down the mountain-side with my cameras as fast as
legs could carry them. Realising that if I did not stop them I
should miss the chance of a lifetime to get a picture at the lip
of a volcano in a state of violent activity, I ran after them,
calling to them to stop. The guide shouted back that we should
all be killed if we did, and they continued their rush down the
mountain-side faster than ever. They raced over the smooth
ash and leapt over stones like deer, regardless of the damage
such a pace might do to my apparatus, which was packed to
suit a more sober gait. Failing to check them with my shouts,
I ran after them, and, being unencumbered, soon overhauled
the man with my hand-camera. Quickly unlashing the camera
from his pack, I returned with another and older coolie—
who had stopped at my bidding—to the crater's lip, and
there hastily I took some snapshots, and then rewarded the
old fellow with a substantial gratuity, much to his satisfaction.

For the remainder of that day the volcano relapsed into a
state of steady activity—thick, black smoke pouring from the
crater. This was the condition for which our host at the hotel
had told us to wait before making the ascent, as when smoke
issues freely it denotes that the vent is clear, and that the
crater may be approached with safety.

The last really great eruption of Asama occurred in 1783,
when a stream of lava poured from the crater down the north-
eastern side of the mountain, and for several miles into the
valley below, overwhelming everything in its path.

The lava-flow spread ruin far and wide through a forest
of pine and maple trees that stood in its path. As one emerges
from the shade of this fair woodland, the barren waste of
distorted shapes into which the molten rock solidified bears
awe-inspiring evidence of the devastating forces pent up
inside the earth.

THE GIRL AND THE LANTERN

CHAPTER XX

THE INLAND SEA AND MIYAJIMA

MIYAJIMA! Even the very name is soft and pleasant to the ear, as is befitting for a queen's; and Miyajima is easily queen of all the lovely isles which grace that fairest stretch of water in the world—the Inland Sea.

I have passed through the Inland Sea by mail steamer half a dozen times or more, and have visited every point of interest on the Sanyo railway, which skirts its western shores; but the most memorable trip of all was two weeks which I spent exploring those beautiful land-locked waters in detail by native coasting vessels and sailing sampans. From a mail steamer one can get only broad effects. Space will not permit herein of a full account of all that I saw, so I will confine myself to a visit, by way of coasting steamers, to the lovely island of Miyajima.

It was from the prettily-situated port of Kobe—which lies at the foot of the Settsu mountains, by the waters of Izumi Bay—that once I embarked on a tiny Japanese steamer for a visit to the far-famed island.

At ten o'clock one summer night we weighed anchor, and soon entered the Akashi Strait, the principal eastern entrance to the famous landlocked waters. The moon was shedding a soft romantic radiance over the motionless sea, and as the little vessel's bow parted a way through the glassy mirror it caused tiny jets of spray to fly upwards and fall back with a hiss on either side. As we glided along past the island of Awaji—which was the very beginning of Japan, the home of the Creator Izanagi and the Creatress Izanami, where they wedded and gave birth to all the other islands of the Japanese

U

Archipelago—we found ourselves in the midst of a fleet of junks, busily engaged in fishing by the light of the moon.

Like phantom ships upon a phantom ocean, they lay in the moonbeams with idle sails that vainly tried to catch a breath of wind—reminding me vividly of that never-to-be-forgotten hour when first I saw Japan.

All next day we were passing through narrow channels, where the tide ran swift and strong, or over sheets of open water which seemed like inland lakes. Junks and fishing boats were sailing everywhere, and the scenery was weirdly beautiful. Grotesque islands of every conceivable size and curious shape —all carved and crannied and pock-marked by the erosion of the swift currents, and studded with fantastic pine-trees leaning over the water, as often as not at angles far below the horizontal—were bestrewn all over the surface of the sea; and our course was altered almost every minute to navigate the tortuous winding channels.

The engine-room telegraph was almost constantly ringing. One moment the helm would be "hard-a-port," the next it was "hard-a-starboard," as the tide came swirling round the rocks, and the steamer heeled from side to side as the currents caught us on either bow. Now and again it seemed almost impossible that we could stem the flood. At one place the little vessel rushed headlong to destruction as she bore straight for the cliffs hemming us in on every side. But at the very moment when it seemed her doom was sealed, the precipice parted asunder and an opening appeared. Quickly, and timed to the fraction of a second, went the word of command. Hard over went the helm, and the staunch, handy little craft, heeling over and nearly standing on her beam ends, strained every bolt and plate as she turned her head to answer, and then swept with a rush through a narrow channel, where the tide was racing like a mill-stream.

We made brief stoppages at many small towns and villages, the most picturesque of which was Onomichi—a pretty little port with plenty of bustling activity about its streets and quays. There is a large island called Mukōjima in front of it, from

which it is separated by a long and narrow strait. This channel
is always haunted by a fleet of old-time junks, though the
ancient native rig is rapidly disappearing from Japanese waters
in favour of brigs and schooners, which can sail a good deal
closer to the wind.

At high-tide the activity of Onomichi's water-front is
strenuous; and when the tide is low, long stretches of sand
lie bare, and hundreds of women and children dig for shell-fish.
Near the town large areas of land are used for growing reeds
for matting, and salt marshes line the shore for miles. The
method of extracting the salt is very simple. The water,
which percolates through sand-beds into pits, is evaporated
in the sun until it becomes concentrated brine; this is then
evaporated again by boiling in iron pans until only the salt,
encrusted on the pans, remains.

A fine old bell at Senkōji monastery, high up in the hills
above the town, sent deep sweet notes trembling to the breezes;
and out in the strait the white-winged junks skimmed continually over its shallow, emerald waters. Fishermen sailed
away to the west as the sun went down, to return with their
spoils at break of day; the laughter of rollicking children
mingled with the murmur of the rippling waves that lapped
the shore; and everything on land and sea seemed to breathe
of peace, as our steamer anchored for the night.

The next day, on another steamer, we had further tussles
with the tide and currents, and though the little vessel fought
them bravely she was baffled more than once. At one place a
great swirling whirlpool yawned before us—fully ten feet or
more in depth—seeming like the gaping mouth of some great
sea-monster seeking whom it might devour. But the little
craft only laughed at it, and swept across its vortex, dispersing
it for a moment as she passed.

Then she throbbed easily along until she came to the
Ondo channel. But here she could not breast the flood which
boiled through the narrow passage. She could not keep her
head to the current; and the moment she wavered it caught
her side and swept her, heeling over twenty degrees, back into

the open reach again. It was an exciting struggle, for though the captain kept her stubbornly to the task and tried three times, he had finally to abandon the effort, and wait for slacker water. Half an hour later, when the tide was running slower, he tried again, and the little vessel fought her way foot by foot up the channel, in the middle of which there was a rock on which a great stone lantern stood. There were villages within biscuit-throw of us on either side—so near that we could look into the windows of the houses, whose busy occupants scarcely turned aside from their occupation to so much as glance at the struggling steamer, so accustomed were they to such sights. On another occasion when I passed through this channel, the tide was running just as strongly in the contrary direction, and a similar conflict had again to be waged against the current.

Then we turned and twisted about for hours through landlocked channels and lakes, amidst seascapes of bewitching beauty. Island after island bobbed up out of the sea—some no larger than the steamer, mere pinnacles of granite, but seldom without a few whimsical pines sticking to some crevice into which they had forced their starving roots. Others were lovely symphonies of colour—great pyramids of green, rising a thousand feet or more above the villages on their shores—and terraced with rice and barley patches to their utmost heights; not an inch of earth was wasted. Every tiny village and hamlet had its temple, sometimes by the shore, sometimes perched upon a knoll; but more often than not it peeped from some clump of pines, far up the mountain-side, where the patron deity might feast his eyes for ever on some glorious view.

As we sped along through all this wonderland, the scenes in the depths below were beautiful as the views above. The sunlight pierced far down into the crystal waters, and by leaning over the bow, where the surface was undisturbed by the vessel's progress, I could see lovely gardens on the bed of the sea.

We were floating over the silent realm of the Nereides,

and could see the beauties of their home as a soaring bird looks down upon the earth.

Sometimes there was nothing but the blue of infinite depth below us; then some submarine peak would stretch upwards, almost to the surface, with great forests of sea-plants on its top, which waved their foliage to us as we passed.

When Aphrodite herself was born and sprang like a lily from a bubble on the sea, that lily could have floated upwards from no fairer spot than this; and as I gazed into the depths, with the spell of their magic upon me, I half expected to see some lovely sea-nymph beckon me with her hand; but instead the sea-trees only waved their branches. There were shoals of fish among the greenery, and in one of the open reaches we ran into a school of dolphins. Scores of the playful cetaceans swam close alongside of us, easily keeping pace with the steamer with scarcely any perceptible movement of their bodies. They seemed to take keen delight in swimming an inch or two ahead of us, and in leaping out of the water across the vessel's prow.

Then the sea began to swarm with jelly-fish. We found them massed in such prodigious numbers as actually to impede our speed. For a mile or more there must have been billions of them, for scarcely any water could be seen for the multitude of the creatures. We were literally steaming through a monster jelly. The Japanese call them kuragé, which means "sea moon." This name is wonderfully appropriate—as indeed most Japanese names are—for a single kuragé in the deep blue water resembles exactly the full moon in the sky.

Then we came to Kuré, the greatest of all the naval harbours—the Portsmouth of Japan. It is said that the hills hereabouts are lined with impregnable forts, but though I have passed them many times, and scrutinised their sides closely with my glass, I have never seen any evidence of a fortification. They exist, however, but are so well and skilfully masked as to be invisible from the water.

The harbour was filled with battleships, cruisers, and torpedo craft; and at Ujina, a few miles further, fourteen transports lay at anchor, and the whole place was busy as a bee-hive.

After an hour's stay we left Ujina, with its feverish activity, and, turning a rocky promontory, beheld Miyajima in all its loveliness ahead. It was now evening, and a faint mist rising from the sea was gradually enveloping the sacred island with a veil, as though its guardian deities—the Sea-king's daughters —were jealous of their trust, and sought to hide its beauty with a garment. It was a thin, diaphanous robe, however, and served merely to add the witchery of enchantment to the charms it could only half conceal.

Now if Miyajima had been in the Ægean Sea the Greeks of old would have called it Delos, and they would have invested it with legend. They would have said that persecuted Latona, condemned by the jealous hatred of Juno to banishment from Olympus, and evermore to rove about the earth, arrived at length on the seashore, and there entreated Neptune to pity her distress. And Neptune would have heard her prayer, and sent a dolphin to bear her to a wondrous floating island which he had raised especially for her from the loveliest depths of his domain. Then when the isle had floated to a certain spot —where the waters were crystal clear, the breezes soft and balmy, and the air all sweet and scented—he would have anchored it fast; and there Latona would have lived happily for ever with Jupiter, her lover.

All this and more the Greeks did say about their legendary isle; but even Delos could not have been more beautiful than Miyajima.

As we approached the matchless isle that summer evening, it seemed too lovely to be real. It was like a dream—a vision of some spectral land which, even as we watched, was slowly melting away into the vapours of the shadowy seas of fable.

But the Queen of the Inland Sea had only thought to tantalise by shrinking thus from view, for as we drew nearer to its shores a sudden change of whim caused it to abandon provocation, and to cast off all conceits and modesty and show its beauty unafraid. We glided out of the filmy enshrouding

mists which lay about the surface of the sea, and fair Delos
of tradition became fairer Miyajima of fact.

Its forest-clad peaks and spires were outlined high against
the twilight sky, and the sweet scent of its pine-trees was
heavy on the air. We steamed along, close under the precipices
which overhung the water, and, as the whistle blew to signal
our arrival, the blast smote the rocks like a blow, and then
went leaping from ledge to ledge up the mountain-side, setting
all the forest ringing, and awaking a thousand echoes in its trail.

Then many lights came into view, and we drew alongside
a little stone pier; but by the time I had engaged a coolie,
and had my luggage loaded on a barrow, half an hour had
gone, and we started off through the village to the Haku-un-dō
Hotel in the dark. I could see but dimly, therefore, all the
beauty we were passing, for the moon had not yet risen above
the island's crest. But I could discern old temple buildings
looming out of the shadows, and the beach was all dancing
with ghostly fire as the ripples broke into attenuated gleams
of phosphorescence on the strand. And there were long rows
of ishi-doro silhouetted against the water; and by the light of
the coolie's lantern I could see deer, frightened by its glare,
skip nimbly out of our way. Then there were fragrant pine-
groves, with turf as soft as velvet; and at last a light appeared
in the heart of the pines, and then a house, and as we drew up
to it there was a chorus of "Irasshai, Irasshai!" ("Welcome,
Welcome!"), from the host and little neisans, who had gathered
round the door as soon as they heard the coolie's shout.

Greetings over, I was immediately taken in charge by one
of the little maids, who, by the light of a paper lantern, led me
over the springy turf, and under the pine-trees, and across a
rustic bridge spanning a murmuring stream, till we arrived at
a neat little wood-and-paper summer-house of two rooms—
all by itself. This, she intimated, was to be my domicile; and
then, after lighting a lamp for me, she pattered off to bring
some tea and cakes. After I had sipped a cup or two she led
me to the bath, and when I emerged therefrom, half an hour
later, she was waiting to conduct me back to my tiny villa

once more. Then she pattered off to bring my dinner—which
was, of course, served on the floor—and she knelt opposite
to me and chatted with me in soft accents in her native tongue
whilst I was having it, asking me many questions about where
I had been and what I had seen.

After dinner she slid open the end of the wall and brought
out bedding—futons, and even sheets, a rarity in Japanese
inns—and made my bed up on the floor. Then she dived into
the wall again and unearthed a huge green mosquito-net,
which she hoisted by means of rings at each corner of the
room, completely filling it. After that she lit an andon (night-
lamp) for me, and, kneeling on the floor, and bowing her
glossy head to the mat, sweetly wished me "O yasumi nasai"
("Honourably deign to sleep"), and then ran off to do a lot
more work before having her own bath and going to bed
herself. It was nearly midnight before I knew, by the shouts
of laughter coming from the direction of the bathroom, that
she and the rest of the hotel staff were having their evening
tub before retiring to their futons.

I slept that night to the murmur of running water and the
chirping of a myriad crickets in the surrounding woods.

The next morning I was up betimes, before fair Miyajima
had shaken off her night kimono of mist. Long shafts of golden
sunlight were struggling with the haze amidst the scented
pines, and deer were browsing on the sweet velvety turf in
front of the hotel. The sea was burnished gold, and junks were
lazily drifting homewards like snow-white swans across its
surface. The night-song of the crickets had given way to the
droning of cicadas; and already, although it was but shortly
after sunrise, the woods were ringing with their drowsy hum.
The prospect was a perfect idyll of peace and beauty.

I went down to the shore for a swim, and found the rocks
all alive with sea-cockroaches. Every island in the Inland
Sea swarms with these curious creatures. They scuttle out of
the way, with much ado, as soon as any one approaches, and
then peep furtively from the crevices in the rocks, and watch
you with great eyes until you go away, when they scamper out

again immediately. I swam about for an hour in the tepid sea, which was so crystal clear that, diving twenty feet deep, I could see and pick up pebbles with perfect ease. The water is always clear here, even in rough weather, for the sand is of coarse decomposed granite; consequently there is no matter to become suspended in the water and discolour it.

For ages Miyajima had been accounted by native connoisseurs one of the three most beautiful places in Japan. The other two of the San-Kei, or "Three Principal Sights," are Matsushima in the north, and Ama-no-Hashidaté on the west coast. Miyajima, however, easily out-ranks the other two. It is one of the holiest of many holy islands in the Japanese Archipelago, being dedicated to three Shinto goddesses—the daughters of Susa-no-Ō, the Sea-king—after the eldest of whom it receives its alternative name—Itsukushima.

Human beings may neither be born nor die within its sacred precincts. Should, however, a birth unexpectedly occur, the mother would be sent to the mainland for purification for thirty days; and in case of a sudden death the corpse must at once be removed to the opposite shore. Dogs are not permitted on the island.

Apart from the great beauty of its scenery, Miyajima's chief attraction is its temple, which is quite unique in Japan, and has furnished inspiration to numerous native artists. The favourite motive is its torii—a colossal one, made of camphor wood—which forms one of the chief features in every view of the sacred island. This torii has been immortalised in every form of Japanese art. From whatever point one looks at it, it is a thing of beauty. At low water it stands on the sand; but as the tide rises the sea comes rippling all around it, until it seems to sail away far out on the bay, and the water is more than a fathom deep under it. Even the temple itself seems afloat, for it is built on piles, sunk deep into the sand, and the rising tide creeps under and all about its galleries and colonnades, setting them all waist-deep in water.

On the "17th day of the 6th moon" great crowds flock to Miyajima, for this is the date of its annual matsuri. Instead, however, of coming on foot and in rikishas, as they do to other religious festivals, the people come in boats, and sail in long procession to the temple, through the great torii which is its main gateway.

A branch of the temple stands on the hill above. It is an enormous building, called Sen-jō-jiki, or the "Hall of a Thousand Mats." A mat being six feet long by three feet broad, the area of this hall is therefore eighteen thousand square feet. Its interior is completely covered—walls, pillars, doors, and all—with wooden rice-ladles. This queer custom was started as recently as 1894, when troops were quartered here preparatory to leaving for the war with China. One of the soldiers one day hung up a rice-ladle in the temple "for luck." Others followed suit, and every one who has since visited the temple has donated a wooden spoon, inscribed with his name, until every available inch of the interior is now covered with this curious form of decoration.

Behind the temple and the town, which is full of shops for the sale of pretty boxes and wood carvings, the mountain isle is covered with a thick forest of pine and maple trees to the utmost pinnacle of its numerous peaks. On the top of the highest of these, eighteen hundred feet from the level of the sea, there is a temple where Kōbō Daishi lighted a sacred flame over a thousand years ago, and this, like the Vestal fire of ancient Rome, is never suffered to go out. During the eleven centuries that have passed since the day when the famous saint kindled it, it is said that the holy flame has been carefully watched by day and night, and has never been extinguished.

Miyajima's forests are broken by gorges and ravines, where limpid streams mingle their laughter with the chorus of the myriad cicadas in the trees. In summer-time the whole island is all a-ringing and a-singing with these sweet voices of Nature in the kindest and most winning of her moods. Deer roam down from the hills to haunt the avenues of mossy granite lanterns by the shore, and to lick the tasty salt from the rocks, or nibble at the biscuits which every visitor gives them. As

one passes the temple, tame pigeons fly from its roofs and settle on one's hand and shoulders, begging to be fed.

The night I left Miyajima was lovely and romantic as a dream. The tide was high, and a sampan came to the beach to take me over the strait. Fiery ripples were breaking everywhere along the shore, and, as we pushed off, phosphorescent flames burst in the water at every stroke of the boatman's yulo. As he stood in the stern, swaying backwards and forwards, with the ghostly wake of the boat burning in the water behind him, his silhouette seemed like some uncanny apparition.

I thought of Charon plying his worm-eaten craft, filled with departed souls, across the river Acheron to Pluto's realm; and I half wished that I had not been able to pay the ferryman's fare, for then perhaps this Japanese sendo would have declined to take me away from entrancing Miyajima—even as Charon made every soul wait one hundred years who could not produce the obolus he demanded as his fare.

As I wrote the notes from which this chapter springs I had the subtle charm and enchantment of Miyajima all around me; and now, as I prepare these final lines for the press, memories of the happy days I have spent in that Japanese Arcadia surge vividly to mind, and a great yearning comes over me to be back there once again.

I long to wander once more among its mossy old stone lanterns; to lie in the shade of its scented pines and watch the passing junks; to hear the croaking of the hoarse old crows and see the lazily-soaring hawks; to roam among its maple woods and listen to the murmur of its hundred waterfalls; to glide at night over the moonlit sea and hear the chants of the boatmen—and to drink to the full of every other pleasure that fair Miyajima has to give. But most of all I long to see once more the burning colours of sunset framed in the beautiful simple lines of its old sea-beaten torii.

THE END

INDEX

PRINTED IN ENGLAND BY J. B. PEACE, M.A.
AT THE CAMBRIDGE UNIVERSITY PRESS

CPSIA information can be obtained
at www.ICGtesting.com
Printed in the USA
BVOW09*2003031117

499469BV00011B/268/P